# 𝕬 𝕳istory of t

# 𝕭rightlingsea

## A Member of the Cinque Ports

Edward Percival Dickin

**Alpha Editions**

This edition published in 2019

ISBN : 9789353602772

Design and Setting By
**Alpha Editions**
email - alphaedis@gmail.com

*350 copies printed, of which this is No.* 48

A

# HISTORY

OF

# The Town of Brightlingsea,

## A MEMBER OF THE CINQUE PORTS.

BY

EDWARD PERCIVAL DICKIN,

M. D.

*Brightlingsea :*
PUBLISHED BY T. W. BARNES.

1913.

## CONTENTS.

### PLATES.

# Prefatory Notes.

I. Though each component of the Town has a chapter to itself, information relating to each will be found outside its own chapter, therefore the reader must not assume that he has exhausted one subject until he has consulted at least the index.

The history of the last few years and the present day conditions are described only when they have some bearing on the past. They are too close to make it possible to select items satisfactorily, and there is too much to be given in full.

Much information relating to Brightlingsea families and properties has been collected; but is too bulky to be given. In order that it may be available to those who are interested, the information in my possession relating to any one family or property will be given to those having a just claim to the information.

II. There are no footnotes. All is included in the text; this impedes the story, but not as much as reference to the bottom of the page necessary, when footnotes are used. References are given to printed works and manuscripts. Each is indicated by letters to which the list given at the end of these notes is the key. A little more trouble will be needed to find the name of the work or MS. to which reference is made, but more information about the source can be given than when the title is given in a shortened form in a footnote. Where possible the volume and page to which reference is made are given in the list of authorities.

Latin and Norman French MSS. have been translated. Fragments of Latin occurring in English MSS. have been translated and are printed in italics. The contractions in both Latin and English MSS. have been extended. Where there is doubt as to the precise form the extension should take, the extended letters are printed in italics.

III. My thanks are due to :—

The Right Hon. the Lord Lucas for access to the Wrest Park MSS., and to Mr. C. F. Argles and Mr. Denley of the Wrest Park Estate Office for their assistance.

The Mayor and Corporation of Sandwich for access to the Corporation Records, and to Mr. J. A. Jacobs, the late Mr. D. Baker, Town Clerk, Mr. Harrisson, Town Clerk, and Mr. John Ewell for their assistance.

The late Sir E. Wollaston Knocker, Seneschal and Solicitor to the Cinque Ports, for assistance in gaining access to the Records of the Court of Brotherhood and Guestling.

The Rev. Andrew Clark, LL.D., for transcribing papers relating to Brightlingsea in a Lieutenancy Book of Essex.

The Urban District Council of Brightlingsea for access to the Parish Records in their charge, and to Mr. W. I. Osborn, Clerk, for his assistance.

The " B.C. Pulleyne" Trustees, Lords of the Manor of Brightlingsea, for the loan of the Manor Court Rolls, and to Mr. Paul Pulleyne, Mr. Gabbert, Steward, and Mr. T. B. Howard, Bailiff, for their assistance.

The Rev. Arthur Pertwee, M.A., R.D., Vicar of Brightlingsea, for access to the Parish Registers.

Mr. J. Horace Round, LL.D., M.A., for much assistance and information given.

Mr. G. Rickword, Librarian, Colchester Public Library, and Mr. A. G. Wright, Curator, Colchester Museum, for assistance given.

To the following ladies and gentlemen for information given, gifts and loans of books, photographs, drawings, manuscripts, and maps, and for permission to take photographs—Mrs. R. Aldous, Mrs. Balding (Woodbridge), Miss K. Jefferies, the late Mrs. James Major, Mrs. F. Miller, Mrs. W. Pannell, and the late Mrs. Wenlock. The Rev. Arthur Pertwee. Messrs. G. W. Crane, J. Sims Earle, F.S.A. (the late), F. D. Girling, A. A. Jefferies, R. L. Jefferies (Colchester), H. Laver, F.S.A., A. W. Norfolk, W. I. Osborn, T. Poole, J. E. Richardson, G. Riches, R. Salmon (the late) C. Wrinch Salmon, E. Southgate, J. Stammers and W. Stammers.

Plate ii. is from a photograph by Mr. C. T. Humphrey of the original water colour drawing in the possession of Mr. A. A. Jefferies. Plate vi. is from a photograph by Mr. C. A. Mathew. Plate iii. is from an old photograph in the possession of Mrs. F. Miller, and plate iv. from one belonging to Mr. A. W. Norfolk. Plate v. is from a copy by Mr. C. A. Mathew of a photograph by Mr. Smith of Sandwich.

# LIST OF REFERENCES.

## PRINTED WORKS.

A,   Statutes of the Realm.   Record Commission.
B,   Testa de Nevill.   297.   Record Commission.
C,   Taxatio Ecclesiastica of Pope Nicholas IV.   Record Commission.
D,   Valor Ecclesiasticus.   I.   Record Commission.
E,   Rotuli Hundredorum.   I.   Record Commission.
F,   Calendarium Genealogicum.   I., 15.   Record Office.
G,   Calendar of Inquisitions Post Mortem.   Record Office.
H,   Calendar of Patent Rolls.   Record Office.
I,   Calendar of Close Roll.   Record Office.
J,   Letters and Papers, Henry VIII.
K,   Historical MSS. Commission : Reports.
L,   Statutes at Large.
M,   Calendar of State Papers, Domestic.   Edward VI., *etc.*   Record Office.
N,   Calendar of State Papers, Domestic.   Charles I., *etc.*   Record Office.
O,   Calendar of State Papers, Domestic.   Charles II., *etc.*   Record Office.
P,   Acts of the Privy Council.   New Series.   Record Office.
Q,   Roxburghe Club : Cartularium Monasterii S. Johannis Baptist de Colcestrie.
R,   B. C. Pulleyne : Synopsis of Records relating to Brightlingsea Manor.
T,   Richard Newcourt : Repertorium Eccles. parochiale Londin.   II.
U,   George Hennessy : Novum Repertorium Eccles. parochiale Londin.
V,   W. Sparrow Simpson : Visitation of Churches belonging to St. Paul's.
W,   Soc. of Antiquaries : Liber quotidianus Contrarotulatoris Garderobae.
Y,   T. K. Cromwell : History of Colchester.
Z,   P. Morant : History of Colchester.
Aa,   John Norden : Speculi Britanniæ pars., Essex.
Ab,   M. Burrows : Historic Towns.   The Cinque Ports.
Ad,   C. R. S. Elvin : History of Walmer.
Ae,   John Lyon : History of Dover.
Af,   F. F. Giraud and C. E. Donne : Guide to Faversham.
Ag,   S. P. H. Statham : History of Dover.
Ah,   W. Holloway : History of Rye. .
Ai,   S. Jeake : Charters of the Cinque Port.
Aj,   W. Boys : History of Sandwich.
Ak,   T. Wright : History of Essex.
Al,   J. Yelloly Watson : Tendring Hundred in the olden time
Am,   D. W. Coller : History of Essex.
An,   P. Morant : History of Essex.   II.
Ao,   W. R. Fisher : The Forest of Essex.
Ap,   J. C. Cox : Royal Forests of England.
Aq,   W. White : Gazeteer of Essex, 1848

Ar,   Nathaniel Salmon: History of Essex.
As,   Pigott's London and Provincial Directory, 1834.
At,   Victoria County History of Essex.  I.
Au,   Victoria County History of Essex.  II.
Av,   C. R. B. Barrett: Essex Highways, Byeways, and Waterways.
Aw,   Carlisle's Topographical History of England.
Ax,   Chapman and André: Map of Essex, 1773.
Ay,   Bristol and Gloucestershire Archæological Society's Trans.  XVIII.
Az,   Essex Archæological Society's Trans.  Old Series.

Ba,   Essex Archæological Society's Trans.  New Series.
Bb,   Sussex Archæological Society's Trans.  IV., 303.
Bc,   Essex Review.
Bd,   Essex County Standard
Be,   Yachting World.
Bf,   British Medical Journal.
Bg,   Brightlingsea Parish Magazine.
Bh,   J. M. Kemble; Saxons in England.
Bi,   F. Seebohm: English Village Community.
Bj,   Royal Historical Society's Trans.
Bl,   John Ray: Collection of English Words, *etc.*  English Dialect Soc.
Bm,   John Ecton: Thesaurus Rerum Ecclesi., pp. xx., 277.
Bn,   White Kennett: Parochial Antiquities.
Bo,   Thos. Fuller: History of the Worthies of England.  I.
Bp,   F. W. Maitland; Domesday and beyond.
Bq,   A Ballard: Domesday Inquest.
Br,   J. E. Thorold Rogers: History of agriculture and prices in England.
Bs,   F. A. Gasquet: The Great Pestilence.
Bt,   E. Arber: An English Garner.
Bv,   G. L. Gomme: The Village Community.
Bx,   English Historical Review.
By,   P. Vinogradoff: English Society in the 11th century.
Bz,   P. Vinogradoff: Villeinage in England.

Ca,   P. Vinogradoff: Growth of the Manor.
Cb,   T. D. Fosbroke: Encyclopædia of Antiquities.
Cd,   M. Bateson: Mediæval England.
Ce,   W. Cunningham: Growth of English Industries and Commerce.
Cf,   J. A. Giles: Anglo-Saxon Chronicle.
Cg,   T. W. Shore: Origins of Anglo-Saxon Race.
Ch,   C. I. Elton: Origins of English History.
Ci,   W. Stubbs: Constitutional History of England.
Cj,   J. Lingard: History of England
Cn,   J. Bosworth: Anglo-Saxon Dictionary.
Co,   J. O. Halliwell: Dictionary of Archaic and Provincial Words
Cr,   S. R. Scargill Bird: Guide to Public Records.
Cs,   L. Wagenaer: The Mariner's Mirrour.  1590
Ct,   N. H. Nicolas: History of the Royal Navy.
Cu,   J. Charnock: History of Marine Architecture.
Cv,   W. Laird Clowes: History of the Royal Navy,
Cx,   M. Oppenheim: Administration of the Navy.
Cy,   M. Oppenheim: Naval Accounts, Hen. VII
Cz,   A. Spont: Letters and Papers relating to the war with France, 1512-3.

Db, The Oyster Dredgers' Petition.
Dc, A. Young: Agriculture in Essex.
Dd, The Division of the County of Essex into Classes.
De, Henry Whitfield: A Sermon preached by, before the Univ. of Oxford.
Df, Sir W. Dugdale: History of St. Paul's Cathedral.
Dg, T. W. Davids: Annals of Evangelical Nonconformity in Essex.
Dh, W. A Shaw: History of the Church in the Civil Wars and the Common-
wealth
Di, List of Non-Parochial Registers, preserved at Somerset House.
Dj, D. Rock: Church of our Fathers.
Dk, F. A. Gasquet: Parish Life in Mediæval England.
Dl, J. C. Cox and A. Harvey: English Church Furniture.
Dm, Essex. A viewe of the state of the Clargie within the Countie of Essex.
Dn, H. W. Macklin: Monumental Brasses.
Do, H. Haines, Manual of Monumental Brasses.
Dp, Royal Historical Society: Cely Papers.
Dq. H. Ellis: Brand's Popular Antiquities.
Dr, N. J. Hone: The Manor and Manorial Records.
Ds, F. W. Maitland: Select Pleas in Manorial Courts.
Dt, H. Atton: The King's Customs.
Du, J. H. Rose and A. M. Broadley: Dumouriez and the Defence of England.
Dv, H. F. B. Wheeler and A. M. Broadley: Napoleon and the Invasion of
England.
Dx, Dictionary of National Biography.
Dy, John Taylor: A Catalogue of Tavernes in the shires round London.
Dz, Journals of the House of Lords. xii., 411, 415.


Ea, C. Creighton: History of Epidemics in Britain.
Eb, Report of the Redhill Exploration Committee, 1906-7.
Ec, F. T. Dollman and J. R Jobbins: Ancient Domestic Architecture.
Ed, T. H. Turner and J. H. Parker: Domestic Architecture.
Ee, G. Jacobs: Law Dictionary.
Ef, Edwardian Inventories for Bedfordshire.
Eg, F. W. Fairholt: Costume in England. II.
Eh, Brightlingsea Directory, 1912.
Ei, Geological Survey Map of Colchester and District.
Ej, Encyclopædia Britannica, 9th edition.
El, Sir W. Dugdale: History of Imbanking.
Em, W. H. Dalton: Geology of Colchester and District.
En, Inquisitiones Nonarum. Record Commission. 322.
Eo, John Wesley: Journal.
Ep, R. G. Marsden: Select Pleas in the Admiralty Court. I., pp. 70, 200.

## MANUSCRIPTS.

PUBLIC RECORD OFFICE.

*Chancery.*

Fa, Patent Rolls. Fb, Close Rolls, Fc, Treaty Rolls. Fd, Inquisitions
Post Mortem. Fe, Miscellanea.

*Exchequer.*

> *King's Remembrancer*—Ff, Subsidy Rolls.  Fg, Depositions taken by Commission, 20 Chas. II., Trin. 10.  Fh, Depositions taken by Commission, David Murray, 1709.  Fi, Special Commission, 2124.  Fj, Book of Decrees, series 4, no. 20.  Fk, Church Goods, Essex, 2,'61.  Fl, Accounts.
>
> *Augmentation Office*—Fm, Particulars for Grants 2386.  Fn, Miscellaneous Book, no. 230, p 188.  Fo, Deeds of Purchase and Exchange, box D, no. 7.
>
> *Exchequer of Receipt*—Fp, Tellers' Roll, no. 61.
>
> *Lord Treasurer's Remembrancer.*—Fq, Recusant Roll, 3, James I.
>
> *Treasury of the Receipt*—Fr, Miscellaneous Books.
>
> *Ministers' Accounts*—Fs, Henry VIII.  Ft, Edward VI.  Fu, Philip and Mary  Fv, Elizabeth.

*State Paper Office.*

> Fw, Letters and Papers, Henry VIII.
>
> *Domestic*—Fx, Edward VI.  Fy, Mary.  Fz, Elizabeth.  Ga, James I.  Gb, Charles I.
>
> *Colonial*—Gc, Entry Book, LXXI., pp. 6, 8, 14.
>
> *Home Office*—Gca, Precedents, I., 50.

*Indexes.*

> Gcb, Palmer's Index, vii., 191.

*Admiralty.*

> Gd, Accountant General's Dept., Registers, Sea Fencibles, Paylists, 25, 26.  Ge, Miscellaneous, various, no 102, p. 5.

BRITISH MUSEUM.

> Ha, Harleian MSS.  Hb, Royal MSS.  Hc, Cotton MSS.  Hd, Additional MSS.

LAMBETH PALACE LIBRARY.

> He, MSS.

GUILDHALL LIBRARY.

> Hf, MS., no. 481, p. 139.

PRINCIPAL PROBATE REGISTRY, SOMERSET HOUSE.

*Prerogative Court of Canterbury.*

> Ia, Vox, 10.  Ib, Horne, 10  Ic, Adeane, 29.  Id, Ayloffe, 7.  Ie, Alenger, 2.  If, Pynnying, 19.  Ig, Goode, 6.  Ih, Chayre, 40.  Ii, Chrymes, 13.  Ij, Lyon, 5.  Ik, Daper.  Il, Daughtry, 5.  Im, Carew.  In, Langley, 22.  Io, Butts.  Ip, Windsor, 39.  Iq, Arundel, 1.  Ir, Leicester, 90.  Is, Sainberbe, 21.  It, Nevill, 91.  Iu, Dixy, 57.  Iv, Montague, 48.  Iw, Bolein.  Ix, St. John, 41.  Iy, Russell, 90  Iz, Goare, 125.  Ja, Lee, 79.  Jb, Harvey, 6.  Jc, Manwarying, 18.  Jd, Porch, Je, Jankyn, 10.  Jf, Thower, 8.  Jg, Dyngeley.  Ih, Cromwell.

*Commissary Court of London, Essex and Herts.*

> Ji, Lowing.  Jj, Fish.  Jk, Pleasant.  Jl, Watts.  Jm, Alderton.  Jn, Saunders.  Jo, Waller.  Jp, Heydon.  Jq, Rickett.  Jr, Hamor.  Js, Porter.  Jt, Mead.  Ju, Original Wills

BODLEIAN LIBRARY.

Ka, Rawlinson MSS., A, 200. Kb, Rawlinson MSS., B, 376.

SANDWICH CORPORATION MSS.

La, Old Black Book. Lb, White Book. Lc, Little Black Book. Ld, Year Book, A and B. Le, Year Book, C and D. Lf, Year Book, E and F. Lg, Year Book, G and H. Lh, Letter Book, OQ. Li, Licensing Book. Lj, Records and Annals of Sandwich. Ljj, Treasurers' Accounts.

RECORDS OF THE COURT OF BROTHERHOOD AND GUESTLING, ROMNEY.

Lk, White Book. Ll, Black Book, p. 59.

LOCAL.

Ma, Liberty of the Cinque Ports' Records, Schedule of Armour. Mb, Parish Registers, 1697-1812. Mc, Parish Papers, bundle 1. Mg, Parish Papers, bundle 7.

MISCELLANEOUS.

Na, Wrest Park MSS., no. 57, in the possession of Lord Lucas. Brightlingsea Manor Court Rolls, 1660-1873; Nb, vol. 1; Nc, vol. 2; Nd, vol. 3; Ne, vol. 4; Nf, vol. 5; Ng, vol. 6; Nh, vol. 7; Ni, vol. 8; Nj, vol. 9; Nk, vol. 10; Nl, vol. 11; Nm, vol. 12. Nn, A Book of Lieutenancy for Essex; in the possession of Dr. C. H Firth, Regius Professer of Modern History, Oxford. No, Colchester Museum MSS.; Wm. Holman's collection for Essex, vol. 11. Np, Colchester Museum, Essex Charters, no. 3. Nq, Diary, 1849, in the possession of Mr. G. Riches, Brightlingsea. Nr. Bill of Sale, 1794, iu the possession of Mr. G. Riches, Brightlingsea.

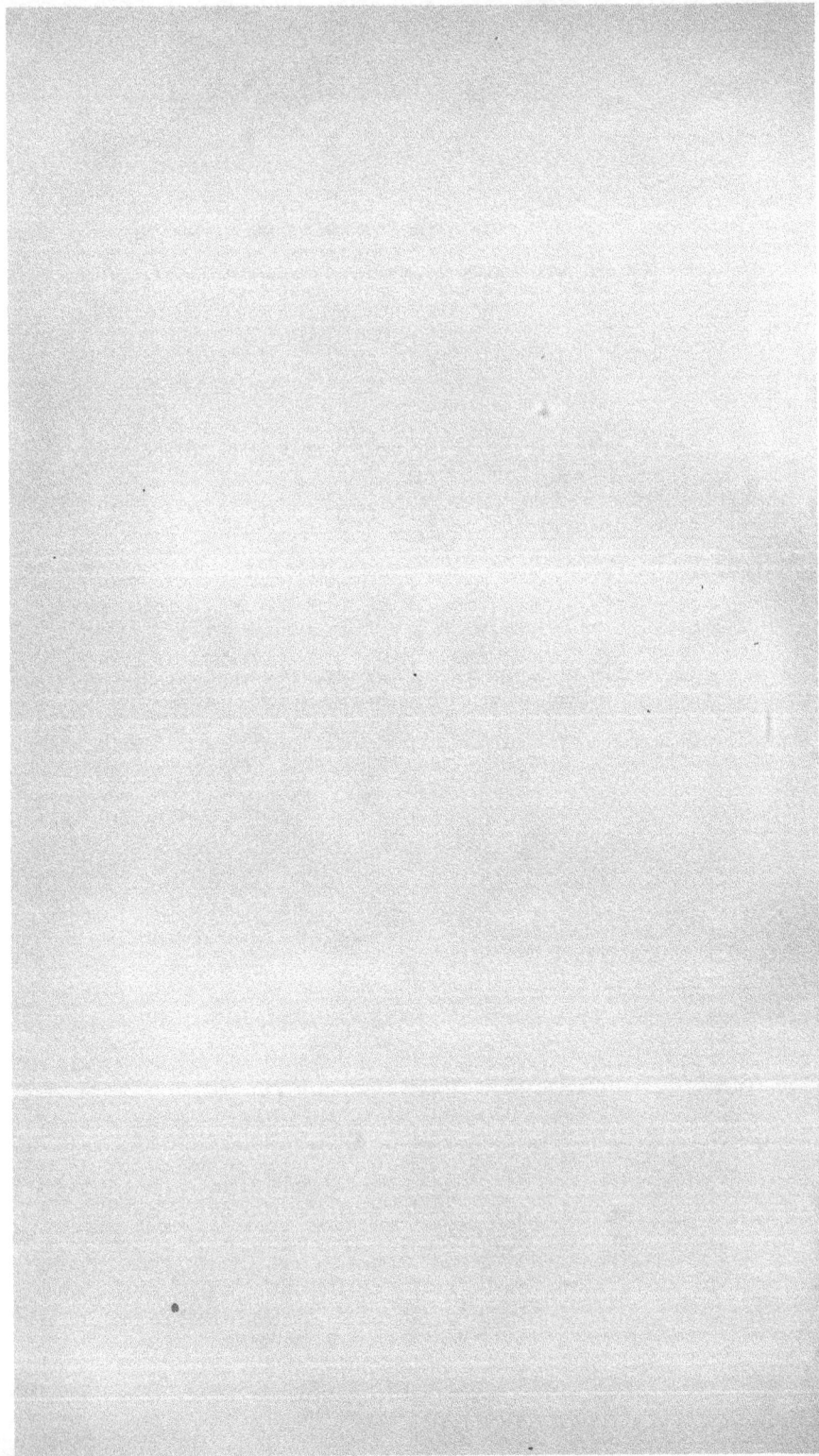

# Chapter I.

## INTRODUCTORY.

1. The name Brightlingsea and its informal conversational form Bricklesey have many variants. It would be wearisome to print the 193 forms I have found. Many of them, however, will be found in the text. When the eccentricities of spelling are eliminated, there are only three forms left—Brightlingsea, Bricklesey, and Brictriceseia (Domesday). If the Norman scribes did not make a mistake over Brictriceseia, as they often did over Anglo-Saxon names, it means Brictric's island. As this form only appears once, probably it was a mistake.

The parish consists of a peninsula, two small islands, and parts of two creeks and the estuary of the river Colne. It was anciently an island, and was described as such in 1295.[1] A map of the second half of the sixteenth century shows it as an island.[2]

2. The main physical features are a central tableland with sides sloping down to wide expanses of marshland, consisting of alluvium or waterborne mud,[3] and in places to deposits of waterborne post glacial gravel.[3] The cap of the tableland is glacial sand and gravel, deposited by glaciers in the Ice Age.[3] The important post glacial gravel deposits are at the Ford, Aldborough Point, the Waterside extending up to High street, the arable field east of the Syndicate Yacht Stores, and on either side of the fleet dividing Brightlingsea from Thorington, where the main road crosses it. The old high-water mark is shown by the junction of the marshland with the sloping side of the tableland. At East End Green and Moverons there are low cliffs. At Moverons, at the foot of the cliff, is a stretch of beach formed of shingle taken by the ebb-tide from the deposit at Aldborough Point. It is grass-grown now, but rabbit burrows show its composition.

Cindery Island, originally a long narrow strip of marshland, has been cut in two by the force of the ebb tide out of St. Osyth Creek

The channel separating the islands from Brightlingsea mainland is
very shallow, compared with the channel on the south, suggesting
that it was originally part of the marshland of Brightlingsea, and
was cut off by the sea breaking through.   The name has given rise
to much speculation.   In a recent lawsuit in which the island was
mentioned, the Judge and Counsel suggested volcanic remains or
the use of the island as an ancient dustbin as the origin of the name.
It is a certainty that there are no volcanic remains there, nor is the
second suggestion probable.   The Brightlingsea native speaks of it
as "the Cindry," thus keeping the form " the Syndry," by which it
was described in a will of 1539.⁴   The form " Sinder Isle " (1674)⁵
explains the native and ancient omission of the modern addition
'island,' and proves the 'y' of Cindery to be the Anglo-Saxon '*ey*,'
meaning an island.   Sinder is most probably the Anglo-Saxon
*synder* or its variant *sunder*, meaning separate or asunder, and
Syndery, the island made by being separated from the mainland.

    3.   Borefleet or Brightlingsea Creek was anciently also called
Balfleet,⁶ Berfliet and Bordfliet.⁷   It has been suggested that it
was called Borefleet because (1) there used to be a bore or tidal
wave on it, 2) that hogs were driven down to it to drink.   If so, it
must have been fresh water then, or the ancient pigs liked it salt.
A more likely explanation is that the 'bord' of the older form is the
Anglo-Saxon '*bord*,' meaning a border or boundary.   At the mouth
of Borefleet is a small fleet, Gandergoose Creek, which used to run
up near to the small green in front of the Station gates.   This
green is no doubt a remnant of the old Gandergoose green.
Gandergoose is an old name for the plant Ragwort, which grows in
open and waste spaces.   Its tall form and bright yellow flowers
have a striking effect when seen in the mass.   It grows in abundance
in Brightlingsea now, and may be seen to perfection in July in the
small field immediately east of " Little Lane."   It most probably
grew on this green, which gave its name to the creek.   Navvy or
Navigation Creek lies east of Gandergoose Creek.   Its form and
name suggests that it is artificial.   It joined the upper part of
Gandergoose Creek to Borefleet, and made a more direct route to
Gandergoose Green.

    There is a small fleet extending from Back Waterside Lane, near
the end of the Coastguard Station gardens, to Borefleet, near
Underwood's Hard.   Before the marsh was reclaimed, it must have
been large enough for boats to come up, to discharge on to the lane.
Lynch's Creek lies further up among the present oyster pits.   It
ends close to East End Green, where there are remains of a small
' hard,' from which an old road, now grass-grown, leads to the green,

It takes its name from some land called Lynch's on the green close by. It was formerly of greater depth than now. Evidence was given in a law suit in 1709 that in its shallowest part there was 12 feet depth at high water.[9]

Cock Fleet is a small fleet lying to the eastward of Lynch's Creek.

4. Originally subject to submersion by high tides, the marshes are now in great part protected from the sea by seawalls, which divide them into saltings or 'out marshes,' and fresh marshes or 'in marshes.' The level of the saltings is considerably higher than that of the fresh marshes, having been built up, since the walls were made, by mud deposited by the tides. When they were made is not known. Land is known to have been so reclaimed by the Romans,[10] but it is believed that there are no Roman seawalls in Essex below Purfleet.[11] The Saxons practised the art, and embankments are known to have existed in the immediate neighbourhood between 1152 and 1170.[12] From the difference in level between the salt and the fresh marshes, already mentioned, most of our sea walls must be of considerable age.

The sea-walls on the north are of the most interest, as they are connected with the question of Brightlingsea being formerly an island. The marshes are well below the sea level, and there would be a very wide expanse of water at high tide but for the walls. Now there is a wall right across each end of the marsh, but they are late additions. There were embankments to protect the marshes, but so placed that there was a channel through which the sea could flow. Traces of these old walls and of the channel can be seen still, and are shown on the map. On the Brightlingsea side, only the west part of this marsh was protected. There is little difference between the levels of the salt and fresh marshes here, showing that these walls are not of early date.

5. Springs. The porous cap of sand and gravel on the high ground and the waterproof London clay below form a natural reservoir for the rainfall, the water eventually appearing at the surface near the edge of the London clay in the form of springs. The most important one is that known as "The Spring." The stream from it has cut a deep channel, showing that the volume of water must have been very considerable before well-sinking cultivation and drainage lessened it. The stream flowed across the marshes to the sea. There are remains of a wall along the east side of this fleet as it crosses the fresh marsh. This embankment may have been a protection against the sea, or part of a mill dam.

There are many other springs, the more important being at Hoglane, East End Green, Jewers, The Hall, and Moverons.

## PREHISTORIC.

There was here one of those interesting puzzles, the Red or Burnt hills, which dot the Essex coast. Stevyn Smith, a Brightlingsea mariner, in 1539, left 3*l*. 6*s*. 8*d*. for "the reparacion of the highway from the green to the burnt owe [hoe or hill] for postes and grauells."[3] No burnt hill, so far, has been located here. The bequest indicates that (1) it was not very far from a green, (2) a roadway connected the two, and strongly suggests that the roadway had to be raised to keep it above water. These points and the usual situation of the Red hills give some guide to its situation. Most probably it was on or near the east end of the "Copperas Grounds," a situation with all the essential surroundings of a Red hill. To this there was a way, Back Waterside Lane, leading from Hurst Green. This is not a new way, for in 1766, in the Manor Court, the Jury presented "that a footway from the Hearse to the Copperas office through the land of Nathaniel Wenlock, which ought to be by him repaired is so ruinous and out of repair as to be a common Nusance, and he is ordered to repair the same." Before the sea-wall was made this way was liable to be tideswept, and after, the fresh-water stream close by would overflow it, unless it were well raised. This site has been cultivated, ditched, and built on, so that trace of a hill may well be lost. Red hills are low flat mounds of varying size and shape. The earth of which they were made was a red burnt earth, which contained fragments of brick flues and fire bars and of coarse pottery.[14] Of the age and purpose of this Red hill no more can be said than to quote the following general conclusions : "That they date from a remote period, and that some at least are prehistoric is proved by the nature of the pottery contained in them. By some they have been regarded as salt works, by others as cattle shelters, human habitations, potteries or glass factories."

[[1] Fe 2/12.   [2] Hd 37024.   [3] Ei.   [4] Jh 15.   [5] Gca.   [6] Ga cxiii. 85.   [7] Q 152.   [9] Fg.   [10] Ab 11, 16.   [11] At 21.   [12] Q 230.   [13] Eb 2.   [14] Eb 1].

# Chapter II.

## THE TOWNSHIP AND MANOR.

### THE CELTS.

7. The Celts inhabiting. Essex were the Trinobantes, who are believed to have conquered the aboriginal race of the country. To the Celts, or, indeed, to any early settlers, Brightlingsea must have presented many advantages as a residence. First it was an island and, therefore, less easy of attack. The creeks surrounding it were full of fish and oysters. The natural landing places, where the post glacial gravel substitutes firm ground for the treacherous mud, were few and so more easily protected, making raids by enemies difficult. Before the sea-walls were made, at high water when the marsh was submerged, they must have jutted out like piers from the land. The one, where the Hard now is, had the additional advantage of being in a creek making a good harbour. That at the Ford had the same advantage.

We may fairly assume that there were two fordable places, one where the Ford now is, and where a gravel deposit provides firm ground, and the other at the gravel deposit where the creek between Brightlingsea and Thorington was narrowest and shallowest, and where the main road now crosses the boundary. There was an ample water supply from springs—a great rarity on the Essex coast. The marsh-land was easily accessible in an almost complete belt round the higher land.

The Celts did not group the habitations of each village close together. They scattered them singly or in several small groups.[1] There was no inducement here for concentration at any one point. By spreading the holdings round the edge of the higher land, they would have easy access to the marshes for grazing, a matter of first importance to them—a pastoral people. Again, concentration at one point would mean leaving one or other of the landing places unwatched and unprotected.

### THE ROMANS.

8. The Romans, under Claudius, in A.D. 43, overcame Essex and established a colony at Camulodunum (Colchester). Roman villas then appeared in the neighbourhood. Dr. H. Laver has drawn attention to the existence of the remains of one at Noah's Ark. Tesserae [small pavement tiles] and bricks have been found

here, but there has been no complete excavation. Probably another villa was placed between the old waterworks and the "Spring," since a collection of Roman red Samian and other pottery, roof tiles, flue tiles, *etc.*, was dug up in Well Street in 1888,[2] and a similar find was made in Spring Road near the "Spring" in 1900. The sites for these villas were well chosen. Each had a spring close by, pleasant surroundings, and was within easy reach of the sea. Whether they were the summer residences of some wealthy Roman or permanent homes cannot be said. A Roman villa was more than a house : it included an estate and its buildings. Perhaps the one near the "Spring" was the home of some official of the Saxon Shore. It would then as now make an excellent look-out station. As a military station the Noah's Ark site was excellent as it commanded the river where it begins to narrow and protected the landing places near. Noah's Ark got its name from a collier so called which was carried over the sea-wall by a north-west gale and an exceptionally high tide, and left high and dry close to Aldborough Point. She was not worth the expense of getting into the water, so windows and doors were fitted and she was used as a cottage. The present cottage retains the name.

The Saxon Shore was that part of Britain under the rule of a high official called Comes Litoris Saxoni, *i.e.* Count of the Saxon Shore. It consisted of the coast from Brancaster on the Wash to the Portus Adurni at the mouth of the river Adur in Sussex.[3] It was so called because its organisation was directed against the attacks of the Saxon raiders, and to keeping in order those Saxons or their allies who made settlements with or without Roman consent on this shore.

There were nine stations scattered along the Saxon Shore holding garrisons for the protection of the coast. Of these stations, Othona has been placed at Bradwell-on-Sea, West Mersea, or Brightlingsea, but there can be no doubt that it was in Bradwell.

[¹ Bp 15.   ² Bg 57.   ³ Ab 23.]

## THE ANGLO-SAXONS.

9. As soon as the Romans left (in A.D. 420) the Anglo-Saxons, and their allies began that series of invasions which ended in the conquest of Britain. By 537 Essex was so far conquered and settled by the Saxons for the kingdom of the East Saxons to be founded. The invaders usually came in tribes, each having a real or supposed common ancestor, from whom it took its name. Brihtlingas was the name of the tribe believed to have given Brightlingsea

its name. Brightlingsea means the island belonging to a Saxon tribe called the Brihtlingas or Brightlings. Kemble has advanced the theory that where there is a place-name ending in *ing* and another place-name similiar but with a suffix, the latter place was peopled by an offshoot of the tribe giving its name to the former.[2] On this theory, the Brightlings of Brightlingsea in Essex were an offshoot of the Brightlings who gave their name to the place called Brightling in Sussex. Wapping possibly got its name from a tribe or part of a tribe of Wæppingas.[3] If so, it could only have been a small settlement relatively.

The houses of an Anglo-Saxon village were placed usually in a compact group.[4] But here the same considerations which would encourage the Celts to spread their holdings over the island, would influence the Anglo-Saxons in the same way. There is some corroboration that such was so. First the name does not definitely indicate the existence of a typical Anglo-Saxon village by calling it Brightlington. There is the suggestion of the settlement of a tribe at Wapping already mentioned. Moverons was described as Moverons, otherwise Morehams, and Moverons, otherwise Morehous.[5] The 's' of Morehams may mean that a man named Moreham once owned it, or it may have got there by mistake.

Morehous suggests a Saxon's homestead, and possibly is derived from *mor*, a hill and *hus* a house. If the 's' of Morhams is a mistake, then ham is the Saxon *ham*, a house or village. The house or village on the hill is an apt enough name for such, where Moverons stand. At Aldborough Point there is a field called Aldborough. Ald is probably Saxon, meaning old, while borough is the Saxon *burh*. A burh was a Saxon fortified place, a castle, town, village, or house. Whether village or dwelling house, it was placed there to protect the landing place and the river. The name old burh suggests a new burh, but there is no indication where it was, if it did exist.

. There are other indications of habitations near this part. Quantities of oyster shells have been turned up by the plough in two fields between Aldborough and Moverons, suggesting the kitchen middens of some ancient houses.

If all these sites were the only places of settlement, we may be sure from their names that the island would never have been called Brightlingsea. The chief settlement or settlements of the Brightlingas must have been in some other part of the island. The invaders with their larger vessels would prefer Borefleet to Alresford Creek. It was nearer the sea. It was wider, deep enough to float their vessels at any state of the tide, and there would not be much trouble in making a landing place to serve at low water. Their chief settlement, probably, was at, or near, what we now call Brightlingsea town.

10. There was a considerable Celtic population left in Essex after the Saxon invasion, and there were enough points in common between the Celtic and Saxon social systems to make a fusion of the two races easy. On the question of this fusion in Brightlingsea, the custom of the manor in the inheritance of copyhold land throws some light. The custom is Borough English or junior right with a variation. In Borough English the youngest son inherits, and the widow has dower, *i.e.* possession of a third or sometimes the whole of the land for life.[6] In Brightlingsea, the youngest son and failing sons, the youngest daughter inherits, but the widow has no dower.[7] The Celtic custom was equal division among the male heirs, no inheritance by daughters, and no dower for the widow.[8] Thus the custom here is in form partly Celtic and partly non-Celtic. Inheritance by the youngest son is not found among the Angles nor Saxons, nor in Scandinavia.[9] The Angle and Saxon rule did not allow daughters to inherit.[10]

11. Junior right was Sclavonic in origin and we must go to "Eastern Germany, to old Slavic lands and German territories, which were influenced by Slavs as the source, or sources, of English junior right."[11] The Frisians were influenced by the Slavs, as is shown in their language, and, among some of them, junior right was the custom.[12] The Wends, who inhabited the south shore of the Baltic, as far as the Vistula, in what is now Pomerania, were Slavs, and among them junior right was the custom.[13] A Frisian tribe might have introduced junior right into Brightlingsea, as they were allies of the Saxons. The Wends, too, were allies of the Saxons, and were well-known as sea-rovers.[14] They were a dark complexioned people,[14] while the Frisians were fair. With the exception of a distinct type of fair men, few in number, and judging from their names of relatively recent introduction, Brightlingsea people are markedly dark complexioned.

The surmise that the custom of inheritance here contains Celtic and Slavonic elements, and that there was a fusion of Celtic and Wendish tribes after the Saxon Conquest fits the facts fairly well. In any case the Brightlingsea folk are an interesting study as they are distinguished sharply from the people of the neighbouring villages.

12. Under Saxon rule there were, most probably, ten families settled in Brightlingsea.[16] The Saxon family, like the Celtic, meant a large family, including even more than married sons and

daughters. Each family would possess a hide,[17] that is a tenement consisting of a homestead, as many acres—usually 120 acres—in the arable fields as a team of eight oxen could plough in a year, a share in the meadow land and in grazing and other rights over the waste land.[18] The arable fields were tilled co-operatively, and the acre strips belonging to each hide were scattered here and there over the fields, and were re-allotted each year.[19] Thus, the strips belonging to one hide one year were held by another hide the next. Not only were the holdings equal in size, but advantage due to peculiarity of soil or situation came to each in turn. The fields were usually cultivated on the two or three field system. In the former, there was an alternate succession of crops and fallow. In the latter, one field was sown with winter corn—wheat; one with spring corn—oats or barley; and one was left fallow.[20] Allowing land to lie fallow was a substitute for manuring.[20] Which system was in use here in Saxon times cannot be said.

From the above it will be seen that the individual tiller had to follow the same routine as the rest.[22] When the seed had been sown, the acres were fenced to keep out the cattle. After the crop was harvested, the fences were taken down and the field was made common pasture until the next crop was sown. The meadow, precious since in the absence of root crops, hay was the only winter keep, was dealt with in a similar manner. When the grass began to grow it was divided into equal strips, each household having an equal number of strips allotted to it each year. They were fenced in until the hay was carried, and then made common pasture until the grass began to grow. The wood was common, whether for feeding pigs on the mast and acorn, or for cutting wood for house-building, fencing, *etc.* The turf was common to cut and dry for fuel. Except for the small closes connected with the homesteads and the land actually under crop, the cattle could roam where they would over the land.

A man might have his house apart from the rest in a remote part of the waste land, and then he had his arable and meadow by his house, in place of a share in the common field and meadow.[23] His share in the use of the waste would be unaffected.

The men of the village met in the village moot to settle local affairs, such as the rotation of crops, the allotment of the acre strips, or the admission of a newcomer into the community.[24]

[¹ Bh i. 459. ² Bh i. 479. ³ Bh i. 476. ⁴ Bp 15. ⁵ No 27. ⁶ Ej iv. 64. ⁷ Ak ii. 770. ⁸ Cg 373-4. ⁹ Cg 149-50. ¹⁰ Cg 159. ¹¹ Cg 151. ¹² Cg 148. ¹³ Cg 149. ¹⁴ Cg 104. ¹⁶ At 434, Ay 290, 313. ¹⁷ Bi 458. ¹⁸ Ca 150 *seq.* ¹⁹ Ca 175-6. ²⁰ Ca 182. ²² Ca 166. ²³ Ci i. 55-6. ²⁴ Ci. i. 90.]

## The Beginning of the Manor.

13. The tribal system decayed, and ideas of private ownership of land grew. Instead of a family holding a hide, individuals began to hold portions of one, but the communal idea was kept up. The portions held corresponded to the oxen of the eight ox team which the holder contributed to the team. Thus the man who contributed four held the land corresponding to four oxen or half a hide. The system of common fields and waste described was not altered.

Grants of larger portions of lands, even villages, were made by the king to private persons or monasteries. The land not so granted was considered the people's land, and so called, folkland. In time the king was considered lord of all land without a lord, and of all men without a lord. The folkland then became royal or ancient demesne manors.

14. The royal manors did not develope quite in the same way as the ordinary manors. The men of a royal manor retained their ancient position as freemen. They paid tribute to the king in the shape of *feorm* or food rents, a custom handed down from Celtic days.[2] The king making progresses through his kingdom, visited his demesne villages, and consumed the food provided for him and retinue by his men there.[3] All the available evidence points to Brightlingsea having been folkland, on which the subsequent manor was from the first a royal one. The king's tenants here paid a yearly tribute of two nights feorm, that is, they found provisions for the king and his retinue during a stay of two days and nights every year. What was provided here we do not know, but in the seventh century ten hides—at which Brightlingsea was assessed —provided 10 dolia of honey, 300 loaves, 12 amphora (72 gallons) of Welsh ale, 30 amphora (180 gallons) of clear ale, 2 oxen or 10 wethers, 10 geese, 20 hens, 10 cheeses, 1 full amphora of butter, 5 salmon of 20 pounds weight, and 100 eels.[4] At a later date the food was sent to the king. This meant a central place where the provender could be stored till wanted,[1] which might be merely a storehouse or a hall or manor house. The king was not likely to have had a residence here, but the hall would be a residence for his steward, with a storehouse, farm buildings, and the land forming the demesne attached to it.[5] The demesne in a royal manor was not so important in Saxon days, as the food rents supplied the produce, which the demesne would otherwise have supplied.

15. At first, the labour required on the king's demesne was obtained from slaves. In the tenth century, and earlier, it became customary for a lord of a manor to settle tenants on his land, giving

them each, usually, a virgate (30 acres), two oxen (the necessary contribution of a virgate to the plough team), two cows, six sheep, and seed for seven acres. He was also to have tools for his work, and utensils for his house. When he died the lord took back what he left.[6] This land might be an original holding, fallen into the lord's hands, or a part of the waste newly taken into cultivation. As long as there was enough waste left for the common use, it was an advantage to both lord and tenants to increase the number of the latter. In return, this tenant, called a gebur, worked on the demesne as a rule, two days a week, and in harvest time, and from Candlemas to Easter, three days a week. He also had to make small payments in kind and money.[7] Some of the land, too, was held by cottiers. They generally had five acres of land, and generally had to work for their lord one day a week, and three days a week in harvest.[8]

The king sometimes made a loan of land on his demesne for the term of a life or lives to a thane as a reward for special military services.[9] Moverons was perhaps so loaned. The ownership of a bell house or mansion was a mark of a thane.[10] Bellhouse was the name of two cottages which stood in Bellfield, near Bell Green. This name might arise from a thane's house. The fact that the land adjoining is part of the lord's demesne lends a little colour to the idea.

Speaking generally, in the Saxon period there was a gradual growth of the manorial system, in which the influence and power of a lord was superimposed on a village community, but which did not destroy it. In the case of Brightlingsea, as in other royal manors, this subjection was modified and delayed.

[[1] Ca 224.  [2] Ca 28.  [3] At 366, 434.  [4] Bi 213.  [5] Ca 225.  [6] Bi 133.  [7] Bi 131-2.  [8] Bi 131.  [9] Bi 168.  [10] Ed ii. 1.]

## THE DANES.

As they attacked St. Osyth and Colchester, it is not likely that they omitted Brightlingsea, though there is no evidence that they ever came here. Speed, in his History of England (p. 331), states that the Danes, after their defeat by Alfred at the battle of Farnham, in 894, fled " ouer Thamesis in passing whereof through ouermuch haste and great feere many of them were drowned and they that escaped fled to an Iland called Breklesey inclosed about by the river Colne." They occupied the island for some time, but Alfred's men " not having any vessels there, could not lay siege to the place, especially as victuals failed them." Morant considered that it was Mersea to which they fled. A careful consideration of the various

accounts of this event and the map bears out Lingard in identifying
the island with Thorney, an island enclosed by the Colne dividing
Bucks from Middlesex.[1]   The only trace of Danish influence here
is the —ness of Borefleetness (West Marsh Point).

[¹ Cj 215.]

## THE NORMAN CONQUEST.

William the Conqueror in 1086 sent commissioners into every
county to obtain information about the taxable property.   From
each township six men were sent to assist in giving the information.
The result was arranged in the MS. volumes known as Domesday
book.   The smaller volume contains the part for Essex, and
Brightlingsea heads the list of the king's lands in Tendring Hundred.
Most of the information is given for three dates, 1066 (before Harold
succeeded Edward), referred to as 'then,' 1086, referred to as 'now,'
and 'afterwards,' when William obtained the manor on Harold's
defeat at the battle of Hastings.

From the entry[1] we learn that Harold held Brightlingsea as a
manor and as ten hides.   In Domesday book it is customary to
ignore Harold as king of England; here he is Harold in contrast
with King William, who follows him as owner of the manor.   As
Edward the Confessor is not mentioned as holding any manors in
Essex, it has been suggested that he did not hold any.   Incidental
references show that some of Harold's manors had been royal
manors.   Havering is described as Harold's, but a reference to it in
another part describes it as the king's manor in King Edward's time.
There is a similar reference to Writtle, another of Harold's manors.
As regards Brightlingsea, the evidence that it was a royal manor or
ancient demesne of the Crown is in the two nights 'feorm' (or farm)
rendered by the manor.   "This archaic system of providing feorm
for the household was normally characteristic of ancient demesne
of the Crown."[2]   Brightlingsea had another peculiarity found in
Essex royal manors; it had an outlying estate or berewick in
another county, joining with it in providing the provisions for the
two nights farm.   The joint produce was worth 25l, but by 1086 it
had been divided, Brightlingsea's share apparently becoming 22l,
and the berewick paying separately.   The berewick was Harkstead,
on the north shore of the estuary of the Stour.

Brightlingsea was held for ten hides, that is, it was assessed at
that number of hides for taxation.   It does not mean that there
were ten hides of land in Brightlingsea then.   Brightlingsea is one
of the few Essex manors which show the five hide system discovered
by Mr. J. Horace Round.[3]   The ancient system was to assess

places as five hides or in multiples of five. When a place was divided, naturally the assessment was divided too; hence only those places which remained intact show this system. A correspondence would be expected between the provisions found (the food rent) and the assessment. Of the five Essex manors paying this farm or food rent, Brightlingsea and Lawford, showing their intact character by their assessment being ten hides, provided two nights farm each. The other three show neither the five hide system nor any correspondence between the assessment and the farm.

18. Usually in Essex, Domesday book shows an increase between 1066 and 1086 in the bordars, but a decrease in the villeins and serfs,[4] Here the bordars increased from ten to twenty-six, and the serfs increased from four to five, but the villeins remained the same in number (twenty-four). The villeins included most probably some men who were personally free, villein socmen or customary free tenants, and who corresponded to the food-rent paying tenants of the Saxon manor, others probably were villeins doing services for their holdings, corresponding to the Saxon gebur. The bordars apparently represented the Saxon cottier, and probably held about 15 acres, though sometimes less.[5] It is supposed that they were employed largely on the demesne for wages, which made up for their small holdings. The ten bordars who held no land are unusual; I believe there is only one other instance in Essex, at Leigh, where there were " five bordars by the water (*super aquam*) who hold no land." Mr. Round suggests that judging from the latter instance, these landless Brightlingsea bordars may possibly "represent a maritime element."[6] The serfs were slaves, and as such were the lord's property; they lived on the demesne and had charge of the demesne plough teams. Usually there were in Essex two to each team, but the numbers of teams and serfs here do not show such a proportion.[7] Possibly the landless bordars just mentioned lived on the demesne and performed similar services to the slaves.

19. The lord had, in 1066, three ploughs on his demesne and two in 1086, and the men (the tenants) had, in 1066, sixteen ploughs between them and eleven in 1086. The reduction in number is one-third of the demesne ploughs, and a fraction over a third of the men's ploughs. The decrease could not be for want of men to look after the ploughs, for the men had increased. Possibly the disturbances due to the Conquest led to a loss of the oxen necessary for the ploughs. The plough here mentioned was the heavy plough needing a team of eight oxen.[8] It does not follow that ploughs with smaller teams were not used. When they were they were

treated for the purposes of the survey as parts of the large team.
The number of plough teams is the index of the amount of arable
land, since no more land could be ploughed than there were teams
to do it, nor would anyone keep more teams than he had land for
them to plough. The estimated amount of land that the eight-ox
team ploughed in a year was 120 acres. There must have been
more than 360 acres of arable on the demesne, for the men's ploughs
would help the demesne ploughs. How much the men's teams
ploughed on the demesne cannot be said, nor can the amount they
were able to do for themselves. But the total can be given. As
there were, in 1066, nineteen ploughs, so the amount of arable land
was 2280 acres. There are about 770 statute acres of marsh land
now in Brightlingsea, leaving 2100 statute acres of land available
for ploughing. There was not enough land for nineteen teams if
the statute acre was the measure, even when leaving out all land
occupied by houses, woods, roads, *etc*. We may safely conclude
that the acre then was not as large as the modern statute acre.

The wood was measured by the number of pigs (one hundred)
which could be fed on the acorns and mast in it. Swine were then
very important stock, and the lord of a manor received payment
known as pannage for the privilege of feeding swine in the woods.

There was a corn mill, almost certainly driven by water. The
only stream at all likely to provide enough water was the brook
formed by the "Spring," but it was quite likely a tidal mill, in
which the mill pond was filled by the flood tide.

By the pasture for the sheep is meant the marshes. Probably
the hundred by which the sheep were reckoned was the long
hundred of one hundred-and-twenty,[9] in which case there was
pasture for seven hundred-and twenty. Cheese was made from the
ewes' milk.[10] The dairies in which it was made are represented by
the 'wicks' which dot the Essex Coast.[11] Probably "Wicks
Wood" gets its name from one.

The live stock mentioned (sixteen beasts, five rounceys, one
hundred-and-sixty-six sheep, and sixty-two swine) was on the
demesne, and the same in number in 1066 and 1086. The beasts
are considered to have been oxen other than for draught.[12] Rounceys were draught horses. The number of ploughs and stock on
the demesne shows that it had become of considerable size, indicating a development of the manorial system from the early Saxon
days when the food rents entirely took the place of the demesne.

At the end of the entry there is the sentence: "In the demesne
are 4 beasts and 5 swine." If this stock were on the Brightlingsea
demesne then the stock already mentioned belonged to the men.

This would be something quite new in the Essex Domesday, where stock mentioned is always taken to be on the demesne, and sometimes it is expressly stated to be so; the men's stock not being mentioned. These four beasts and five swine are about the number found on the demesne of a very small manor or estate and are far too few for a demesne of three ploughs. It cannot apply to Harkstead, as the numbers do not correspond with those given for Harkstead in the Suffolk Domesday. The simplest explanation is that this is the end of the entry of another manor, the rest being omitted unintentionally, or, more likely, of another manor or estate belonging to Brightlingsea. Accepting such an explanation there might be some such words as these:—" In Brightlingsea there is 1 hide which was held in King Edward's time by . . . . now King William holds it. Then as now 1 villein, then 2 bordars now 3. Then and now ½ plough on the demesne and the men have ½ plough. Pasture for 20 sheep. It is worth 20s. which is included in the above valuation. In the demesne are 4 beasts and 5 swine."

The following is a translation of the entry as given in Mr. J. Horace Round's article on Domesday in the *Victoria County History of Essex* (vol. i.).

" Brictriceseia was held by Harold as a manor and as 10 hides. Now King William (holds it). Then as now *(semper)* 24 villeins. Then 10 bordars; afterwards 11; now 16 bordars; and 10 bordars who hold no land. Then 4 serfs; now 5. Then 3 ploughs on the demesne; afterwards and now 2. Then the men had 16 ploughs; afterwards and now 11. (There is) wood (land) for 100 swine. (There is) now 1 mill. Pasture for 600 sheep. Then as now (there were) 16 beasts *(animalia)* and 5 rounceys (runcini) and 166 sheep and 62 swine. Then Brictriceseia and Herchesteda [Harkstead] between them rendered 2 nights' ferm *(noctes de firma)* and when P[eter] received them 25 pounds; now 22 pounds. But that outlying estate *(berewite)* lies in Suffolk. In the demesne are 4 beasts *(animalia)* and 5 swine."

[¹ At 434.  ² At 336.  ³ At 338.  ⁴ At 359, 362.  ⁵ At 361.  ⁶ At 434, 532
⁷ At 361.  ⁸ At 365.  ⁹ At 309.  ¹⁰ At 369-71.  ¹¹ At 369.  ¹² At 367.]

### EUDO DAPIFER AND THE ABBEY OF ST. JOHN'S,
### LORDS OF THE MANOR.

20. How long after 1086 Brightlingsea remained a royal manor is not known, Unless William II.'s charter to St. John's Abbey in 1096 is spurious,¹ it was by that date the property of Eudo de Rie, or Eudo Dapifer—(the Steward), as he was generally called. He

was a favourite of William I. who made him steward of his household and gave him many manors. He retained the favour of
William II. and Henry I. He founded the Abbey of Saint John the
Baptist in Colchester, and gave the Abbey the manor of Brightlingsea. When he made the gift is not clear. There is the charter of
William II. which confirms the gift;[1] a later charter of Henry I. in
confirming Eudo's gifts to the Abbey omits Brightlingsea,[2] while it
is said that Eudo made the grant of Brightlingsea on his death-bed,
in late 1119 or early 1120.[3] It appears that he had some trouble
with the monks and the endowments of the Abbey,[4] and he may
have had taken possession of Brightlingsea again and regranted it.
In any case, the Abbot and Convent, that is, the Abbot and Monks
of the Abbey of St. John the Baptist at Colchester, more conveniently
referred to as the Abbot, held the position of Lord of the manor in
1119, and their possession of it was repeatedly confirmed to them by
royal charter.

When lord of the manor, the king must have had a court in
which criminal and manorial business was done, Eudo Dapifer, too,
must have had a similar court, but it is of the Abbot's court that we
have definite information. At this time (twelfth century) manor
courts were not divided into court leet, court baron, and customary
court, as they were later. The business pertaining to the three
was done in one court. The criminal jurisdiction of the court was
the result of the custom begun in Saxon times of giving the lord of
a manor the profits of some of the criminal jurisdiction over the
men of his manor. This naturally led, in time, to the proceedings
being taken in the lord's own court instead of in the hundred court.
Those who managed the hundred court could not be expected to do
the work and someone else take the profit. The Abbot had grants
of the profits of jurisdiction over many offences in Brightlingsea.
He had the right to hold courts (sac and soc) ; the right to the fines
paid for,—neglecting to serve with the fyrd (the national army)
(feardwite), neglecting to serve as watch or ward (weardwite),
taking provisions in fairs and markets before the king's pur-
veyors are served with necessaries for him (forfeng), assault on
the highway (foresteall), bribery (feofeng), bringing an unjust action
in law (miskenning), and breach of the peace in a man's house
(hamsokna).[5] In Anglo-Saxon law a breach of the peace in a man's
house was a more serious offence than if committed off such
premises ; there was the additional offence of breaking the owner's
house peace.[6] The Abbot was given power to punish thieves, who
robbed and were taken in Brightlingsea (infangthef).[5] If they
escaped from his possessions he could not capture them. The

abbot could hang the thief on his own gallows. If the culprit was a woman she was buried alive.[7] The goods and chattels of thieves became the Abbot's, as did those of fugitives from justice.[5]

21. We get a reminder in some of these jurisdictions of an outstanding feature of pre-Conquest law, the association of men into groups of ten as sureties for each other's good behaviour. It was the business of the hundred court every half-year to see that all males of twelve years and upwards were placed in these groups. Each group of ten was called a tithing and had a headman, a "capital pledge" or "tithingman." If one broke the law, the other nine had to produce him, or prove that they had no part in his escape, or pay compensation for the harm done.[8] The Abbot had the grant of "frythsokna" which entitled him to place his Brightlingsea men into tithings in his court, and he took the fines and a share of the compensation paid for default under this system (burh bryce).[9] Putting the men into these tithings was called the "view of Frankpledge." Arising out of the same idea of joint responsibility was the fine paid to the Abbot when a felon escaped from prison, by those responsible for him (uthleap),[9] and when a thief was hanged without judgment (hengwite).[9]

In Anglo-Saxon law a man's life was valued according to his rank; a proportional sum of money called his 'were' was payable by the murderer or those responsible for him. The Abbot had a grant of "weargyldweof,"[9] apparently a right to the royal portion of this 'were.'

Trade was a source of profit to the Abbot. Fairs were the principal source from which people obtained those things they could not supply themselves. He had the right of taking tolls in fairs on goods sold (toll)[10] and payment for permission to remove goods bought in Brightlingsea to where the purchaser wished (hleastings).[10] His rights in the fair were protected. Merchant strangers wishing to expose goods for sale had to pay for permission to do so (sceawinge).[10] Thus there was no chance of evading the fair dues by bringing goods at other times.

These privileges were granted by Henry I. to the Abbot to have "on land and in water, and in city and without, in house and without, in town and without."[11]

The abbot claimed in 1274 to hold pleas of "namare vetito" A lord of a manor might order his bailiff to distrain on the goods or property in another manor. If the lord of that manor forbade the distress, the distrainer might demand satisfaction for the injury. This franchise gave the Abbot the right to deal with a case in his own court, and incidentally to make a profit out of it.[12]

B

22. The Abbot had other privileges in Brightlingsea as regards
the harsh forest laws. The forest of Essex was made to include the
whole of the county, probably by William I. Part, if not the whole,
of Tendring Hundred was disafforested by Stephen,[12] but was
afforested afresh by Henry II.[13]  In 1228 it was held to be outside
the forest, but, in 1250, Henry III. had foresters and other forest
officials in Tendring Hundred. It appears that, in 1277 and 1292,
the crown still claimed Tendring Hundred as part of the forest of
Essex.[14]  However, royal grants freed the Abbot's lands from the
forest law. In Brightlingsea, the Abbot and his men might hunt
and take in his demesne the beasts and birds of the warren,[15]
usually held to be the hare, rabbit, fox, pheasant, partridge, and
woodcock.[16]  The cat was included here, for in Henry III.'s
charter (1253) permission was given to hunt it in Brightlingsea.[17]
This grant of "free warren" prohibited any one from hunting in the
Abbot's land without his permission under a penalty of ten pounds.[18]
A special privilege allowed the Abbot to keep greyhounds *(canes
leporarii)* for taking hares in his warrens for the use of the infirm
monks.[19]  These hounds are believed to have been more like a
deerhound than the modern greyhound.[20]  He and his men might
also keep "unlawed" dogs.[19]  All dogs in or near the forests had to
have the three claws of each fore-foot cut off (called lawing), to prevent
them chasing the game.[21]  If the Abbot's hounds, in hunting the
hare, the fox, or the cat, went beyond the bounds of the warren,
and took nothing beyond, he was not to be fined.[22]  The Abbot, and
the monks, were "to be quit of vexations of foresters if of their
wood they should take anything."[23]  Apparently, this means that if
they took any game (in their wood) which was not classed as of the
warren, they were not to be fined.

[[1] Q 18.  [2] Q 4.  [3] Q xviii.  [4] Q xv.  [5] Q 10, Ee ferdwit, forfeng, miskenning, hamsoken, Cn foresteal, R wardwite.  [6] Bp 99.  [7] Br i. 12.  [8] Ci i. 94 *seq*.
[9] Q 10.  [10] Q 10, Ee toll, lastage, scavage.  [11] Q 11.  [12] E 163, Ee vetitum
namium.  [13] Q 32.  [14] Ao 25-7.  [15] Ap 26.  [17] Q 56.  [18] Ap 3.  [19] Q 20-1.
[20] Ap 48.  [21] Ap. 47.  [22] Q 56.  [23] Q 45.]

## THE NORMAN MANOR.

23. After the Conquest, the process of manorial development
ended in the complete subjection of the peasant class to the power
of their lords. The four classes, ceorls, geburs, bordars, or cottiers,
and slaves found on Saxon manors in Edward the Confessor's time
were fused into one class of villeins.[1]

The lord of a manor in legal theory owned the bodies of the villein, his wife and children, his land, his cattle, in fact all he had was his lord's. If he left the manor he could be brought back again. He held his land at the will of his lord, and the quantity and quality of the services he rendered to his lord could be varied by the latter.[2] When he married his daughter, or made his son a clerk, he had to pay a fine. He had no remedy against his lord in a law court, as his lord could plead, as a bar to the action, " that the plaintiff is my villein and I need not answer him."[3] But for custom which smoothed some of the legal harshness, the villein would have had a very poor time of it.

In the manor of Brightlingsea, this development was arrested. It had been a royal or ancient demesne manor, but when it came into private hands it ceased to be royal but continued an ancient demesne manor. As tenants in ancient demesne, the villeins of Brightlingsea had very important privileges. No one could deprive them of their lands. Their services were fixed, their lord could not vary them at will.[4] They were protected against their lord by special writs, which enabled the case to be removed to the royal courts. A plaint was made first to the king, and he issued a little writ close or writ of *monstraverunt* directed to the bailiff of the manor.[5] The plaintiff then sued his lord in what had been the king's court, but which was now the lord's manorial court; from there " the process could be taken up to the public courts and went on under their inspection." Thus, though they held in villeinage, they were free from the worst features of villeinage, and were personally free. Strictly, these privileges only applied to villeins holding land which had been villein land in 1066, villein holdings created later being excluded; but this distinction was not always enforced.[6]

24. Other privileges came to Brightlingsea men as being tenants in ancient demesne. They were free from toll in all markets and custom houses. They were free from enforced attendance at the County Court of Essex (not to be confused with the modern County Court) and the Hundred Moot of Tendring. They were not assessed with the rest of the county for danegeld, nor with the hundred for the murder fine. They were exempt from the sheriff's jurisdiction, and did not serve on juries and assizes before the king's justices. As they were not taxed with the county, they had no representatives in the early parliaments.[7] When the king taxed the tenants of the royal manors, the tenants of Brightlingsea could be taxed in the same proportion, but the Abbot took the tax, not the king.[8] If a villein escaped from a manor, and resided for a year and a day in Brightlingsea, he became free, and his lord could not claim

him, nor enforce his return to the manor.[9] It was customary in
ancient demesne manors for the court to decide as to the admission
of strangers.[10]

The steward of the manor representing the lord was president of
the Manor court, which was held every three weeks.[11] All freeholders, villeins, and cottagers had to attend the court, and were
fined if absent without valid excuse. Each "capital pledge" would
bring his tithing. The court might have been held in the hall of
the manor, in the nave of the church, or in the open air,

[[1] Bz 132.  [2] Bz 77.  [3] Bz 46.  [4] Bz 89.  [5] Bz 94, 102.  [6] Bz 114.  [7] Bz 92.
[8] Bz 93.  [9] Bz 86.  [10] Bz 117.  [11] Hd 19985.]

## THE TENANTS' SERVICES.

25.  The freeholders paid a rent to the lord for their lands. The
freeholders of Brightlingsea paid, in addition, an "aid" of 2s. to the
lord every third year.[1] In harvest time, the freeholders came to the
Abbot's demesne farm, and helped in the work. This was considered
a concession, and so was called bean, or boon work. In return, the
abbot gave the workers a meal or meals.[2]

The statute *Extenta Manerii* required lords to make detailed
accounts of their manors. A list of the tenants of this manor
exists giving details of their holdings and services. It is part of
such an extent probably.[3] It is not dated, but may be assigned to
a date about 1300.

From it we learn that Geoffrey Snow held a 'native' tenement
called Snows. For it he had to plough each year on the demesne
farm 2 acres for wheat, 2 for fallow (the field which was to lie
fallow each year was ploughed), and 2 for oats. For each acre
ploughed he was to have the reward for "two works." If he
neglected to do so he paid 6d. for each acre unploughed. He had
to do also on the demesne farm each week except two weeks at
Christmas, a week at Easter and at Whitsuntide, two works, as
follows. He might have to thresh and winnow three bushels of rye,
four of wheat, four of barley, level measure or one quarter of
oats, each counting as one work. If he did hedging, haymaking,
straightening straw for thatching, carrying water for thatching, or
hoeing, he was credited with one work, for each half day he was so
employed. He might be called by the bailiff or other minister of
the manor to come to the farm with a horse, cart, and man to cart
manure on to the field *(extra campum)*.

He had to reap in autumn, 2 acres of rye or 2 of oats, without
receiving any allowance. This service was called "Gavelrep."

He had also to reap through the whole autumn while the Abbot had corn standing on the Brightlingsea demesne, half-an-acre of rye or half-an-acre of oats a working day, if required to do so. He had an allowance of two works for each acre reaped. These allowances or rewards for work done were payments in food most probably.

The Abbot had three meadows in Brightlingsea called Newemad, Melnemad, and Herboldmad. Certain customary tenants had to mow on these meadows when it should please the lord, and not otherwise, nor anywhere else. They were not allowed to count this as 'works' but had in lieu, the second best sheep in the abbot's fold at that time, and the second best cheese in the dairy house without anything to pay for them. They were to have a cartload of brushwood and the large room in that house *(moot)* in which the cheese was made. The wood, no doubt, was to cook the mutton with, and they had the room in which to enjoy the feast.

He had to carry with a man and horse any Sunday a year, if need should be, from this manor to the Abbey, Greenstead, or Weeley (possessions of the abbey), three bushels of rye, four bushels of wheat, three bushels of barley, or six bushels of oats, which had grown on the Brightlingsea demesne. For each carrying he was to have sufficient bread *(panem coquinam)* and ale for his 'levener' *(jentaculo)*. Every year he found four bushels of oats as foddercorn, that is, as fodder for the Abbot's palfrey's or horses, at the Feast of the Purification (February 2nd). He also gave the Abbot twenty-five hen's eggs at Easter, and 8s. of silver a year at the four terms of the year in equal portions.

26. Many of the customary tenant's services were lighter. John Gor held a messuage called Maundeviles, for which he did similar services, but did not plough, carry manure, nor carry to Colchester, Greenstead nor Weeley. He gave two bushels of oats as foddercorn, five eggs and 6d. a year.

John atte Forde held a tenement once Alice atte Fordes. He hoed for seven half days and reaped in autumn 3½ acres of oats without receiving any allowance. He came to the lord's meadows with his own fork to make hay, to the lord's farm *(firmar')* with his own fork to fill the carts with manure when summoned. He rendered 20d. and five eggs a year.

John Schypman held a messuage and one acre once Richard atte Ford's. He came to the lord's field with his own rake to spread manure *(simos extra carriare)* and to the lord's meadows to gather the hay when summoned. Any one Sunday in the year he carried a load on his back from the manor to the Abbey, Greenstead or

Weeley, if the lord pleased.   He received for this sufficient bread
and ale for his ' levener.'

Three tenants had only to fill the lord's carts with manure and
make hay.   Seventeen other tenants in addition paid two eggs
instead of ploughing 2 acres.   Four tenants spread manure and
gathered hay for the lord as John Schypman did, but did not carry
to the Abbey, etc.   Many of the tenants did not work for the lord,
but rendered foddercorn, eggs and a money payment, while others
rendered eggs and money, and some money only.   Eight bushels
was the largest and half a bushel the smallest amount of oats
rendered as foddercorn.   Twenty-eight eggs was the most paid,
while one tenant paid one third of a hen's egg, this fraction was
the result of dividing a small holding.   One tenant rendered a hen
and a pullet at Christmas, and another a capon at Easter.   The
Abbot received yearly forty-seven-and-a-half bushels of oats, three-
hundred-and-seventy-two eggs at Easter, one hen, one pullet, one
capon, and 12*l.* 10*s.* 7*d.* from his customary tenants besides their
services.   One tenant paid 12*d.* instead of ploughing 2 acres and
another 6*d.* for 1 acre, which they would otherwise have had to
plough free.

27.  The size of the holdings and the services and payments
rendered for them varied very much, but there is a correspondence
between the size of the holding and the renders, when they are
considered together.   If the holding was large and the services
light, the payments are heavy, and *vice versa.*   While some of the
tenants had their work spread over the year, most were required
only at certain times, when the hay was made, or when manure had
to be carried on to the fields.   The small size of so many holdings
explains this partly.   There were only seventeen messuages having
ten or more acres.   The area of some is not mentioned, and they
perhaps should be added.   There were ninety-three messuages and
cottages with less than five acres.   Such small holdings would not
need ploughs, carts, oxen, nor horses.   Hence the simple service
with a fork or rake, instead of ploughing.   For the same reason
the small holder carried a load on his back instead of taking a
larger load on his horse's.   Some of the holdings were as small as
half a rod, and only paid a money rent.   Probably these belonged
to men who went to sea ; they could not cultivate a large holding,
nor give labour services.

Many of the holdings were parts of larger tenements leading to
absence of uniformity in size.   Any opinion as to the size of the
original villein's holding is a point at which it is difficult to arrive.
There are a few holdings of 15 acres and 7½ acres, which suggest

the half and quarter virgate. There were ninety-two customary messuages and tenements and thirty-six cottages; the rest of the one-hundred-and-fifty-three entries were crofts or other small pieces of land. There are given one-hundred-and-four different names of the customary tenants. In some cases where the same name is repeated, it is indicated that it is the same man. In other cases it may be another man of the same name. The customary tenants held not less than 580 acres exclusive of the common land. Three freeholdings were named, one, Moverons, of which the acreage is not given, and two of which the acreage was 10 acres between them.

As regards the work he had to do for the lord, the Brightlingsea customary tenant or villein was very fortunate. It was quite usual for a villein to have to work three days a week for his lord without payment of any kind. The gavelrep most probably represented a Pre-Conquest service in lieu of a portion of rent. The foddercorn too was probably Pre-Conquest in origin. The origin of the light rewarded services probably lies in the Saxon food-rent system which prevailed on this manor till after the Conquest. The food-rent system was not convenient to the Abbot, while the services on the demesne were, and we may well imagine that an agreement was made between the Abbot and his men that the food-rent should be commuted for labour on the demesne and a money rent. The villeins were in a position to bargain and so obtained advantageous terms.

28. Part of the demesne was held by tenants.[3] Nineteen acres of Boardland (land to provide for the lord's table) with seven messuages and cottages were held at yearly rents of from 6d. to 4s. The holdings are described as Longelandscot, Warhous, Cowpers, Godryches, Morgenescroft, Smyths, and Clerks. A field of four acres called Grymes can be identified with part of the demesne by reference to a later MS.[4] Similarly three parcels of a lane (venelle) called Hadeslane or Hadyslane were parts of the demesne and rented for 5d. Parts of a lane being rented as part of the demesne suggests that the Abbot had enclosed part of a roadway and made it his demesne. Probably some of the other land held by money rents was part of the demesne.

The Hall or Manor-house was the centre of the estate, and would have farm buildings, sheds, barns, dovecotes, fishponds, orchards, and gardens around it. Anything like a park round a manor house was unknown then.[5] The Abbot did not reside here, but he or any monks when visiting Brightlingsea would stay in the Manor house, and so would the Steward of the Manor, when he came to preside in the manor court.

The duties of the Steward have been indicated. The Bailiff appointed by the Abbot, was the next in importance. He had to see the ploughs yoked, and that they did their work, and supervise the work on the demesne generally. The Reeve was elected by the villeins from among the best husbandmen. He had to supervise the work done by the villeins and arrange their services. The Hayward had to supervise the sowing and take care of the meadows, corn, and woods. He overlooked the mowers and reapers. The Constable chosen in the court had "to summon juries, arrest vagabonds, and nightwalkers" distrain on the goods of defaulters, and generally to preserve the peace in Brightlingsea.

## THE MANOR AFTER THE BLACK DEATH.

30. The Black Death had a very marked effect on manors generally. We have no direct evidence of its occurrence here, but we know that it visited Colchester in 1348, and probably it was here about the same time. It is estimated that half the population died. This meant that labour became very scarce. The lords of manors tried to enforce to the utmost the services of their villeins, while the Statute of Labourers by limiting the wages to be offered and received, attempted to set a maximum wage limit. Then followed the peasant revolt under Wat Tyler in 1381, in which Brightlingsea men do not appear to have been implicated. The result was the hastening of the inevitable commutation of labour services for money rents, and the emancipation of the villeins.

Sometimes a formal deed of emancipation was given, in which the lord gave up all his rights over his villein. A copy of such a deed given to a Brightlingsea man has been preserved.⁶ This is a translation of it :—

" To all the faithful in Christ to whom the present writing shall come, Walter by divine permission, Abbot of the Monastery of St. John of Colchester and the Convent of the same place, Greeting in the Lord everlasting. Know ye that we with the unanimous assent of all our chapter by our present writing have manumitted and made free from all yoke of servitude, nativity, and villeinage, have freed absolved and quitted claim in Richard Haukyn, son of John Haukyn, the elder of Bryghtlynsey, our native by tenure and service in our manor of Bryghtlyngsey aforesaid in the County of Essex, with all his descendants born and to be born, and all his goods and chatells. Willing and conceding for us and our successors that the same Richard with all his following born and to be born to live free and in free condition and wheresoever it shall please him to remove with all his goods and chattels without claim and challenge by us or our successors. Thus that neither we nor our successors can vend or sell anything in the body of the aforesaid Richard or any of his descendants born or to be born. In testimony" *etc.* Dated 1488.

[¹ Q, 627. ² Q 626. ³ Na. ⁴ Ft, 771. ⁴ Br, ii., 55. ⁶ Na, 234b.]

## THE DISSOLUTION OF THE ABBEY.

31. In 1536 it was decided to dissolve the monasteries of less than £200 yearly value. St. John's escaped as the abbey's income was above that amount. Pressure was put on those remaining to surrender. Thomas Beche, the abbot of St. John's, resisted. Sir John Seyntcler (who owned Moverons) took a leading part in dealing with the abbot. He wrote to Cromwell giving an account of an interview he had had with the abbot on 20th November, 1538, whom he told that the abbot of St. Osyth had acted like an honest man, for he, the latter, said "I am the Kynges subject and I and my house and all is the Kynges wherefore if yt be the Kynges pleasure I as a trewe subject shall obey without groge" (grudge). The abbot of St. John's replied "I will not saye [so] for the king shall never have my howse but agayn my will and agayne my hart for I know by my lernyng that he cannot take yt by right and lawe." Sir John concluded by saying "My lorde I like not the man. I fere he hath a cankred harte for he whas accused but late of traitorous words by one William Halle but he hade no witnesse."¹ Sir John Seyntclere was one of those who examined the witnesses against the abbot, and was one of the commissioners before whom the abbot was tried for treason late in 1539.² The abbot was found guilty and hanged 1st December 1539.³

In consequence of his attainder, the property of the abbey escheated to the crown. Henry VIII. made a grant of Brightlingsea manor, on 20th April, 1540, to Thomas Lord Cromwell, together with other manors, late the property of St. John's Abbey and St. Osyth Priory.⁴ The grant was a general one. The manors and their franchises are not stated individually, but an extensive list of possessions and privileges is given, followed by an important clause that the manors and privileges were "to be held as fully freely and wholly and in as ample manner and form as the last abbot of the said late monasteries of . . . . St. John of Colchester." None of the criminal jurisdictions granted to the abbot are named. They had become obsolete by then. Cromwell was to have his manorial courts, leets and views of frankpledge, and the profits of

these courts, heriots, reliefs, escheats, goods and chattels of felons
fugitives from justice outlaws persons attainted and suicides.
Customary rents were secured to him and customary services,
though the latter, as far as Brightlingsea was concerned, meant
little, if anything, by that time.  He was discharged of all payments,
as regards Brightlingsea, except an annual rent of 6l. payable to the
hospital of St. Mary Magdalen, Colchester.  Cromwell was Great
Chamberlain and Keeper of the Privy Seal, and on 18th April,
1540, was created Earl of Essex.[5]  He soon lost favour with the
king.  He was arrested in June on a charge of treason.  He was
condemned to suffer as a heretic or traitor at the king's pleasure
and forfeit all property held since 31st March 30 Henry VIII.  His
sentence, to be hanged and quartered, was exchanged for the milder
punishment of being beheaded (29th July, 1540).[6]

32.  As a result of his attainder, the manor was in royal hands
again.  The accounts kept by the king's officers give some information about it for this time.  The tenants were paying rents of
assize (quit rents) amounting to 21l. 5s. 2¼d.[7]  The increase beyond
the 12l. 10s. 7d., which they paid about 1300, represents the money
paid in place of the eggs, corn and labour services given then.
When this change was completed cannot be said precisely.  We
get too, instances of another result of the scarcity of labour, the
letting of the demesne lands to farmers.  The demesne farm and
the farm called Jewers, part of the demesne, had been so let.  The
Abbot had let to William Heckford in 1531, the "manor place
called Brightlingsey Hall with all the demesne lands meadues
leasures pastures inmarshes and owtmarshes to the said manor
place belonging . . . . and all manner of tythes to the said manor
place of right and old custom in any wise belonging . . . . with all
the Rents of the Bord lands then being owt of the chardge of
the Collectour of the said Lordship " . . . . for twenty-one years
paying 26l. a year, the Abbot providing for the repairs and allowing
the tenant half-an-acre of brushwood for firing a year.[8]  This
estate is represented now by the Manor house, the Park, and the
Lodge farm.  Of the payments made in the manor court, we learn
that 6s. 8d. was paid as a common fine.[9]  Sums from 13l. 12s. to
2l. 15s. 7d. are accounted for as "fines of land," and "issues of
land" amounted to 3s. 4d. in one account.  These, most probably,
were payments for admittance to holdings, and heriots.  "Per-
quisites" not specified amounted to 8s. 7d.[9]  Fines for offences
such as absence from the court, assault, brewing bad beer, or using
false weights, probably made up the latter.  The steward's expenses
for holding the court are stated to be 10s. 10d. on one occasion,[9]

while on another they were nil as they were borne by the farmer, who was bound to "finde and prepare at the said Manor place meat drynck and Lodging suffycyent and convenient for our officers their servants and horses for one daie and one night when so euer thei shall repare thither for the keaping of our Courts there."[11] The bailiff received 20s. a year for the fee of his office.[12] The court was not held every three weeks then. Two a year seems the usual number. The manor was worth 55l. in 1561, that is the profits of the courts, reliefs, fines, quit-rents, heriots, etc. brought in that amount.[13]

33. William Beriffe, in his will, dated 1542, bequeathed to his son, a parcel of land called Turners, on the condition of "keaping a dryncking on gang Munday at the crosse in turners," and required that " who so euer shall enjoye the said lands and tenements shalbe bounde to keepe the aforesaide dryncking on Gang Mundaye at the saide Crosse."[14] Gang Monday was the Monday before Ascension Day, when the parish bounds were beaten. Turners is a field south of the road leading eastward from East End Green. The cross may have been a pre-Reformation wayside cross. It could not be a parish boundary mark in such a position. Mr. Pertwee has suggested that the drinking was part of the proceedings of the beating of the bounds. There are two other possible explanations. Meadow land, from early times, was divided up and allotted to the tenants of a manor, and this is known to have been done here in the thirteenth century[15] (see section 12). In certain places one share was called the drinker, and was held in turn by each tenant, who had to provide a drinking for the rest,[16] Possibly the drinking here originated in a similar division of the meadow, and was continued as a charge on the land after the communal method of allotting it in strips was abandoned. In some places, part of the common land was let to provide a general drinking feast.[17] Possibly Turners was a piece of land so let, and the burden was transferred with it when it became private property.

[[1] Q, xxvi.  [2] Q, xxvii.  [3] Q, xxxiii.  [4] R, 45.  [5] Ej, vi. 605.  [6] J, xv, 458 [7] Fs, 976.  [8] Fn.  [9] Fs, 923.  [10] Fs, 923, Ft, 771.  [11] Ft, 771, Fn.  [12] Ft, 771. [13] Fm.  [14] If.  [15] Q, 626.  [16] Bb.  [17] Ch, 390.]

## SIR THOMAS HENEAGE, LORD OF THE MANOR.

34. The manor remained in royal hands until Queen Elizabeth granted the Manor to Sir Thomas Heneage and others in 1576.[1] The grant was made more in detail than in that to Cromwell. The new lord was to have the rents of assize of the free and customary

tenants, amounting to 21l. 6s. 0¼d., the manor place called Brightlingsey Hall, and all houses, buildings, structures, barns, stables,
dovecotes, yards, orchards, gardens belonging to the manor place,
all demesne land belonging to the lordship and manor of Brightlingsey, all lands, tenements, meadows, leasows, pastures, marshes,
in marshes, out marshes, all manner of tithes issuing in the premises
called the Manor place and of the demesne lands, and all rents of
the Borde lands being without the charge of the collector of rents,
that is excluding the part anciently rented to tenants, whose rents
were collected by the Reeve. Also all lands, tenements, meadows,
feedings, pastures, marshes as well salt as fresh in Brightlingsea
and Thorington, which had belonged to the Abbey, and all woods,
woodlands, and groves in the tenure of John Barker, formerly part
of the possessions of the Abbey. These were the lands bought or
given to the Abbot, not being part of the demesne. (There is a
wood called "Barker's Grove" near to Morses at the present time).
He was to have stolen goods when abandoned by the thief in his
flight (chattels waived), cattle found straying in the manor and not
claimed after proclamation within a year and a day (estrays), the
goods of felons failing to appear when called upon on five county
court days (exigent), the implement or other inanimate thing
causing death (deodand), fairs, markets, wreck of the sea, shipwreck,
flotsam (floating wreckage), jetsam (goods thrown overboard to
lighten a vessel), and ligan (goods sunk but marked by a buoy) of
the sea, fleets, creeks and banks. These rights were to be held as
fully and as freely as the abbey of St. John's had held them. The
Bailiff was to be paid yearly 25s. for exercising his office. All other
profits except 3s. 6d. a year were to be the lord's.

Sir Thomas Heneage was M.P. for Essex from 1585 till his death.
In 1589 he was made vice-chamberlain and a Privy Councillor.[2]
On his death in 1595 his daughter Elizabeth became lady of the
manor.[3] She married Moyle Finch, who was made a Baronet in
1611.[3] She was made Viscountess Maidstone in 1623, and Countess
of Winchelsea in 1628.[3] She sold the manor to Richard Wilcox of
London.[3] He was succeded by his eldest son George, and he by
his brother Thomas,[4] who was of the Bodyguard to Charles I.[5]
Colonel George Thomson became lord of the manor in 1660.[4] The
court rolls that remain begin in this year.

## THE COURT ROLLS.

35. They show the working of the courts. The view of frankpledge and the general court baron were held together once a year,

at first in April, then in June, and after 1740 usually in September
or October.  Sometimes a court baron was held earlier in the year
as well.  All the ancient business of the view of frankpledge, the
placing men into tithings already explained, had completely disappeared.  The only feature of that system left was the common fine
of 6s. 8d., which the Jury state was payable by them at the view
once a year.  This common fine was originally paid by the capital
pledges or the headmen of the tithings.  We get a reminder of this
in the roll for 1722, when fifteen capital pledges take the place of
the jury, the only instance of their appearance in these rolls, and
possibly due to a revival of an old tradition.  The business actually
done under the heading of the view of frankpledge is that of the
court leet, and the name leet or court leet often appears in the
entries.  We are reminded that in the court leet jurisdictions were
exercised, which had been transferred from the king's courts, when
we are told in 1661 " the names of the jury impannelled to inquire
for the Lord the King."  Generally there was a jury of thirteen for
the leet, and a homage in the court baron of from four to thirteen
appointed separately.  No hint is given how they were chosen, but
they would be chosen by those present in the court from among
themselves.  As attendance at the court was required of all tenants,
the next business was to receive the excuses of those absent, offered
by someone on their behalf.  Those absent and not excused were
fined.  In 1661 twenty-one resident free tenants were fined 3d.
each for absence.  In 1718 eight customary tenants were fined 2d.
each, while in 1724 the fine was made 2s. 6d. for each resident
within the leet absent.  This 'suit' of court and the quit-rents were
then the only links connecting the free tenants with the manor.

Some of the leet jurisdiction had no essential connection with the
manor, it was part of the township court's business.  Of this we
have some reminders.  Two constables were appointed in 1661 for
the town of Brightlingsea.  In 1721 the constables, aletasters, and
common drivers were to execute their offices within the precincts of
this leet, that is within the town of Brightlingsea.  There is nothing
manorial about these duties ; there is no connection between them
and the dominion of the lord over his servile tenants.  The lord
had no voice in their appointment, it was the men who formed the
court who chose them, as they were chosen in the ancient town
moot.  The chief duties of the constables have been described
already (section 29).  Their duties were performed in Saxon times
by the capital pledges or headmen of the tithings.  In the period
covered by these rolls, the ale and bread tasters do not appear to

have done more than test weights and measures. In 1724 they were presented for neglecting their duties, and were fined 1s. each. They were active at times as these entries show :—

1735. "The homage aforesaid present that Daniel Shipman before this Court hath made and sold within the Jurisdiction of this Manor a wheaten Loaf of insufficient weight, to wit of the weight only of two Pounds and six Ounces."

1736. " And also at this Court the Homage aforesaid present William Shipman for using and keeping four bad and insufficient weights to wit, a quarter pound weight, two ounces weight, one ounce weight, and half an ounce weight, and the same being found defective were taken away, and the said Shipman is amerced two shillings and sixpence."

In 1739 they had neither weights nor measures with which to test. Although little is heard of them after this date, they must have been supplied with the necessary implements, for their scales were in existence a few years ago.

The common drivers is a very ancient office, going back to the early Saxon township days, if not earlier. He had charge of the commons, and had to see that the regulations relating to them were observed. In early times, he drove the cattle to and from the commons, as his name suggests. In 1661, the jury presented that " a certain [blank] being a Common Driver when leading a horse to the pound of the Lord for the Manor aforesaid to impound it, a certain William Lucas came with great violence, and violently took and rescued the horse aforesaid. Therefore he is in mercy of the Lord five shillings " (is fined 5s.). Three men in 1666 were fined 10s. each for assaults on the common driver. The common drivers were fined 1s. each for neglect of duty in 1724. The water servers had charge of the public water courses, and were to see that they were kept clean and free from obstruction. It was not only a question of drainage, but also of water supply. Fines were inflicted for fouling the watercourses, obstructing the flow, or improperly taking water from them by making a drain from a course to a well in a yard. From the well in Hoglane, supplied by a spring, an open watercourse ran down Hoglane to the corner where it joins High Street. It went along the north side of High Street, nearly to where St. James' chapel now stands, when it passed under the road and discharged into a pond. This watercourse was deepened and widened at intervals along its course to form reservoirs of a few feet deep, from which the householders obtained a supply. The remains of one of these reservoirs exists under the grass in front of

THE TOWNSHIP AND MANOR.

53 High Street, as may be seen after a spell of hot weather, when the form of the brickwork is shown by an annular scorching of the grass.

36. Other misdeeds were dealt with besides those relating to the offices just described. Fences had to be kept in repair under penalty, and fleets had to be kept well scoured. In 1661, a tenant was presented for not making his "shie," or groyne, as a protection against the sea.

Attention was paid to the highways. In 1661, a tenant was fined 5s. for making a "whoolfe" (channel) in the highway. In 1735 making a "grip" in the highway led to a fine of 20s. There were several instances in which manure placed on or near the highway was ordered to be removed. A "hogs coat" and a butcher's shop placed on the highway had to be removed. The surveyors of the highways were presented for neglect of duty in 1725. A footbridge over the fleet, between Brightlingsea and Thorington, in 1756, was reported to be out of repair, and, in the same year, a tenant was fined 20s. for pulling up a footbridge near Copperas House. In 1673 complaint was made of a man fixing a gate in and obstructing Hoglane, and the highway was obstructed by laying timber on it in 1754.

Assaults came within the court's jurisdiction. In 1666, an assault with drawing of blood led to a fine of 3s. 4d.; 39s. was the fine inflicted for an assault on a child in 1733. This was the heaviest fine the court could inflict.[1]

37. An unusual feature was the jurisdiction exercised over maritime affairs. Three men were presented in 1720 for placing stakes in the channel near their oyster beds, and so preventing boats from passing up and down. In the same year there was a complaint made that smacks were hauled up on to the land out of Borefleet. Laying anchors on the waste led to a fine of 20s. in 1754. The manorial court proper, in the normal course of development, became two courts, the court baron for the freeholders and their affairs, and the customary court for the customary tenants and their affairs. Here no such division had taken place. The court baron was attended by the customary tenants, and the business relating to their lands was dealt with in it. In fact, it was the customary tenants' court, for the manor had lost nearly all hold over the free tenants. In a court baron, the free tenants were the judges, while in the customary court the steward was the judge.[1] Here the customary tenants were put on a level with freemen in that their affairs were settled in the court baron.

On the death of a copyhold or customary tenant, the homage presented that the death had occurred "since the last court and before this present Court," and that the deceased had held a house with all thereto pertaining by copy of court roll and that his youngest son or other was his heir. The heir usually came to the court "in his own person," that is he himself appeared, instead of sending a representative or attorney, and sought to be admitted to the property. The lord, through his steward, then delivered possession by the rod, "according to the custom of the Manor by rent and services thereof before owed and of right accustomed.' The later entries add "at the will of the Lord," probably at the instance of a steward guided more by the standard practice in other manors than by local custom. The new tenant paid a "relief" to the lord for his admittance, and did fealty to the lord. It was more usual for a copyhold tenant to do homage.

The transfer of property through the symbol of the rod is a custom which is not manorial in origin. The Salic law provided that a man wishing to transfer his property to another, should call in a middleman, and in the presence of witnesses transfer the property by handing a rod to the middleman, who then handed the rod to the new owner, thus completing the transfer of the property. In the manor court the steward is the middleman and the members of the court are the witnesses.[5]

When the heir was a minor, a guardian was chosen by or for him, according to the custom of the manor. A minor was formally admitted and did fealty when twenty-one. It was the rule for some proof of age to be given. Usually some, one came to the court, stated that he remembered the tenant's birth or baptism, and corroborated it by a remembrance of some such occurrence as having broken his leg then, or his old cow having died. The rolls contain one proof of age.

"1738. At this court Mary Middleton came and in open court did make oath that William Pain (who was admitted to an oister-laying the second day of October one thousand seven hundred and thirty three) was born nineteen years ago last June at Hawkin's Farm in Brightlingsea, and which the said Deponent did very well remember having at that Time lived as a servant to the said William Pain's Mother."

38. When a copyhold property was sold, the transfer was made in open court by the vendor surrendering it "by the rod by the hands of the steward" into the hands of the lord, who by the rod and by the hands of the steward, gave possession of it to the purchaser, to

hold by copy of the court roll etc. If a man and wife holding a copyhold property jointly, desired to sell it, before the transfer was made in the open court, the wife was first "solely and secretly examined by the steward as the manner is" to ascertain that she really consented to the sale.

A frequent entry is that of conditional surrender as security for payment of money. In 1661 Elizabeth Upcher surrendered to John Smith her cottage on condition, that if at or before the next court she paid him 35s. 6d., the surrender shall be void.

Sometimes a surrender was made out of court in the presence of the Bailiff or his deputy, and two customary tenants. A man sometimes surrendered his property "to the use of his will." It descended then to those whom he wished should inherit, otherwise it would descend according to the custom of the manor. One disadvantage of copyhold tenure was that permission to let copyhold property had to be obtained from the lord. An example is given in 1733. Simon Hutt Scarlett paid 5l. 5s. for licence to let to Nathaniel Wenlock some copyhold lands for twenty-one years, "saving to the lord and lady their just rights."

It will be seen that the court rolls provided a means of recording proof of ownership, and it is said that a freeholder was so convinced of this advantage that he made his freehold copyhold.

39. Four interesting entries may be quoted here:—

1786. "The Lord of the Manor with the consent of the copyhold Tenants doth grant license to John Lappage a Copyhold Tenant of this Manor to erect a chimney to a certain Building now placed on part of the waste of this Manor, he the said John Lappage, his Heirs and assigns paying the Sum of sixpence per annum as a quit-rent for the same so long as it continues on the said waste." The addition of a fireplace raised it to the dignity of a house, to be treated accordingly.

1747. "And at this Court Baron it is presented by the Homage that J . . . S . . . late a customary Tenant of the said Manor hath been indicted and convicted for ffelony and murder and hath been executed for the same at Chelmsford in the County of Essex whereby all his lands and tenements holden of this Manor by copy of Court Roll are become forfeited to the Lord of the said Manor according to the custom thereof and the same are now in the Hands of the Lord accordingly." This forfeiture was a violation of the privileges of ancient demesne. Probably this was a case of ordinary manorial law being applied to Brightlingsea by a steward ignorant of the fact of its being ancient demesne. Cases of execution for

c

felony were not common enough here for the tenants to have pre-
cedents to guide them as to the custom of this Manor.

1740. "The first general Court Baron of John Colt Esquire,
Lord of the Manor . . . At this Court came John Tabor [and 12
others] severally attorned Tenants to the Lord of the Manor and
paid him each one shilling in the name of attornment."

"And also at this Court it is presented by the Homage aforesaid
upon their oaths that the customary Tenants of this Mannor
according to the custom thereof give to the Lord of the said Manor
at this his first Court four pounds of lawfull money of Great Britain
called Palfrey money to be paid and had out of the customary
Lands Tenements and cottages holden of the said Mannor."

The meaning of the first part is that John Tabor and his fellows
on behalf of the rest of the tenants acknowledged John Colt as their
new Lord. The palfrey money is probably a relic of the time when
the King claimed the use of horses belonging to the men of the
royal townships to carry his goods, *etc.* from one township to
another.[7]

40. Some copyhold property in Brightlingsea was heriotable.
On many manors the most valuable chattel or beast was taken as a
heriot, but cattle only were claimed here. If a man left his
heriotable property to his widow for her life, the heriot was seized
by the bailiff and valued by the tenants. The widow then had the
use of the heriot till her death, finding sureties to the court for the
true payment of its value at her death. The fact that some copyhold
property is heriotable and some is not, is interesting when the origin
of the custom is considered. Some copyhold property was in
existence before the practice of settling tenants on land, and providing their outfit began. And some was made after this custom
had ceased. It was known in the 9th century and it does not seem
likely that it continued here later than the 12th.

According to Morant (i. 455) tenants here were not punishable for
felling timber on their customary tenements. He does not give any
authority for the statement, which, however, is quite in accordance
with the privileges of ancient demesne. In the court roll for 1739
a customary tenant is stated to have felled trees without license of
the lord, contrary to the custom of the manor, and he was judged to
forfeit his lands, but the forfeiture was respited on his paying 21s.
In 1842 some trees had been cut down on some copyhold land, but
as the timber had been used in the repair of the copyhold building,
no thirds were due to the lord. These two entries do not agree,
there is a great difference between forfeiture of the holding and

payment of 'thirds,' probably the third of the value of the timber. Manorial'law allowed a copyhold tenant to fell trees for housebote, hedgebote, and ploughbote, that is for repair of his house, hedges, and ploughs. Probably the instances quoted are the result of the steward using ordinary manorial law instead of the actual custom of this manor.

41. Borough English, a custom of this manor, has been spoken of in sections 10 and 11. The explanation given until recently, connected it with the lord's infamous *jus primæ noctis.* The custom of the youngest son inheriting is a much older institution than manorial lords. One explanation is that the elder sons had gone out into the world, and had made their homes, and the youngest, being the least able or least likely to do so, inherited his father's house. Another possibility is that the youngest son was most likely to be present at his father's death, and could arrange for the burial, a highly important matter. This view is corroborated by the fact that in ancient communities the inheritor of the deceased's property was he who performed the funeral ceremonies. The conclusion is arrived at "that the oldest customs of inheritance in England and Germany were in their remote beginnings connected with a domestic religion and based upon a worship of ancestral spirits, of which the hearth was essentially the shrine and altar."[3] (Indications of the protection of the sanctity of a man's house by Saxon law is shown in section 20 and of the importance of a hearth in a house in section 39.)

The custom of merchet, a payment to the lord on the marriage of a villein woman, was held to be a payment for relief from the *jus primæ noctis.* Modern research, however, shows this to be a myth. The payment was no more than a marriage license and a compensation to the lord for the loss of the services the woman might have to render as a villein. It may have originated in the custom by which a woman's kindred in ancient days received payment on her marriage, and have been continued as merchet,[4] the lord of the manor taking as the head of the community the place of the kindred, and receiving the payment or part of it.[5]

In *More Letters of Edward Fitzgerald* (p. 190) he speaks of a Brightlingsea custom not described in the court rolls or elsewhere. A lady proclaimed her right to some land in Brightlingsea "by walking up the Church with a dog and a hunting whip."

[[1] Ee, Court Baron.  [2] Bh, ii., 61.  [3] Ch, 211.  [4] Ca, 347.  [5] Bz, 372-3.]

## THE COMMONS AND THE OPEN FIELD SYSTEM.

42. The common lands, once very extensive, were more and more taken into cultivation as time went on. The lord added part to his demesne, and settled tenants on part. The Statute of Merton (1263) allowed a lord of a manor to enclose the common land of his manor for tillage or woodgrowth, if he left enough to provide the pasture to which his tenants were entitled.[1]  The legal theory is that the common land belonged entirely to the lord, and the use of it was by his grant.  Historically, the village community was the real owner, and the lord was the encroacher.  In spite of the legal theory the tenants, representing the village community, share with the lord in the waste and common lands.  This share is recognised in these court rolls as this entry shows:—1721.  "The Jurors aforesaid present that Joseph Wilkinson without license of the Lord and the tenants of this manor aforesaid dug and opened an old oyster pit in the Lord's waste.  Therefore he is in mercy one shilling which he pays to the Steward in the Court."

The free tenants formerly had rights over the common land as well as the copyholders.  When they dropped out of the manorial organisation, they naturally lost what had become rights exclusively manorial.

Common right was of two kinds, common appendant, and common appurtenant.[2]  Common appendant arose from the ancient husbandry system.  Arable land required cattle to till and manure it, and cattle required pasture.  Therefore to all ancient arable land right of pasturing on the commons such cattle as are indicated above (horses, oxen, and sheep) was appendant.[2]  Common appurtenant arose from custom, and the right was attached to buildings or land not arable, and applied to animals not required for the arable, such as goats, swine, and geese.[2]

When the common land was extensive, there was no need to limit the number of cattle each tenant put on the commons, but as it diminished, it became necessary to do so.  Each tenant here was allowed to put on the commons one-and-a-half sheep for every acre he held and as many hogs as he might reasonably keep, to be lawfully ringed and yoked (to keep them from rooting up the ground with their snouts).  Every cottager might keep one barrow pig.[3]  No mention is made of the number of horses and oxen that might be pastured.  Possibly because no one was likely to keep more than his holding required, while to sheep and hogs, being beasts kept exclusively for killing or selling, there was no such natural limitation, hence the need for "stinting" them.  Geese do not appear to have been allowed on the common here.  Some of the tenants were careless about their stock as this entry shows:—1768.  "At this Court the Jury aforesaid also present J . . B , . J . . B . . and J . . M . . respectively for a Nuisance by each of them in keeping Hogs severally, and letting them go about the street and the parish unyoaked contrary to the custom of the said manor, and they are amerced ten shillings each."

43.  In close relationship to the enclosure of the commons is the abandonment of the open field system.  This system persisted in many parts of England until the Enclosure Acts of the eighteenth and nineteenth centuries, but in Essex it was largely abolished before then. Large tracts of common land were enclosed in Great Bentley, Weeley, Thorington, and Alresford, early in the nineteenth century, but in Brightlingsea there was then none to enclose but the greens.  The scattering of the holdings in Brightlingsea would help the enclosure, and the prosperity of the place in the fourteenth and fifteenth centuries must have given it an impulse.  In any case, it appears to have been effected earlier than in the neighbouring villages.  In some of the sixteenth century wills of Brightlingsea men, property is mentioned as lying in the town and fields of Great Bentley and other neighbouring places, while land in Brightlingsea is described then as lying in the town or parish of Brightlingsea. This suggests the continuance of the open field system in Great Bentley and elsewhere in the sixteenth century, and its cessation here.  The process of its decay was gradual; instead of the yearly change of ownership of the scattered strips, they remained

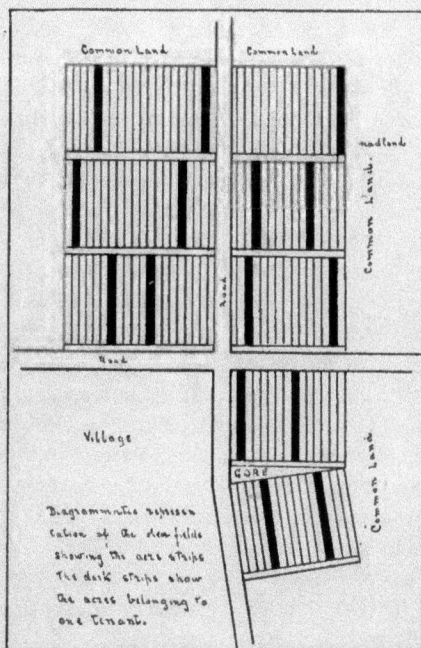

FIG. 1.

in the same hands. Then by exchange each owner got his strips
together or at least in parcels. When the strips were in compact
groups, it was but a short step to enclose them entirely. Then the
open field system disappeared, for laying open the fields for common
pasture, after the crops were harvested, was an essential of that
system.

The old system had the advantage of equality and convenience
when co-operative tilling was practised, but it had the grave disadvantage that there was little encouragement to improve the land,
since others were as likely to benefit by it as the tiller, and when
individual farming came in, the wide separation of the acre strips
led to a great waste of time.

44. Of the open fields here we have only a little direct evidence.
From the Extent of about 1300, we learn that the three field system
of rotation of crops was in use. Gores and the "hlinch" are mentioned
in it. A gore was a corner of a field which could not be ploughed
in the regular acre strips. A linch was formed in ploughing the
acre strips on sloping ground. The plough always turned the sod
downhill, returning idle. Thus in time the soil was removed from
the higher side of the strip to the lower, so that each strip formed a
level terrace separated from the next by a steep bank covered with
rough grass.* There are hints of the system in the court rolls. A
messuage and ten small closes called Feriers suggest a house and
ten strips belonging to one owner in the open fields. In some cases,
a quite small piece of land has the name of several owners attached
to it. As an instance, two cottages and gardens near the Spring
were called Rogers, Teysells, Mendhams, and Freysells; Also 4
acres, 1 rood, 8 perches of land near Morses is called Fords, Long
Harrises, Taysellers, Christians, and Rogers: in the Back Road is
a house, barn, and five acre field called Fords, Long Harrises, Taysellers, Christians, and Rogers. Mention of single acre pieces of
land are naturally rare, when the late date of the rolls is considered,
but there is mentioned one acre called Rogers and another called
Warrens. The small parcels of land having several names suggest
a number of acre strips each with the ancient owners name still
attached being fused into one. The above examples also show the
same owners name appearing several times in different parts of the
parish, pointing to the scattering of the acre strips. Another
example of a number of names belonging to a small piece of land is
found in a certain 10 acres, part of which was known as Locks,
Reeves, Hunts, Millin Chases, Marshalls, or Pupletts. Mention
has been made of the scattering of the holdings and houses, and

instances of it were given in the Moverons end of the Island. In the eastern and southern parts this scattering was very marked. It has only been in comparatively recent years that there has been concentration at one point, forming a town in the modern sense. Not only were there houses round Lower Green, Hurst Green, and the Street, but there were no less than seven round East End Green, and at least three round Bell Green. There were not less than four in the Back Road. In Church Road there were three in the lower part, and two by the Malting Farm and Stranges Corner, and seven on the Boardlands close by. Morses and East Marsh Farm each had at least two other houses round them. More than half the known houses were outside the town as we now know it. The houses were not close together even in what we call the town. There were only twelve known houses in what is now called the High Street.

45. To return to the owners of the manor, it changed hands several times before it came into the possession of Nicholas Magens in 1763. It remained in his family until 1860 when John Dorrien Magens sold it. There is a very large and elaborate monument to Nicholas Magens in the Chancel of the Church with an inscription eloquent as to his virtues. It mentions his literary works. He is entered in the British Museum catalogue as having written in German an essay on insurances and an English edition of the same work.

46. Part of the manorial jurisdiction was superseded by the Police Acts. In 1832 the Tendring Hundred Magistrates wanted to appoint additional constables. The parishioners objected, as the appointment of constables had always been a privilege of the Court Leet. At length it was agreed that the additional constables should be appointed by the Leet.[5] A special Court Leet was held in February to swear in six constables additional to the two previously appointed. Eight were appointed at the next court. In 1842 the appointment by the Leet was abolished. The rest of the juris-diction was allowed to lapse. The vestry superseded the manor as a controller of local affairs to a large extent. The cage in which the prisoners were confined used to stand in High Street immediately east of the site of the Bank House. This was superseded by a small brick building in Spring Road, still in existence and recognisable by its barred windows. It is considered fit only for wheelbarrows now; evildoers are temporarily rested in a handsome spacious building in Ladysmith Avenue.

The manor had the misfortune to be for a time in the hands of those who took no interest in its history, nor cared for its ancient

records. The late Mr. Benjamin Colet Pulleyne while lord of the
manor took a great interest in its history and recovered some of the
lost records.

The view of frankpledge and court baron are held still, at which
the ale and bread tasters, water servers, common drivers, and reeve
are appointed. The copyhold tenants do not work for their lord
now, not even in harvest time, but ancient custom is kept up in
that they receive "the food of the lord" in the shape of an annual
dinner.

[¹ Dr, 113.  ² Bz.  ³ Ak, ii., 770.  ⁴ Bi 5.  ⁵ Mg.]

## The Manor House and the Demesne.

47. The lease of the Manor place or Brightlingsea Hall to John
Heckford in 1531 has been dealt with in section 32. A similar lease
was made to John Locke in 1552 for thirty years at the same rent.
The manor had passed into private hands before the lease had
expired, and we hear no more of the Manor house being let. It has
been held often that what we now call Brightlingsea Hall was the
original manor house, and the description "Manor place or Brightlingsea Hall" favours that idea. But such can hardly be the case,
as will be seen when Brightlingsea Hall is considered. A more
suitable site for the Manor house could not have been chosen. It
is placed in the exact centre of the Island, making it convenient for
supervising the manor. As a residence it has the advantage of
being on the gravel soil, and enjoys a beautiful view of the estuary
of the Colne and the bay beyond. The fishponds belonging to it
point to it having been a house of importance before the Reformation. Of late years the house has been restored and enlarged by
the present owner, Mr. Herbert Sullivan, of whose uncle, the late Sir
Arthur Sullivan, the house contains many interesting reminiscences.

The demesne farm which was connected always with a manor
house is now represented by the Lodge Farm. It was on this land
that the lord's meadows, Newmad Melnemad and Herboldmad
would be, on which the customary tenants mowed the hay. They
would be most likely near the stream running from the spring,
because it was usual to flood the meadows when the crop was
growing. Melnemad probably means mill meadow, corroborating
the idea that it was near a stream. 'Her' in Anglo-Saxon means
army, and 'bold' a house, so Herboldmad might have been a
meadow by a fort or watch house. The site was suitable for a fort,
but such a derivation must be received with considerable reserve.

The field now called Curd Hall perhaps got its name from a dairy house placed on it, in which the cheese was made from the ewes' milk, and where the customary tenants had their feast after the mowing. Hards and Sharps (a field) and Wayhill Marsh are names of which the meaning is not clear. The name Sheepcotes, a field on the higher ground, is self explanatory. Stranges field, the present allotment field, represents in part the ancient Boardlands.

Another part of the demesne was the farm now called Ruffell's, but anciently Jewer's. It was let to William Beriff for thirty-six years from Michaelmas, 1528, at a rent of 7*l*. a year, the tenant doing all repairs, and the Abbot finding sufficient wood for them.[1] It was sold to Hugh Hollingshead by Queen Elizabeth in 1561.[2] The recorded description of the farm states that at this time it was of the clear yearly value of 7*l*., and that the price of 154*l*. was at twenty-two years purchase.[x] Part of it, known as Culre pightle Brumble field and East field, had been separated from it by 1630.[4]

## The Fixed Names of the Free and Copyhold Properties.

48. The properties have still, in most cases, names, which appear to have been given to them long ago. They were the official names by which they were described in the manor court rolls, and sometimes differed from the names by which they were generally known. In many cases they may be traced back to the Extent of about 1300, and from it, it appears that then some of these names were not new, but had been in use for a now unascertainable time before then. There are very few descriptive names; they were nearly all the owners' name, with a possessive " s " added. Often there are several names to one property, due to the fusion of several properties. Sometimes, in such a case, the names are separated by " or." This was probably added through the writer of the court rolls misunderstanding the significance of the many names. In the following list, the names quoted are found in the court rolls from 1660, a rental of the Manor dated 1685, and the Extent of about 1300, except where the reference given shows otherwise. The Extent is referred to as 1300.

*Beasts.* There was a house and 13 acres called Beasts on the south side of East End Green, and east of the present East End Green farmhouse. Another house (111 High Street) and land was called Beasts or Edens (Edynes, a tenant in 1300). 74 to 86 High Street, and 3 to 9 High Street, were called Beasts or Beastons. In 1300, William Biesten held a customary house and 25 acres

called Biestes. Richard Biesten held a free house and 7 acres
called Biestes, and John Biesten held a house and 4 acres once
belonging to Geoffrey Biesten. The name arose from their residence,
By East End. The form Beaston is a corruption of Biesten. The
name got shortened into Beast, and then into Best.

*Bellhouse*. A cottage and land abutting on Bell Green, to the
south-east. The land was known as Bellfield, or Bellhouse field,
or the Warren.

*Boardlands. Shotenslade*, part of the Boardlands, was leased to
James Beriffe in 1586.

*Brickhouse*, or *Edriches, Mandevils, Linches*, or *Gills*, or *Levers (or
Linings) or Turners*. The property now known as East End Green
Farm. As the names imply, several old properties are joined
together. In 1300, there was a house and 18 acres called Edriches,
a cottage and ½ rod once belonging to John Lynings, a house and
1 acre called "le hlynch," and a house and land called Maundeville.
Two fields belonging to this farm are called ' Linen field ' and
' Holy ground' in the tithe commutation map.

*Brockmans*. On the south side of the Back Road, near East End
Green. 1300, John Brockman's house and 2 acres.

*Brooks, Tylers, and Long Johns*. 1300, John att Brooks held a
house and 20 acres called Bysouthes.

A house and croft called *Caprons, Broadfield* 4 acres, *Notts* 5½ acres,
meadow and 2 acres called *Capons*, a house and 5 acres called *Swifts*,
a cottage and 1½ acres called *Souths*, a tenement and 3 acres called
*Patches*, a house and 4 acres called *Edriches*, 3 acres called *Pipers
Hatch*, and a meadow called *Wisbeaches*. These properties had been
joined together and then divided, so that their individual identity
cannot be ascertained. Part are what is now the Malting farm,
and part the land lying west of Victoria Place and Station Road,
and south of Spring Road. The Malting farmhouse is probably
Patches, and Edriches probably is now represented by 37 and 39
Victoria Place. Capons, Notts, Paches, and Edriches all appear
in 1300.

*Chamberlyns*. House and land lying by the church gate, leased
to John Beriffe.[5] Most probably part of the rectory estate.

*Chickens*. A house and garden on the west side of Hurst Green.

*Clarkes*, or *Wells*, or *Wests*. A cottage and land on the west side
of Queen Street, on the site of 27-31 Queen Street. In 1330, John
Clerke held a cottage and 1 rod, once Ralph atte Welles.

*Clarkes* or *Woodrows*. A house, garden, barn, and two fields,
butting on the north-west corner of East End Green, and on the
south of the Back Road.

*Crosses.* A cottage and garden in the Southend. 1300, Robert at Crosse's cottage and curtilage.

*Dyams.* Site not known, but probably part of land lying immediately east of Regent Road. 1300, Nicholas Dyam's house and land.

*Dyers.* "The Ship," and 7 and 8 Victoria Place.

*East Marsh, Paramours, Minnetts* or *Hurrells, Bushey Close* or *Bishops.* Now form Folkard's farm. Paramours and Minnetts, had each a house at one time. The name East Marsh, and that of the next two properties on the list, almost certainly originated from a family named Estmar, or Estmer, who flourished here in 1300, at which time there were three properties called "Estmars," and also Paramours.

*East Mersey.* A house and garden on Hurst Green, now the "White Lion."

*East Mersey* or *the Lawn (or Loun).* A house and 14 acres on the site of the present Coast Guard Station.

49. *Ffaires and Ffarheires.* The first name is probably a corruption of the latter. The site has yet to be identified. Richard Fairhair was living here in 1320.[*] In 1300, two properties of Ffayrhairs are mentioned.

*Fontys and Salters.* In 1539, there were a house and parcels of land in the Northend called Fontys and Salters, the exact site is not known. In 1300, a house and land, Geoffrey Fonte's.

*Fords, Long Harrises, Taysellers, Christians, and Rogers.* About 5 acres of land lying immediately west of the road to Morses; also another 5 acres with the same names immediately south of the Back Road, west of the entrance to Folkard's Lane. 1300, a house and land, Richard at Fords.

*Franks and Ranspotts.* A house and land, site not identified. 1300, a cottage and land, Matilda Franks.

*Gales.* Land, site unknown. 1300, a house and land called Gales.

*Goodriches.* A house and land on the north side of High Street, the site of the present No. 1. Goodriches, or Wildes, or Guyers, land on the east side of New Street. 1300, three properties called Goodriches.

*Greenwindows.* A cottage, outhouse, and yard on the west side of the Backwaterside Lane, north of the Coast Guard Station.

*Hatches* or *Campnells.* 1300, a cottage and land, atte Hache's.

*Hawkins.* A house and land on the west side of Hurst Green, Nos. 16, 17, and 18. 1300, a house and 13 acres called Hawkins.

*Holbrooks.* A house and 3 acres on the west side of Victoria Place and Station road. Belonged to Lord Skelmersdale in 1847.[7] 1300, a house and 3 acres, Henry Holbrook's.

*Jacobs.* A house and land on the south side of High Street (nos. 44-54). It was owned by the Beriffes from before 1496 until after 1624. There was also a cottage and land of the same name on the north-east side of East End Green. Morses was also called Jacobs. 1300, a house and land called Jacobs.

*Jenkins.* Houses and land on the site of 49-53 High street.

*Kings, Little Kings.* House and land on the site of 27-33 High street. The land extended to the east and west, but how far exactly is not known. Possibly Little Kings was part of Kings, which possibly included the "Swan" and its land. 1300, John King's house and land.

*Lamplees, Champnells, Chapples, Smarts, Picardys, Clarks, Shanks,* and *Curtis*; now known as the Redbarn farm. 1300, house and land, Smarts; land, Clarks; house and land, Shanks; house and land, Roger Curteys.

*Lilberds* or *Libberds.* A house and land on the north side of Hurst Green (no. 33). 1300, Walter Liberd's cottage and land.

*Lumpkins* or *Pammets, Crossfield* and *Kitchenfield.* Nos. 38-42 Queen street and land belonging lying to the east. A house on the west side of Queen street, below the old "Anchor," was also called Lumpkins or Pammetts.

*Morses,* late *Jacobs.* Part of the farm now called Morses. The present farm includes Warrens, Millers, Moreffs, and Fullers, and the land described under the heading Fords. It belonged to the Beriffes.

*Patches* or *Marks.* Land on which a house stood, on the north side of the road from East End Green to the marshes, and close to the green. 1300, John Pach's house and land. William Beriffe "at the Brook," who died in 1527, lived in "Patches." Probably this was the house. The meaning of "at the Brook" is not clear, possibly it refers to a stream running from a spring adjoining this property.

*Pennylesse* or *Pennals.* A house and land on the north side of Victoria Place (no. 51 Victoria Place).

*Pitwaters, Whippatts* or *Finches.* A house and land on the north side of High Street, west of Hoglane (nos. 67-77). 1300, William Petywalter's house and 5 acres.

*Raggs.* A cottage on the north side of the Back Road, immediately west of Folkard's Lane.

*Richardsons.* A house and garden in the South end, exact site not known.

*Rogers, Teysells, Frisells* and *Mandams.* Two houses and land on the east side of Spring and Church Roads, on the site of Walnut

Tree House and nos. 2 and 4 Church road. The land lying near the above, to the north-west and bounded on the north by the Back Road, had the same name.

*Shanks.* A field on the north side of the Back Road near " Love Lane." 1300, Hugh Schankk's land.

*Salcots, Silcots.* Land lying between Station Road and New Street. Belonged to the Beriffes. 1300, Walter Salcot's house and land. Included in Salcotts were Locks, Reeves or Hunts, Millin Chases, Marshalls or Puppletts, probably small estates absorbed into it.

*Stormes,* or *Stornes* or *Shermers.* A house and land on the north side of Hurst Green, now nos. 27-30.

*Stormes* or *Coopers.* A house and land, nos. 12 and 13 Victoria Place. 1300, Ralph Cowper's house and land.

*Stranges.* A cottage and garden. Exact site not known ; probably near Stranger's Corner.

*Sturges.* A house and 14 acres near Hurst Green. Probably lying west of it.

*Turners.* Freehold land, part of the present " Freelands," lying south of the road from East End Green to the marshes. This and Chapmans, also freehold, belonged to the Beriffes.[8] A house stood on each in their time.

50. *Wallows, Swallows, Soffield* (? Southfield), and *Bridgland.* The farmhouse and land lying east of Back Waterside Lane and south of Hurst Green including the marsh adjoining. 1300, a house and land called " Walhawes."

*Wisbiches.* A house on the west side of Victoria Place, about the site of nos. 33-36. Also a meadow lying west of this site.

*Woodrows and Carons.* Land, and formerly a house, lying on the south side of the road between Little Lane and East End Green.

[[1] Fs, 976. [2] Gcb. [3] Fm. [4] Ju, Ellis Markant, 1630. [5] Ju, John Beriffe, 1542. [6] Ff, 107/10. [7] Nr, 388. [8] Ha, 1603, 1-2. Ih. Ig.]

## MOVERONS.

51. The evidence of an estate at Moverons has been mentioned already, and also the possibility of the last sentence of the Domesday entry about Brightlingsea being a reference to a small estate such as Moverons might be. Accepting such a theory, Moverons might have been this estate, a part of the demesne, too far to be managed with the rest of the demesne, and so let.

We know that Osbert de Brightlingsea died in 1247[1] in possession of an estate, afterwards called Moverons, for which a rent of 28s.

was paid, and that Alexander de Brightlingsea, his father, had it before him.[2] Alexander had held two virgates (60 acres) of free-land in Brightlingsea at a rent of 28s. which identifies it with Moverons.[3] Sixty acres is small compared with the present acreage of Moverons, but the 60 acres was only the arable land, the marshes and waste land belonging to it being understood. Alexander de Brightlingsea was a man of some importance, he was a knight and held the important office of verderer of the forest of Essex.[4] When, after a heavy gale, Henry III., in 1223, ordered the windfall wood in the forest to be sold, Alexander de Brichtlingese was one of the four chosen to do it. He was one of the twelve knights who made perambulations of the forest in 1225 and 1228.[5]

Osbert de Brichtlingeseye left his three sisters, Aveline, Johanna, and Rose (Roysia), his heiresses.[1] As a family name " de Bright-lingsea " then disappeared here, but there was a Thomas Briklingseie at Southampton in 1393-4.[6] Rose was the wife of Richard Mun-viron. The Abbot gave a charter to him and his wife, confirming them in the possession of this estate. A second charter similar, but more in detail was given to them as well by the Abbot, which stated that they were to hold " all the lands and tenements with all their appurtenances, which Alexander or Osbert de Brightlingsea held of our ancestors in the town of Brightlingsea as fully and freely as they held the same in the days, in which they were alive and dead in homages, rents, services, reliefs, escheats, in meadows, pastures, marshes, woods, plains, paths, and roads, waters, fisheries, fishponds, hedges, free entrances, and exits, and all other things with all appurtenances and free customs to the aforesaid lands and tenements pertaining," paying yearly the rent of 28s. 8d.[7] The terms of this charter do not contradict the idea that it had been demesne once. John de Moverons who succeeded Richard, received a grant of free warren in his lands in Brightlingsea and Haylesley in 1263.[8] When he died is not known, but it must have been some time prior to 1331 (see below). Assuming that he was fifteen when he received this grant of free warren he would have been eighty-three in 1331, a most unlikely age for those days. In the subsidy rolls for 1319[9] and 1327[10] " Magister Moueron " appears as paying in Brightlingsea 8s. for a twelfth, and 3s. 7¾d. for a twentieth. He is the only one styled Magister (Master) on the Brightlingsea list. John de Moveron's daughter and co-heiress, Mariota, in 1331 made a release to William Harewold and Cicely his wife (presumably Mariota's sister) of her lands in Brightlingsea.[11] John Harewolde who was mentioned in the Inquisitio Nonarum for Brightlingsea in 1340-1 possibly belonged to this family.

52. The property is next heard of in the Seyntclere family. John, son of Thomas Seyncler, knight, in his will dated 12th July, 1410, mentions his manor of Mouerons in Brightlingsea.[13] These Seyncleres had a residence, Seynclere's Hall, in St. Osyth, where they had considerable property. John Seyntclere died in 1493. He held the manor of " Marons " in Britlyngsey.[14] He instructed his executors " to sett my children to scole and sett them forthe and mary my daughters as they think best."[15] His son, Sir John Seintclere, took a leading part in local affairs. His share in the dissolution of St. John's, and the trial of the last Abbot was referred to in section 31. He played his part in the Court too. He was one of the knights who 'lined the route' at Blackheath where Anne of Cleves met Henry VIII., when she came to marry him.[16] Seintcler died in 1546. Moverons was worth at the time of his death 20 marks (13l. 6s. 8d.). He held it by fealty and suit of court of the manor of Brykelsey, and paid 28s. 8d. a year in lieu of all services.[17] His son John succeeded him. Laurence Warren was the next owner, and he disposed of it to Thomas Darcy. It remained in the Darcy family until Sir Thomas Darcy sold it to Robert Barwell.[18] Brian Darcy, who was deputy in 1642 and 1649, probably belonged to this family; Brian was a favourite name with them.[19] He may have lived at Moverons, and probably was the " Mr. Darsy " imprisoned in 1644 for not paying his tithes.[20]

Robert Barwell's son sold it to John Colt in 1718. Nicholas Magens purchased it in 1763.[18] Since then being in the same hands as the manor of Brightlingsea, it has lost its identity somewhat. In 1871 it was purchased by the late Mr. John Bateman.

The present house of Moverons is partly of recent date and partly of ancient timber work. There are the remains of a moat near it. The fishpond close by suggests an important house in Pre-Reformation times.

[[1] F.  [2] Q, 665-6.  [3] B.  [4] H, i., 399.  [5] Ao, 24-5.  [6] K, Southampton, iii., 73.  [7] Q, 665-6.  [8] An, 455.  [9] Ff, 107/10.  [10] Ff, 107/12.  [11] 5 Edw. III., pt. i., m18d.  [12] En.  [13] Hd, 36273 A.  [14] G, Hen. VII., 382.  [15] Ja.  [16] J, xv., 4-5.  [17] Hd, 19985, f. 118d.  [18] An, 455.  [19] Ak, i., 776.  [20] Hd, 15669, p. 38.]

# Chapter III.

## ECCLESIASTICAL.

### EARLY CHURCH HISTORY.

53. We have no direct evidence of the existence of Christianity in Brightlingsea during the Roman or Saxon period. Possibly the Brightlingsea people were converted soon after Mellitus became Bishop of London in 604, and when Sabert, King of the East Saxons, embraced the faith.[1] On the death of Sabert, Christianity was driven out. In 653 Cedd and another priest were sent to preach in Essex.[1] They visited various parts with great success. He was made Bishop, and ordained priests and deacons to assist him, built churches, and had two centres of activity in Ythancester (Bradwell-on-Sea) and Tilbury,[2] Ythancester was quite close, and Brightlingsea may well have felt Cedd's influence. At first parish priests were not appointed; the priests belonged to the diocese, and were sent to minister to the people as occasion demanded. Though there might have been no resident priest, there might have been a church. It is almost certain that each village had its pagan temple; these were not destroyed, but were transformed into christian churches.[3]

It was laid down (735-66) that every church should have allotted to it one complete holding (a hide), which was to be free from all but ecclesiastical services.[4] A hide was sufficient for the maintenance of the priest and his assistants. The priest receiving such a holding did not mean dispossessing any one; it only meant so many more acres being added to the common fields from the ample waste. The scattered acre system of the common fields was adapted for the convenient payment of tithes. Every tenth acre was allotted to the church's estate.[4] The tithe was distributed one part to the repair of the church, one to the priests, and one to the poor.[5] The payer of the tithe could and did decide where it should go. Normally it went to a ' Diocesan fund,' and was distributed as needed.[6] When private enterprise began church building it was usual to give one-third to the parish priest, and spend the remainder on church repairs and the poor.[7]

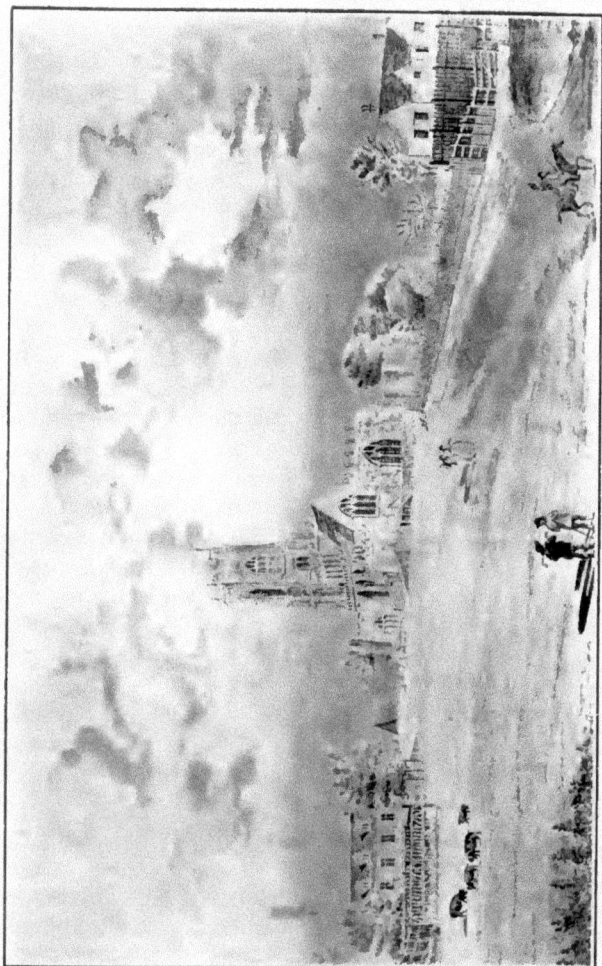

From a water colour drawing, dated 1801, in the possession of Mr. A. A. Jefferies.

*Vicarage.*     *Tithe barn.*               *Hull.*

*Pound.*

THE CHURCH (ALL SAINTS') AND GREEN, 1801

(Plate ii.)

54. It is almost certain that there was a church in Brightlingsea before the Conquest. Domesday does not mention a church here, it only mentioned churches in Essex incidentally.[8] It is hardly likely that one of the most populous places in Tendring Hundred at that time would be without a church. It is not likely that in the troublesome times just after the Conquest, that church building would flourish; therefore a church mentioned soon after the Conquest is almost certainly of Saxon foundation. In the Chartulary of St. John's there is a charter of William II.'s (said to be about 1096) which confirms Eudo's grant to St. John's of the manors of Brightlingsea, Weeley, and Hallingbury, with their churches and their appurtenances, and two parts of the tithe of the demesne and mills, all tithe of the pannage of his woods, and all other benefits ecclesiastical and lay.[9]

In Henry I.'s charter (1119 or a little earlier) the grant of two parts of the tithe of Brightlingsea was confirmed.[10] From the grant of two parts of the tithe to the Abbey, we may infer that the custom of giving one part to the parish priest and spending the other on the church and poor was practised here. When the Abbot received the tithe, he became responsible for the church and poor. Eudo only transferred the tithe of his own property, such as his demesne, mills, pannage of his woods, and the foals of his mares.[10] He could not transfer his tenants' tithes. No doubt they soon followed his example. The advantage of giving tithe to a monastery was great; there was a good spiritual return in the prayers to be said perpetually for the repose of the donor's soul.

Eudo further granted the proceeds of all his chapels on this side of the Thames to the Abbot on condition, that the monks officiated in them on feast days.[11] These chapels were probably connected with his manor houses. A chapel in Brightlingsea is mentioned as being in the Abbot's estate *(territorio)* in 1237,[12] but in 1165-71 it is a church which is situated in their estate *(fundo)*,[13] so the chapel might be the church itself, but as a church is mentioned in 1237 as well as a chapel,[12] and there was a Chapel-field here about 1300,[14] it seems more likely that there were both church and chapel.

The evidence we have connecting the present church building with these early times is the doubtful Saxon or Norman recess immediately west of the south door. This had been bricked up and plastered over. It was discovered by Mr. Pertwee and restored, except that a column was left in the centre for support. In fact it is as easy to believe that there was a Saxon church, perhaps built of wood like that at Greenstead, and replaced by a stone one built in the Early English period (1200-1300). There are examples of

D

this style of architecture in the lancet windows in the north and
south walls of the chancel, now blocked up, and the south doorway.

An annual payment of 60s. from Brightlingsea church was confirmed to the Abbot in 1165-71[13] and again in 1202.[15] This was
possibly the priest's third and such payments as altarage or burial
dues.

55. The religious services were performed by either monks from
the Abbey, or by resident chaplains. We heard of a chaplain,
Peter the Cleric of Brightlingsea, through his owning land here.
His grand-daughter gave a charter to the Abbot quitting her claim
to land, which he had held in Brightlingsea.[16] The charter was
made before 1247, so he would be alive in the latter part of the
twelfth century, about the time of which we are speaking. This is
an instance of a married priest. These marriages were illegal, but
were often overlooked. In 1179 the Abbot was confirmed in his
right to elect a parish priest for Brightlingsea, and to present him
to the Bishop of London. The bishop would commit to him, if
found worthy, the cure of souls. The priest was to answer to the
bishop for spiritual affairs, and to the Abbot for temporal matters.[17]
The Abbot would pay what he chose and remove the priest at his
will. Such did not meet with approval, and after the decision of
the Council of Oxford in 1223, the bishops insisted on definitely
ordained vicarages.[18] In 1237 the Dean and Chapter of St. Paul's,
with the consent of Roger, Bishop of London, made this ordinance :

" We ordain that in the church of Brightlingsea a vicar be instituted for ever by the Bishop of London who for the time shall be.
Of which church we make a vicarage to the value of ten marks, a
suitable vicarage house adjoining the said church to be assigned,
all the residue of the said church with a yearly payment of 60s.,
which the said Abbot and Monks receive from the same church, to
the lights of the church of the blessed Paul of London forever
being assigned entire, with the houses to the said church belonging
and all other things to the same church pertaining, saving never-
theless the tithes to the said Abbot and Monks, which they possessed
in that parish."[19]

This ordination made the Dean and Chapter Rector of Brightlingsea. It will be noted that certain houses already belonged to
the Church, of which apparently one was to be the Vicarage house.
The last sentence apparently means the tithe of the demesne and
other property actually possessed by the Abbot.

The parish priest was now a permanent official appointed by the
Bishop, with a fixed salary and no longer at the caprice of the
Abbot. He had a house and a salary of 6l. 13s. 4d. a year, which

might be augmented by voluntary offerings, but from the ordination
all compulsory ecclesiastical dues went to St. Paul's. 6*l*. 13*s*. 4*d*.
do not seem much, but it was good pay at a time when a priest
could be obtained for five marks a year or two marks and his
board,[20] and was sufficient for the vicar to maintain himself and
exercise a certain amount of hospitality. There were no inns then;
the parish priest provided lodging for wayfarers.

56. The Vicar's stipend did not remain at this figure. It had
become 17*l*. 0*s*. 4*d*. by 1537.[21] Possibly the Black Death by
making the clergy scarce, had been the cause. It was difficult then
to get any one to take a vicarage for ten marks a year.[20] There
is a notice of an early vicar in the Chartulary of St. John's, in
which a grant of land in Witham was made to Henry, Chaplain,
Vicar of Brightlingsea. He granted the land to the Abbey in a
charter in which he is described as Henry de Bluntestone, perpetual
vicar of Brightlingsea.[22] The charter is not dated. Most likely
he was earlier than the next name as John de Moueron, who
witnessed the charter, was old enough in 1263 to receive a grant of
free warren. John de Chishull is described as parson of Brightlingsey on the Patent Rolls for 1294.[23] Edward I. was then in
great need of money for his wars, and had summoned the clergy to
meet him on 21 September, 1294. He told them, after they had
offered two tenths for one year, that they must pay half their entire
revenue, or be outlawed.[24] John de Chishull complied, as on 18
October, 1294, he received a patent of protection for one year,
stating that he had granted the King a moiety of his benefices and
goods.[23]

John de Banstead de Barking (1332)[25] is the next known, but
there must have been one or more between him and the next, John
Ware (1362-5).[26] The Black Death killed off many of the clergy
in 1348. The Bishop of London's Registers are missing for this
period, so no information is available. Ware was followed by
Roger Vencroft (1365), Nicholas Eastheye (1365).[25] and Richard,
Vicar of Brightlingsea, whose name occurs in the list of those who
took the oath against annulling any of the statutes passed in the
then parliament (1387-8).[27] Next came John Hubard de Lithing-
ton (-1398), John Symond (1398-9), William Pecock (1399-), Roger
Shelton (1414-35), Thomas Caumbrigge (1435-52), John Abbott
(1452-), John Roston (-1458), Richard Rolfe (1458-69), Richard
Strother (1469-1470), John Jeffrey (1470-80).[25]

In 1293 the dean and chapter's "spiritual" profits in Brightlingsea
church were 6*l*. 13*s*. 4*d*., while the Abbot received 2*l*. as "spiritual"
profit.[28]

57. During the thirteenth century, the nave and aisles as far as the present line between the south and north doors were built. The arches have the plain chamfered moulding and octagonal shafts usually found in village churches in this, the Decorated period. Traces of a pavement lower than the present one were found in 1878,[29] pointing to the existence of a nave and aisles of the Early English period or earlier.

The churches belonging to the Dean and Chapter were visited by the Chapter's officials. Records remain of visitations made in 1297 and 1458. Brightlingsea only appears in the 1458 visitation. The Dean and one of the Canons visited Brightlingsea on July 31st, when five Brightlingsea men formed a jury, and informed the Dean that the chancel (which as Rector the Dean and Chapter should repair) was defective as to the tiles of the roof, and that they should be removed to repair it afresh. The hall of the rectory was half destroyed, because of defects in the underpinning. A chamber at one end of the hall was defective in its tiled roof and wall, and in the floor, because of defects in the underpinning. A chamber at the other end of the hall was quite destroyed. Two other chambers or outhouses *(domus)* at one end of the hall were nearly destroyed. The barn there was burnt in the time of Roger Feryer, the farmer there; another was defective in its walls and tiled roof. There was a cattle shed well and suitably repaired. The enclosure (fence or wall) round the rectory was destroyed. The enclosure round the granary was wanting, and the seawall on the marsh on the west part required to be repaired and heightened.[30]

The rectory was more than a house, there were farm buildings attached to it. Cattle sheds meant pasture, barns and a granary meant arable land. No land, except the marsh, however, was mentioned, because there was no occasion to do so. This land, no doubt, represented the hide and its appurtenances, which belonged to each Saxon Church.

The Dean and Chapter were granted protection by the king for one year in 1322 in their manors, of which a long list is given, and Brightlingsea appears among them.[31] As the manor of Brightlingsea did not belong to the Dean and Chapter, it can refer only to this estate. The protection was from the dreaded purveyance; nothing was to be taken for the king's use from the Dean and Chapter's corn, hay, horses, carts, carriages, victuals, or other goods. There is nothing unusual in a rectory estate forming a manor. The rectory of East Mersea was a manor with a court baron and copyholders.[32]

58. Here, as elsewhere, there was a great increase in church

building in the fifteenth century. The nave of the church was lengthened by the addition of two bays to the west. The old tower, the foundations of which were found when the church was restored, must have been pulled down and the present fine Perpendicular structure erected. The tower contains a belfry and belfry chamber, a large room with recesses in the walls which, provided with doors, would make cupboards. Beneath there is a gallery opening on to the nave through the east arch of the tower. New Perpendicular windows were put in the north and south aisles, and the south porch was built at that time. In 1497 some new work had been begun on the tower, but whether it was ever completed cannot be said.

[[1] Au, 1.  [2] Au, 2.  [3] Bh, ii., 424.  [4] Bi, 115-6.  [5] Bh, ii., 502.  [6] Bh, ii., 510.  [7] Bn, Tithe.  [8] Au, 3.  [9] Q, 18.  [10] Q, 6.  [11] Q, 3.  [12] Q, 94.  [13] Q, 86.  [14] Na.  [15] Q, 66-7.  [16] Q, 249.  [17] Q, 61.  [18] Au, 6.  [19] Q, 91.  [20] Bs, 205.  [21] D, 442.  [22] Q, 482.  [23] H, Edw. I., iii., 117-9.  [24] Ci, ii., 131.  [25] T, 93.  [26] Bg, 325.  [27] Fe, 18/8.  [28] C, 23.  [29] Bd, 3 Aug., 1907.  [30] V.  [31] H, Edw. II., iv., 52.  [32] Ar., 438.]

## THE SIXTEENTH CENTURY.

59.  " Sir " Thomas Wright was Vicar from 1480 to 1509.[1]  Unlike some of the vicars he appears to have resided here. He was here at the bishop's visitation in 1495,[1] and witnessed John Beriffe's will in 1497. The title " Sir " does not mean that he was a knight. Some priests were styled master *(dominus)*. It is said that the latter were graduates at a university, and those styled "Sir" had not graduated.[2]  John Denny (1509-30)[1] appears to have been resident. Reginald Baynbrigge seems to have been non-resident, for in 1534 he did not sign the clergy's acknowledgment of the King's supremacy, while Robert Kyng signed and described himself as "stipendarius de bryklyngsey,"[3] a description equivalent to that of curate.

There was a chantry here with its priest. When it was founded cannot be said, but William Bolle was chantry priest here in 1420.[4] A chantry was an endowment made to pay a priest to say mass for the repose of the founder's soul and those of others, generally his relatives. An altar, other than the high altar, was often dedicated for this purpose. There was an altar in the south chapel of the church, which possibly was so used. An inscription in Latin, " Pray for the Soul of John Mors and Dionisia his wife, and for the souls of all the faithful," now partly obliterated, suggests it.[5] The Lady chapel on the north side would have an altar also. In addition to saying these masses, a chantry priest acted as curate in his parish, and often as schoolmaster. The chantry here is mentioned in the *Valor Ecclesiasticus* as producing nothing, and reference is made to a lawsuit touching it in 1548.[6] In 1548 the churchwardens stated that they had spent some of the money made by the sale of some of the church goods in defending a suit concerning a chantry presented to be in the parish.[7] As in other places, no doubt the chantry was dissolved by the parishioners who, foreseeing confiscation, diverted the proceeds of the chantry for other purposes. Sir Robert Kyng, "prest" and Sir Robert Smyth, curate, were witnesses of a will in 1521, and the former was appointed to sing masses by the same will. He was similarly appointed in 1525 and 1538. In 1525 he was described as parish priest, as also was John Letheby in 1537.[8] Probably King was the chantry priest.

There was a place called Brightlingesbregg. In 1371 Alberic de Vere, Earl of Oxford, held in it a quarter of a knight's fee, worth 25s., as of his manor of Great Bentley.[9] Sometime between 1422 and 1461 or between 1470-1 the Earl of Oxford still held a quarter of a knight's fee in Bryghtlyngbregge.[10] In 1470 there was a chantry in Brytlingisbregge, of which William London was the priest.[4] Bregge means no doubt bridge, so we have Brightlings bridge and Brightlings island, presumably close together. The exact site of Brightlingsbrigge cannot be said. It might have been the piece of land which belonged to the Earls of Oxford, and was situated near the "Lady's Bridge," to which reference will be made later. An objection to this idea is the fact that this piece of land was very small to be worth a quarter of a knight's fee.

When the manor came into Henry VIII.'s hands in 1540, it was apparently considered desirable for the rectory to be in the King's hands too. In 1544 an exchange was arranged between the King and the Dean and Chapter, in which the rectory, with all its " Ryghts membres and appurtenances," was transferred to the king.[11]

[[1] T, 93. [2] Do, xcvii. [3] J, vii., 1025. [4] Hd, 35096. [5] Bg, 308. [6] D, 443. [7] Fx, xix., 64. [8] Jc, Id., 1, Ig, 7, 25, 27, Jh, 12. [9] Fd, Edw. III., file 222. [10] Ha, 7356. [11] Fo.

## The Pre-Reformation Church.

60. The south doorway was the people's entrance to the nave, the people's part of the church. It was associated with the more secular parts of the church's work. The first part of the marriage service was performed in it. The bride's dower was paid there. In it business matters were arranged. Because of this a porch was built to provide shelter. In 1835 Thomas Turpin, of Wivenhoe,

surrendered certain property to Edward Harvey, of Elmstead, if he did not pay the latter 28o*l.* at or in the church porch of Brightlingsea in March "next."[1]   Inside the doorway on the right will be seen a niche, which contained the holy water with which the people sprinkled themselves on entering.   A stick called a holy water sprinkler was usually provided for this purpose and was chained to the wall.   Pews were not usual till late in the fifteenth century.[2]   The floor was covered with rushes on which the people knelt or stood.   The nave of a church was used for secular purposes as well.   Business meetings of various kinds were held in it.

The chancel contained the altar, the essential part of the church furniture, and held in special reverence.   Hence the chancel was sharply defined from the nave.   In Saxon churches a wall divided them, in which was but a small archway, and this was closed by a veil.   The wish to have the altar more in view led to wider central arches, and to side arches as well.   The veil was done away with, except at the more solemn time of Lent.[3]   The idea of seclusion was kept up by a screen.   We have to imagine the centre chancel arch here filled as high probably as the springing of the arch, with a wooden structure consisting of a solid base carrying shafts forming compartments with tracery at the upper part, each compartment being like an unglazed Gothic window.   An enriched cornice completed the screen.   Most probably the side arches were treated in the same way.   Supported by the screen was the roodloft, a narrow gallery to which access was gained by a flight of steps.   The roodloft supported a rood or crucifix (sometimes so large as to be called lifesize) with images of the Virgin Mary and St. John the Baptist, at the sides (John xix. 25), to which it gave access.[4]   Candles were kept burning on the roodloft before the rood.   John Street in 1531 left a cow, the profits of which were to be spent in keeping a light burning before the roodloft.[5]   Candlesticks, which stood on the loft, were confiscated in 1552.[6]   During Lent the rood was covered.[7] The "roode cote of old red velvet" here was probably so used.[6]   In Saxon churches the altars were generally of wood; stone altars came into use about the eleventh century.[8]   The altar was covered with cloths, of which there were six here, of diaper and plain work.[6] Here a cloth hung in front made of Bruges satin.[6]   On the altar stood a crucifix usually with figures of SS. Mary and John at the sides.   Two crosses belonged to this church, one of silver with SS. Mary and John, weighing 52 ounces, and one of silver gilt of 109½ ounces.[6]   One of these crosses may have been used as a processional cross.   An ornamented background to the altar called a reredos was an enrichment, for which William Beriffe left 2o*l.* in

1527.[9] He described it as an awter table. On the south side of the altar was the piscina, where the silver cruets for wine and water provided here[6] were placed for use at mass, and which was provided with a basin, from which the water used for washing the priests hands could drain into consecrated soil.[10] This piscina appears to have projected from the wall, and to have been hacked off. The consecrated wine and bread were contained in a chalice and paten. Here there were two silver gilt chalices and patens weighing 13½ ounces and 11¾ ounces, and two silver ones.[6] It was the rule to keep the sacrament reserved for use in emergencies, suspended over the altar in a receptacle called a pix. There were three pixes here, one silver gilt and two silver.[6] The pix was covered with a cloth called a canopy cloth.[11] Richard Piper in 1539 left 20s. to buy one. Associated with the altar were various other ornaments. "Sacryng" bells, of which there were three,[6] were rung during mass to mark the stages in the ceremony. A silver censer was used in which to burn incense.[6] Silver chains were provided by which to carry it.[6] Before 1250 a direct kiss of "mutual salutation and affection" was given at the end of the mass. After that date, the use of the pax replaced it. It was in the form of a plate with a handle. It usually represented on the face the Crucifixion. Here there were three paxes made of silver.[6] It was kissed after the Agnus Dei by the celebrant and the others who assisted in the service, and then by the congregation in turn.[12] In the south chapel the remains of the reredos of the side altar may be seen. Its piscina is intact in a hollow in the south wall. As the Lady chapel was enlarged eastward sometime after 1521, there is no trace of the original altar. The remains of the later altar's reredos may be seen.

61. On the north side of the chancel was placed the Easter sepulchre. It was sometimes a permanent structure, and sometimes erected temporarily each year, and decked elaborately with rich hangings. On Maundy Thursday a consecrated wafer was placed in a pyx, put with a crucifix into the Easter sepulchre, over which the priest and people watched and prayed till Easter Sunday. At dawn the priest removed the sacrament from the sepulchre to the usual place over the altar.[13] John Street in 1531 left 13s. 4d. to provide each year "a taper of wax of six pounds weyght to brene [burn] at the sepulchre in the said churche."[14]

The font was usually placed at the west end of the church. Fonts were ordered to be made of durable material, usually stone, and to be kept covered and locked to preserve the baptismal water, which was consecrated on Easter Eve.[15] These font covers were often elaborately made in wood. In addition embroidered covers were used sometimes.[16] A bequest of 4*l*. in 1527 for "a covering for the font" was probably for an embroidered cover.[17]

The walls were usually coloured and adorned with scriptural pictures. The roof here was decorated. William Beriff in 1527 left 20*l*. to the painting of the roof.

When officiating at mass the priest wore an amice, alb, maniple, stole, and chasuble, put on in the order named.[18] "The amice was a rectangular piece of fine linen" worn over the shoulders.[19] The alb was a long white linen gown reaching to the feet, and secured with a girdle. It was ornamented at the neck and wrists with embroideries.[19] The maniple was a narrow strip of embroidery, originally a napkin used for wiping the chalice. It was carried on the left wrist.[19] The stole was a narrow embroidered scarf long enough to reach to the ankles, worn over the shoulders, and crossed over the chest.[19] The chasuble, varying in material and colour, was circular in form with a hole in the centre, through which the head was put. It fell in folds over the arms and body, and reached to the knees.[19] Possibly the amice and stole were included in the "vestments," of which there were several.[6] To perform high mass in its entirety required a deacon and sub-deacon in addition to the priest.[20] Two dalmatics or tunicles, tunic-shaped gowns, the distinguishing marks of deacons and sub-deacons, were among the vestments here.[6] The vestments for services unconnected with the altar, were the surplice, almuce, and cope.[21] The surplice gets its name from the Latin superpelliceum, implying that it was worn over a furred garment. It was a large unornamented alb without a girdle.[22] The almuce was a furred hood having long ends which hung down in front of the dress. It was worn for warmth in cold weather.[19] The cope when flat was semi-circular. It had no sleeves, and was fastened by a clasp across the chest.[19] These were the most costly vestments, as may be guessed from the fact that one of the copes belonging to the church was made of cloth of gold,[6] a material sold at 80*s*. a yard in 1481.[23] Another cope was made of red purple velvet,[6] which cost 16*s*. a yard in 1481,[23] and one was of white damask,[6] sold in 1526 at 7*s*. 6*d*. a yard.[24] John Piper might well consider that 12*l*. was needed, when he decided to bequeath a cope to the church in 1527.[25]

62. On the three days before Ascension Day, priest and people went in procession from the church preceded by a cross, and accompanied by a banner special to the occasion, perambulating the parish and its bounds.[26] The service was of a two-fold nature, to beg a blessing on the fruits of the earth, and "to preserve the rights and properties of the parish."

A "brass pot for holy water" was among the church furniture.[6] This was used to hold the holy water, with which the altars, priest, and people were sprinkled. Houses too were sprinkled with it.[27]

A funeral was an elaborate ceremony. The body, laid on a bier, was carried to the church. In the procession were holy water and cross bearers, the sexton ringing a bell that those who heard it might pray for the dead, the priest in alb and almuce followed by the bier with torch bearers, and last the chief mourners dressed in black cloaks and hoods.[28] John Pyper in 1539 left 16d. to be given "to four men to bear me to church."[29] In the church the bier was covered by a pall or "herse cloth" (here made of Bruges satin) with a wax taper at each corner. A long service in the church preceded the committal to the grave.[28] Masses or other services for the repose of the soul were often arranged by will. In 1496 John Beriffe ordered that a priest should sing masses for his soul for four years immediately following his decease.[29] Between 1506 and 1538 there were many similar bequests for periods of from three months to four years.[30] There was a regular rate of payment of ten marks for a year's masses.[30] The memory of the deceased was perpetuated also by gifts of bread and ale or bread alone, the prayers of the recipients being given in return. The distribution was made on the day of burial, the seventh day after, the month day or thirty days after, and the obit, year day or the anniversary. The poor were generally specified as the recipients. Joan Benet in 1537 left ten marks to be distributed on her burial day, seventh day, month day, and year day.[31] John Piper two years later left 6l. to be spent at his burying day, seventh day, and month day.[32] Another of John Street's numerous religious bequests extended over twenty years. Bread and ale were to be distributed on his burying day, seventh day, month day, and year day, each year.[33] Before distribution, the food was blessed in a religious ceremony. On the eve of the obit day, it was usual for the bell man to go round asking his hearers to pray for the soul of him, whose obit was to be kept, and announcing the services to be held for his soul's benefit. On the obit day the church bells were tolled, and the grave was covered with a pall.[34]

Another way in which prayers for the departed soul were obtained was the beadroll. It was a list of names of those who had made gifts to the church. Every Sunday prayers were asked for those "that have honoured the church wyth light lamp vestment or bell or any ornaments by the whyche the service of Almightye God is the better maintained and kept, and above all for those soules whose names be accustomed to be rehearsed in the bederoll." On special days, such as All Saints' day, the roll used gave the names of the benefactors, and specified their gifts.[35] John Ayer in 1537 bequeathed " for me and my frendes to be praide for in the bedroll as longe as my Wiffe doth lyve, iiij*d*."[36]

63. Bequests to the church were very numerous. It was the rule for a bequest to be made to the high altar " for tithes and oblations forgotten or negligently withholden." The cathedral church of St. Paul's (" Mother Church of Powles ") was sometimes remembered.[37] Possibly a remembrance of the time when tithe, *etc.*, was paid to the cathedral. Sometimes a bequest was made to " Paul's Pardon."[38] Apparently it was connected with St. Paul's in some way. There was a chapel and chantry of note attached to the cathedral called " Paul's Pardon." Possibly it was to this chantry that the bequests were made.[39] In addition to the bequests for religious purposes, other bequests were made for the fabric and furniture of the church. The following bequests are additional to those already mentioned.

1496. John Berif the elder. " Also I leave to the buying of two new bells 100 marks [66*l.* 13*s.* 4*d.*], which William Bownde and Robert Barlowe owe me for one parcel *(pacco)* of salt, Provided always that the parishioners of Brikilsey aforesaid are willing to do entirely, and to complete in all things the new work of the bell tower there weil begun as they promised me, wherefore if they refuse, then I will that they shall have nothing therein." (Mr. Pertwee has drawn attention to the very large amount of money left for the purchase of these two bells.[40] It was also a very large sum to be owing for one parcel of salt. At the average price in 1497 it would mean 363 quarters of salt.[41] Possibly there was a mistake in writing or copying the will, or Bownde and Barlow were not expected to pay many shillings in the pound.)

1506. Richard Patrike, priest. To " reparacions " 6*l.* 13*s.* 4*d.*[42]

1513. John Cowper, mariner. " Vnto the byldinge of a vestrye in my parrisshe Churche thre parts of a Ship called Mary and John, paying of the same to James Garton vij[li.][43]

1518. William Beriffe. " I will that the Church haue xxx[li.] to bye a crosse for me and my sisters and all good ffrendis,"[44] (that they might be on the bederoll).

1521. John Beryff. " I bequeath to Brightlynsey church towarde the lengthing of our Lady Chapell according to the chauncell iij. quarters of the ship called the Trinite, if God send hir well home. . . . . And if she come not well home which God forfende, than I give and bequeth to brightlynsey church xl[li.] sterling to the use aforesaide owte of the barbora and the maryflower, if God send them well home."[45] (The chapel was to be lengthened, so that its east wall was continuous with the east wall of the chancel. It had only reached about half the length of the chancel.)

1521. John Adam. To Bryklingsey church, 3*l*. 7*s*. 8*d*.[46]

1524. Annes Martin. "I geve x*s*. to by a Baner cloth to the Church."[47] (A banner was carried in the Rogation day procession).

1527. Thomas Pynell. To Brekelingsey church, 5 marks.[48]

1531. John Street. To the churche of brylingsey, xx. nobles.[49]

1534. Henrie Benet. "halfe ye v[li.] for the thing that have moste nede in the chyrch of Brightlings."[50]

1537. John Payne, mariner. "I gyve . . . . as myche monye as will by a greate bell called a tenour."[51]

1537. John Ayre, mariner. To the church, 3*l*. 13*s*. 4*d*.[52]

1538. Thomas Chaundler, mariner. "To buy a gravestone to lye afore the stone of William Beryff to the quere [chancel] warde and a thousande pavement Tyle for the path afore the quere dore [the door in the rood screen] as far as it will goo."[53]

1539. Richard Sayer, mariner. To the church, 6*l*. 13*s*. 4*d*.[54]

1539. John Piper, mariner. 20*l*. to the church should his sons die before they were twenty years of age.[55]

1542. William Beriffe. "I give to the reparacions of the saide churche twenty poundes sterling yn discharging of myselfe of all oother wills and bequests."[56]

1542. John Beriffe, repairs, 40*s*.[57]

Taking the cost of building the vestry to be equal to that of building the Beriffe chapel, in the forty-two years ending 1539, 250*l*. was bequeathed to the fabric and furniture of the church, a considerable sum, and equal to about 3000*l*. now-a-days.

[[1] Nk, 304. [2] Dk, 61. [3] Dk, 170-1. [4] Dk, 55-6. [5] If. [6] Fk. [7] Dk, 170. [8] Dl, i. [9] Id, 26. [10] Dk, 51-2. [11] Dk, 48. [12] Dl, 50. [13] Dk, 177-8. [14] If. [15] Dk, 63-4. [16] Ef. [17] Id, 21. [18] Do, lxiv. [19] Eg, ii., amice, *etc*. [20] Dk, 101. [21] Do, lxxiv. [22] Do, lxxv. [23] Bz, iii., 500. [24] Bz, iii., 505. [25] Id, 21. [26] Dq, i., 197. [27] Dk, 155. [28] Dj, ii., 378 seq. [29] Ib. [30] Ic, Id, Jc, Jd, 21, 26. [31] Jg, 7. [32] Ie. [33] Jf. [34] Dj, iii., 80. [35] Dk, 223-4. [36] Jg, 25. [37] Jd, 30. [38] Id, 26, 36, Je. [39] Df, 92-3. [40] Bg, 299. [41] Bz, iii., 340. [42] Ie. [43] Id. [44] Ju. [45] Jc. [46] Jd, 36. [47] Ju. [48] Jd, 30. [49] If. [50] Ju. [51] Jh, 12. [52] Jg, 25. [53] Jg, 28. [54] Jh, 15. [55] Ie. [56] If. [57] Ju.]

## THE REFORMATION.

64. The first step was the repudiation of the Pope's supremacy in 1534. In consequence, the first fruits (the profits of a benefice for one year) and the tenths (of the yearly income), which had been paid to the Pope, were now paid to the king. A new valuation, called the Valor Ecclesiasticus, was made to replace the Taxatio of

Pope Nicholas. The rectory was valued at 6*l*. 13*s*. 4*d*., and the vicarage at 17*l*. 0*s*. 4*d*.[1]

The Bible was published in English in 1535,[2] and in 1538 Cromwell ordered that every parish should procure a copy of the ' Great Bible.'[2] A book of homilies containing reformed doctrine was ordered to be used in all churches.[2] This the churchwardens here bought, for they paid 12*d*. for " an omylye that ys deuydyd [divided] in partes."[3] In 1548 a service in English was added to the Latin mass.[3] 6*s*. 6*d*. was paid for " a boke of ye communyon and for Erasmus's Paraphrase " (of the Bible), and 4*s*. for " a boke cawlyd the ordynery of the churche."[3]

65. The confiscation of the property of the monasteries, and the change in religion made the people doubtful of what would happen to their church property. Evidently they believed, that selling it and spending the proceeds on the repair of the church or other local matter would be better than allowing it to be confiscated. In this Brightlingsea was at least as forward as her neighbours. In consequences of the sales, certificates of the sale or embezzlement of church plate, *etc*., and of the appropriation of the proceeds were required from the churchwardens throughout the diocese.[4] Our churchwardens sent this certificate,

" Brytelingsey.

Thomas Spysall } Churchwardens doo say that they by the
John Hubbarte } advyse of the parryshe there haue solde of the churche plate and ornamentis there three parcels folowinge *namely*, A crosse of Syluer and gylte xxvj*li*. vis. viij*d*., a chalyce a senser two paxes and a pyxe xxi*li*. vis. viij*d*. and two copes a vestemente and two tynnacles [tunicles] vj*li*. xiiij*s*. iiii*d*., whiche money was hollie spente and layed owte in repayringe the steple with the two yles [aisles] of the said churche, in amendinge two bridges there leading over the salte water, and in defending a suyte concernyng a Chauntre presented to be founded in the same churche."[5]

The total amount received was 55*l*. 5*s*. 4*d*., equal to about 660*l*. in present value; which seems a large sum for the work done. By 1552 there had been further sold for 26*l*. 4*s*. 8*d*., a broken chalice, a broken "senser," two "lytyll crewetts," two paxes, a "lytyll basen of siluer," weighing in all 65 ounces.[2] This was done by the advice of the parishioners. Other goods sold were three old copes, a vestment, a piece of old velvet, and two silver clasps 1*l*. 8*s*. 4*d*.; a silver pix, a silver bell, and two candlesticks, apparently silver, weighing 57½ ounces, for 12*l*. 18*s*. 9*d*.[3] The two silver chains weighing 13¾ ounces, belonging to the censers previously sold, fetched 1*l*. 6*s*. 6*d*.[3]

66. A saints *(sanctus)* bell had been removed, and was in 1552 in the king's storehouse in Brightlingsea. A valuable cope of cloth of gold had been given to the Earl of Oxford with the consent of the parishioners.[5] No doubt the Earl desired it, and the parish thought it well to please so powerful a neighbour. In March, 1551, the Privy Council declared that as the king had need of money, commissioners would be appointed to take into the king's hands the remaining church plate, *etc.*[6] On 24th September, 1552, John Lucas, Sir John Seyntcler, and John Teye, Commissioners for the confiscation of the church plate, visited Brightlingsea, and by their direction the following goods were delivered to Thomas Beryf " of the sayd Towne" for the king's use. A silver cross with SS. Mary and John, 52 ounces, a chalice and covering (paten), parcel gilt, 13½ ounces, a pix, silver gilt, 6¾ ounces, a cope of red-purple velvet and a vestment and alb, a green damask cope, a red Bruges satin cope, eight vestments, good and bad, with their albs, stoles and vaynels (maniples), two chasubles belonging to one of the above vestments, a cloth of red Bruges satin used to hang before the altar, a rood cote of old red velvet, a herse cloth of Bruges satin, four bells in the steeple "cawlyd a ring," three little brass "sacryng" bells, two great standing brass candlesticks, two small brass candlesticks, eight broken candlesticks, and certain candlestick heads " which dyd stande apon ye rode loft," twenty-four lead organ pipes, a pair of organ cases, three or four pounds of old wax, "a payle of brasse standyng in the font with wayter, with a pot which was for holye water," and a purse.[3]

67. The Commissioners delivered to the churchwardens for Divine service a silver-gilt chalice and covering weighing 11¾ ounces, a white damask cope, a green Bruges satin cloth used at weddings and churchings, eight towels, six altar clothes, two old surplices, and eight old hutches.[3] The Commissioners were more generous than usual. Their commission implied that a chalice and surplice were ample.[7] Sir John Seyntcler, being the owner of Moverons, perhaps in consequence was generously inclined.

The churchwardens' accounts, apparently for the three years preceding, since the rent for the church house was entered for three years, were audited by the Commissioners.[8] The church house was an important feature of parish life. In it a variety of parochial business was transacted. Churchwardens in want of money brewed ale and sold it at a convivial meeting ("church ale") called for the purpose in the church house. The rent here was 12*d.* a year,[8] probably the manorial quit rent. It was probably a timbered house, for 2*s.* was paid for "dawbing" (plastering) it. In the same account is an item for "ten tunes[tons]of timber to repare the churche which ys like to fall" 3*l.* 6*s.* 8*d.*, and another for washing the church "clothes" 4*s.*⁵ It does not state whether this is for a year or more.

Removing the stone altars and "makyng cleane the churche" cost 4*s.* 6*d.* This, no doubt, meant the removal of the rood, roodloft, images and stained glass, and obliterating the wall paintings, as was ordered in 1547.⁸ 23*s.* 4*d.* was paid for the communion table to take the place of the altar, and four forms "with the carryeng ye Same."³ Probably these forms were for the communicants to sit on round the communion table. A seame and a halfe of "whyte lyme" (2*s.* 6*d.*) was, no doubt, for the whitewash used to obliterate the wall paintings. A "baldryke for the belles" to make which half a horse hyde was obtained (3*s.* 6*d.*) was probably used to assist in removing them from the tower.⁸ The Commissioners disallowed 7*l.* 13*s.* 4*d.* paid to Thomas Randall "for makyng of the steps." There is nothing to show what these steps were. Who and what he was, is difficult to say. 4*s.* 8*d.* was also paid to him "for his fee," and 2*s.* 4*d.* was paid to William Tarre due to "Thomas Randall the Mr. for his fee.⁸ "Mr." may mean minister, as suggested by Mr. Pertwee. The vicar of that time was named Bainbrigge, but he may have been non-resident, and Thomas Randall may have been his substitute, or he may have been the master builder and William Tarre his workman.

68. The influence of the Reformation is shown in the wills. The bequests to St. Paul's and the high altar for tithes forgotten were omitted, though once (1563) a bequest of 2*s.* 6*d.* was made to the vicar for tithes.⁹ Bequests to the church were rare, even for the repair of the fabric. There was no need for ornaments in the reformed faith, but the fabric needed repair whatever the faith. Bequests for masses were omitted, and gifts to godchildren were much less frequent. Gifts to the poor were not so common. There was as selfish a reason for their omission as there had been previously for their presence; the new faith did not believe in prayers for the dead. There was no invoking the mediation of the Virgin and the saints, when the testator commended his soul to God. Thomas Spisall's will (1551) shows the change; he bequeathed his "soule unto almightie God who became a lyvelie sacrafice upon the awter of the crosse for the same."¹⁰ Richard Wade (1575) committed his soul "into the handes of God our hevenlie father hopinge to be saved throughe the meritis of Christ's deathe and passion."¹¹

1553 saw Mary on the throne and the old forms were soon re-enforced. The clergy who had availed themselves of the permission

to marry given in 1547, were deprived of their benefices.[12]  Reginald
Baynbrigge, who was vicar from 1530 till he died in 1555,[13] evidently
had not married, and, further, managed to fall in with the change
to and from the reformed faith.  Aristotle Webb (1555-9)[18] saw
the change made again, for, on the accession of Elizabeth in 1558,
the reformed faith was re-established, the altars were pulled down
again and replaced by communion tables, while the surplice was
the only vestment required to be worn.[14]  The clergy had to agree
to Elizabeth's supremacy or lose their benefices.[14]  Persecution,
even to death, came to those who opposed the ordered faith.  It
must have been these persecutions or those of Mary's reign, which
led Henry Ffroste in 1571 to leave the reversion of his house for
the benefit of "afflicted members of Christe, I mean those which
have suffered persecution for his Worde, and are nowe in
necessitie."[15]

69.  The clergy were often not well educated, and many were
unable to preach.  Endowments were made to provide lecturers
or preachers in addition to the rector or vicar in some parishes.
Apparently Thomas Simpson (1560-84) was not able to preach, as
although there does not appear to have been any perpetual fund
here for a preacher, Thomas Beriff in 1563 left "towards the paines
of a preacher for making and preaching twentie sermons within the
parishe Churche afforesaid," 3*l.* 6*s.* 8*d.*[16]  Making and preaching
sermons was paid for at a higher rate than saying masses; twenty
sermons were equal to one year's masses.  A minister named John
Horton was a witness to a will dated 1575.[17]  As there was a
resident vicar then, this minister was probably a preacher.  Thomas
Addy "person" in 1576,[18] and John Woddy "clerk" in 1590 were
witnesses to wills, and may have been preachers here.  Provision
was made for the funeral sermon.  Henry Blacke, in 1565, left
"towardes the paines of a precher for an exortacion to be made at
the assemble at burial or otherwise," 5*s.* 8*d.*[20]  [Brian Atkinson,
vicar, 1586-94.]  The Protestantism of this period did not please
the Roman Catholics nor the Puritans, and the law dealt very
severely with those who stayed away from church.  Brightlingsea
folk, as a rule, like their vicars, appear to have kept clear of religious
differences, but two at least paid a penalty for their recusancy.  In
1605 the vicar, churchwardens and sidesmen of Brightlingsea presented "that Thomas Barwicke gentleman nowe of their parish
refuseth to come to their churche to dyvine Servis of God, and that
he and Margaret his wif have forborne to come thither three yeres
togither nowe last past."[21]  In the same year they were each fined
40*l.* for this offence.[22]

Hugh Jackson, vicar from 1594 to 1609,[23] was resident, and was described as "a diligent and sufficient preacher." The living then was worth 40*l*. a year.[24] Thomas Wheeler[23] followed Hugh Jackson and was succeeded by William Smith at a date not later than 1614, when he (Smith) witnessed a will.[25]

70. In 1640 began a series of changes by which the Church of England was so altered as to justify the statement that it was abolished. The bishoprics, spiritual courts, Book of Common Prayer, thirty-nine articles, psalter, *etc.*, were abolished. The churches were visited for the purpose of demolishing and removing all images, altars, communion tables placed altarwise, and "other relics of idolatry." Churchwardens were also ordered to remove the communion table to some convenient part of the church, and take away the altar rails, and level the chancel.[26] Whether Brightlingsea church was so visited cannot be said. If it were the inscriptions on the brasses asking for prayers for the souls of the departed, considered superstitious and therefore to be removed, were overlooked.

The clergy, too, were abolished in most instances. Robert Pettit, who became vicar in 1626,[27] was ejected for "sundry dismeanours" now unknown.[28] While some of the clergy were unfit for their office, very many were ejected for their political beliefs. Taking "the archbishop to be a wise holy man," or not praying "for the Parliament till late" cannot be considered serious offences, yet were put forward as reasons for ejecting clergy.[29] Richard Hutton was minister for a time. He was removed to Cumberland by the Committee for Plundered Ministers, and was succeeded by George Wilkinson, "a godly and orthodox divine," on 29th November, 1649.[28] A fifth of the profits of all sequestrated property and offices was allowed to those from whom they were taken. George Wilkinson was ordered to pay Mrs. Pettit a fifth of the profits of the vicarage, being 8*l*., but only paid 6*l*. and refused to pay more. The Committee for Plundered Ministers, on 18th March, 1647, ordered the Committee of Parliament at Colchester to enquire why. On June 22nd the committee reported that they had ordered him to pay the 8*l*. and the arrears, or he would be removed from the vicarage. By 10th July, 1647, he had paid her in full, and she was ordered to leave the vicarage house, part of which she had occupied to his annoyance. She evidently was not satisfied for, on 14th August, 1647, she again petitioned the committee, but they would not hear her till she had left the vicarage house.[30] Wilkinson had left here by 1657 for James Backler was minister then.[31] Pettit, although out of the living, was in trouble for, on 29th June, 1649,

E

the Standing Committee in Essex ordered him "to be sent for by a Trooper to answeare to such misdemeanours, as are objected against him.[32] What his offence was does not appear.

In place of the system abolished, Presbyterianism was introduced with assemblies of great power, but subordinate to Parliament. There were parochial "classes," and provincial assemblies. There is extant a list of "classes" for Essex in 1646. Brightlingsea is in the Tendring Classis.[33] The confession of faith took the place of the thirty-nine articles, while the Directory of Worship replaced the Prayer Book. Many other changes were made: for instance, Christmas Day was not to be kept as a holiday, nor might mince pies be eaten then, as they were supposed to favour superstition.[34] Presbyterianism held its ground for a time only. The Independents obtained the sway, and voluntary associations were formed to promote their religion.[35] The Essex Association was formed sometime before 1658.[36]

71.  One feature of the new church system was a committee of trustees for providing maintenance for preaching ministers. Where thought necessary they made additions to the ministers' salaries. In 1657 the trustees ordered that, as yearly payments from Ardleigh, Horndon and Sampford rectories amounting to 9*l*. 12*s*. to the minister of Brightlingsea could not be obtained, 9*l*. 12*s*. was to be paid yearly from the profits of Steeple Bumpsted rectory to James Backler, minister of Brightlingsea.[31] On another occasion a grant of 40*l*. was made to the minister here.[37] There were passive resisters then. In 1644 "Mr. Darsy [Darcy] and Mr. Samford, parishioners of Britlingsea" were ordered to be kept in safe custody until they paid their tithes."[38]

In 1660, on the return of Charles II., the Church of England was restored. By the Act of Uniformity of 1662 acceptance of the Book of Common Prayer was required of all who held church livings. Many Puritan ministers preferred leaving their comfortable positions to changing their religious beliefs. How the vicarage became vacant at this period I am unable to say, but Robert Pettit had been restored before 1668.[39]

Many harsh laws were enacted against the Nonconformists, and they obtained no legal relief until the Act of Toleration. It does not appear that licenses for preachers or meeting houses were applied for in Brightlingsea, when they were allowed in 1672.[40]

A minister, ejected from Stapleford Abbots in 1662, was named Lewis Callendrine. In 1661 Lewis Callendrine, "Clericus," was presented in the manor court of Brightlingsea for non-attendance, he being a resident. He owned the farm we now call Redbarn

THE CHURCH, 1877.

(Plate iii.)

farm, in 1685.[41] Whether this was the ejected minister, or another of the same name, is difficult to say.

On the accession of William and Mary many of the clergy refused to take the oath of allegiance; Christopher Bateson, the vicar then, was not one of them. Holman gave this account of him. "Christopher Bateson, Clerk, was instituted vicar here 19 June, 1671, and dyd 1699. He was of Queen's Colledge in Oxford, an admirable Scholler. He accompanied John Hebden, Esquire, envoy extraordinary from King Charles the 2 to the Emperor of Russia in 1678 in quality of Chaplain and Latine Secretary to his Excellency and left an exact Diary of his Journey into Moscowe."[42]

[[1] D, 360. [2] Ej, viii., 376. [3] Fk. [4] Au, 27. [5] Fx, xix., 53. [6] Au, 29. [7] Au, 30. [8] Au, 27. [9] Ih. [10] Ju. [11] Im. [12] Au, 32. [13] T, 93. [14] Au, 38. [15] Ik, 24. [16] Ih. [17] Im, 4. [18] Im, 36. [19] Ju, Ric., Jollye. [20] Ii. [21] K, x. 10. [22] Fq. [23] Bg, 325. [24] Dm. [25] Ju, Humphrey Hastler, 1614. [26] Dh, i., 104-6. [27] Bg, 325. [28] Dg. [29] Au, 58. [30] Hd, 15670 f. 106, 15671 ff. 64-5, 80, 114-7. [31] He, 993 f. 392. [32] Ha, 6244 f. 84. [33] Dd, 18. [34] Am, 117. [35] Dh, ii , 98. [36] Dh, ii., 161. [37] Dh, ii., 496-7. [38] Hd, 15669 p. 38. [39] Fg. [40] Au, 69. [41] Np. [42] No. 52.]

## THE EIGHTEENTH CENTURY.

72. Holman's MS. notes of Essex (about 1709 with additions dated 1747) give an account of the Church. It is described as a lofty stately building; the height of the tower is stated to be 94 feet. He gives an account of the brasses, which is especially valuable, as it gives the inscriptions now missing. They are thus described[1]:—

(1) "In the North Isle of the chauncell [Lady Chapel] is a gravestone of gray marble, on it the Effigie of a Venerable Man in Brasse in the habit of a Mayer, his Hands folded in token of Devotion, underneath on a plate of Brasse, this inscription in Gothic letters: John Beriff of Jacobes died the xx. of Maye Anno 1542. Here lyeth William Beriffe his eldest sonne who hath bene Deputie of Bryghtlyngsee xii. yeres, who had Isue by Anne his wiffe ii. sonnes and ii. daughters, who died ye ix. of Maie Anno Domini 1578. (Plate viii.)

(2) "Upon a flat stone in the chancell praye for ye soule of Sir Thomas Knight [Wright] Sometyme Vicar of this Chirch who dyed 2 day of October 1509 on whose Soule Ihesu have mercy Amen. This monument is now—1747—removed into the Church Porch and there set in the floor." [A stone now in the porch has the matrix of a small figure and plate for inscription.]

(3) "Upon a flat stone in the Beriffe Chapel a man betweene his 3 wives Sans Arms [without coat of arms]. *Here lies John* Beryfe

*Margaret Amy and Margaret his wives who died      day of the month of*
*March 1496.  Whose souls God Pardon."*  (Plate viii.)

(4) "Another *there* [Beriffe chapel].  Of your Charitie pray for
ye Soule of Dame Alyse Beryff which dyed ye last day of October
1536 and for ye Soule of Margaret her daughter whose Soules God
pardon."  (Plate viii.)

(5) "Another *there* [Beriffe chapel] pray for the Soules of John
Beriff of Jacobs Mary and Alys his wifes which John deceased 26
Aug. 1521 on whose soules Jhesu have mercy."  (Plate viii.)

(6) "Another *there* [north aisle].  Pray for ye Soule of Margette
Beriffe who died 1514.  This monument 27 August 1747 is now (as
I apprehend) in the church porch and was removed about 14 yeares
agoe with the other of Sir Thos. Knight [Wright] as the present
incumbent informed me F.B.  The effigies in brass is now—1747—
kept in the Chest in the Vestry."

(7) Another *there* (north aisle)—"*God be merciful to the soul of*
*Mary Beriff and to the souls of all the faithful dead and all her sons that*
*they may rest in peace.  Amen.  Who died on Michaelmas day 1505."*

(8) "Another in the midd Isle of the church very fayre.  Of your
charite pray for the Soule of William Beryff marriner and Johann
his wife which William deceased 2 Sept 1527 on their Soules Jhesu
have mercy."

73.  Holman does not mention the fine bracket brass in the Lady
Chapel.  The four stepped calvary, part of the shaft, the three pairs
of trefoils springing from the shaft, and part of the bracket are
missing.  The present effigies (no. 4) did not belong to this bracket
originally, as they do not fill the matrices, which have the outline of
priests wearing vestments.  Probably the priests brasses were cut
down, and engraved on the reverse for the Beriffes.  In Margaret
Beriffe's brass the outline of her gown is contracted about the level
of the knee, done no doubt to adapt it to the priest's brass narrow
at that part.  Holman mentions this coat of arms as hung in a
frame in the chancel,—"Argent, a fess gules with a lion currant or,
between six trefoils stalt vert 3 2 1."  This coat of arms, now disappeared, is similar to the Beriffes, and may be a variant of theirs,
belonging to another branch of the family.  The trefoil appears on
the bracket brass as well as in the Beriffe arms.  Did the Beriffes
make the trefoil their badge to explain their appropriation of the
bracket brass?

In a window of the "Isle" was a shield, argent, bearing a plain
cross gules.[1]  A shield bearing a "garb" (sheaf) appeared several
times in the roof,[1] apparently part of the decoration.  Francis
Wheeler's (of Colchester) tombstone, then in the "middle Isle," is

now in the organ chamber.   There was a hatchment displaying
Wheeler's arms, "Sable, a bar engrailed argent, between three doves
argent, impaling argent on a chief sable three mullets or, a chevron
chequey or and azure between three cross crosslets fitchey."[2]
Francis Wheeler, father of the above, was a man of position here,
and judging from his will wealthy.[3]   He was an Assistant in 1635.[4]

David Murray, vicar from 1708 to 1724, began a lawsuit in 1709,
to recover tithes on certain lands, and oysters and oysterlayings in
Borefleet, but in 1713 judgment was given against him with costs.[5]
Complaint was evidently made to the Bishop, that he had bribed a
witness in the case.   An affidavit made in 1713-14 contradicted it.
There was some fear that the Bishop might remove him, and in
1721 twenty-six parishioners signed this petition[7] :

"These are to certifie The Right Reverend Father in God John
Lord Bishop of London, That David Murray, Viccar of the parish
of Brightlandsea in the County of Essex hath lived with us near
twelve yeares.   During which tyme he behaved himself as becometh
his Holy professione being exactly conformable to the doctrine of
the Church of England in his publick preaching, in his conversatione
sober exemplary and obliging, and in the private exercise of his
calling (visiting the sick which is with us of great value) diligent
and careful ; and that (of late) we have been so much deprived of
his company, we are much troubled for it, and if your Lordship
thinks fitt to remove Mr. Murray wee beg leave to recommend
Mr. Ley to your Lordship who in Mr. Murrays absence has taken
all ye possible care of us that he could and is minister of the next
parish to us."   He was not removed.

74.   Thomas Luck's influence (1724-61) is shown by the parish
registers.   He must have looked after his congregation well, for
there was a big increase in the number of baptisms registered,
directly he became vicar ; many of them were youths and adults.
His tombstone in the Lady Chapel bears witness to his devotion in
these words : " Here lieth the Body of Thomas Luck A.B. Vicar of
this Parish upwards of Thirty seven Years (and of this only) and
that too purely voluntarily."   He is best known as the founder of
the school.   [John Smith, vicar, 1761-67].   Henry Whitfield, 1767-
78,[8] is the only known vicar to have had the degree of Doctor of
Divinity.   A sermon he preached before the University of Oxford in
1773 has been handed down to us.[9]   The text is " Where shall
wisdom be found ? and where is the place of understanding ? "
(Job, xxviii. 12).   He remarks that " wisdom is unquestionably the
truest epitome of human perfection, and such is its excellency, that
not only those that have attained it, but also those also, who never

will, nor never can attain it, make equal pretensions to it." His final conclusion that wisdom and understanding are to be found in the University of Oxford is only to be expected. William Wade, M.A. (1778-1809),[10] was curate here at a salary of £30 a year before becoming vicar.[11] John Robertson (1809-36) held the living also at Great Bentley, where he lived. He used to ride over for one service a Sunday.[10] He must have had assistance in his work here, for the parish register records the burial of Robert Bewick, curate of Brightlingsea (1806), and Joseph Territt, officiating minister (1827). The living is in the gift of the Lord Chancellor. For a short time it was in the hands of the Bishop of Peterborough, and previously in the Bishop of London's.

75. In 1703 Queen Anne's Bounty was founded. The scheme provided a fund into which the first fruits and tenths were paid, and from which small livings were augmented.[12] Brightlingsea vicarage was discharged from the payment of first fruits and tenths, and received an augmentation of 200l. in 1737.[13]

William Whitman left 7l. a year in 1730 to the vicar on condition that he preached two sermons every Sunday from Ladyday to Michaelmas, and resided with his family in the parish for that time.[14]

In 1747 there were two bells and a saint's bells in the tower, and there was a frame for five.[15] One bell was sold about 1816[16], and there is now one bell and a saint's bell unhung. The bell bears this inscription "Dulcis sisto Melis Vocor Campana Michealis Wm Ffounder me fecit,"[17] which may be translated "I appear sweet and honeylike. I am called the bell of Michael. William Founder made me." This bell most probably is of fifteenth century date.[18] In 1552 the church bells were confiscated. Probably they were restored during Mary's reign. There is a tradition that some of the bells were sent by sea to be repaired, and the ship was lost. Another explanation is a churchwarden in financial difficulties early in the eighteenth century had them sent away, and pretending that the ship was lost at sea sold them and kept the proceeds.[18] This would account for there being only two bells and a saint's bell in 1747. The saint's bell was for a time used at St. James' Chapel, but has been returned to its original home.

There are some details extant relating to the work of the church for 1773. There was then one service every Sunday, and communion four times a year. There were fifty communicants from the one-hundred-and-twenty houses (approximately) which the parish contained. The children were catechised in summer.[19]

76. On 29th March, 1814, the original roof and clerestory of the church fell in with a crash, heard as far away as the Lodge Farm.

THE CHURCH, 1877.

(PLATE iv.)

Two arches between the nave and the south aisle, and the aisle itself were damaged.[20] It was estimated that 919l. 10s. would be required to repair it, and that 326l. would be received for the old lead from the roof of the nave and aisle. The parishioners were given a royal brief to enable them to receive contributions, and make a house-to-house collection throughout England.[21] One of the bells was sold at this time to raise money, and it is said of one churchwarden that he was willing to sell the steeple, if anyone would buy it; the origin, no doubt, of the local saying that " Brightlingsea people had sold the bells, pawned the church, and promised the steeple."

There is a stone slab at present under the arched recess in the south wall of the Lady Chapel, where it was removed from the chancel steps. It is 75 inches long, 27 in breadth at the head, and 19 at the foot. Incised on it is a large cross flory supported by a shaft rising from a plain round arched base. The lines were cut by some pointed tool. There are also five small incised crosses irregularly arranged on the slab. The shape suggests that it was used as a coffin slab, while the five small crosses suggest an altar stone. It may have been an altar stone cut down to make a coffin slab.[22]

The chancel, west gallery, tower arch, and west window were restored through the generosity of the late Mr. T. Nevinson, of Leicester. There was a general restoration of the church by public subscription in 1878. In 1886 the tower was restored by the late Mr. F. C. Capel. Judging from a drawing of 1801, the pinnacles, if not the parapets too, of that date were at some time replaced by some of a simpler type, which in turn were replaced at this (1886) restoration by pinnacles and parapets, lighter and more ornate as were those of 1801.

[¹ No, 46.  ² No, 52-3.  ³ Jb.  ⁴ Le, 298.  ⁵ Fj.  ⁶ Kb, 42.  ⁷ Kb, 273.  ⁸ Mb,
⁹ Dl.  ¹⁰ Bg, 325.  ¹¹ Hf.  ¹² Cr, 104.  ¹³ Bm.  ¹⁴ Ak, ii., 771.  ¹⁵ No, 46.
¹⁶ Bg, 316.  ¹⁷ Bc, vi., 45.  ¹⁸ Bg, 315.  ¹⁹ Hf.  ²⁰ Bg, 309.  ²¹ Hd, Charters,
Bv, i., 3.  ²² Ba, vii., 376.]

## THE RECTORY AND VICARAGE.

77. The old differentiation between the Manor and the Rectory estate has disappeared. The latter has lost its name and identity. As the Rectory house was the residence of the priest before the vicarage was instituted, it may be expected to be found close to the Church, and the land not far away. Brightlingsea Hall and the Hall Farm represent the rectory house and land. In a suit for tithe, begun in 1709, it was shown that John Skinner and others

combined with Elizabeth Brand, widow and devisee of Isaac Brand, late owner of the great tithes and lord of the manor, to refuse to pay tithe for certain land as being ancient glebe land, and alleged that "within ye memory of man noe small tithes or any composition in lieu thereof have been paid to the vicar" for this land. It was claimed that the rectory or parsonage land was freed from payment of small tithes, and that the vicar could not by the provisions of the ordination of the vicarage claim more than the annual payment of ten marks in lieu of his small tithes for the manor. The defendants alleged that the parsonage farm, in the occupation of John Skinner, was all of it ancient glebe land. The court ordered that the plaintiff's case be dismissed with costs, but John Skinner was to pay the 6l. 16s. tendered. So the above statements made by the defence were accepted as true, except that apparently there was due a payment of ten marks to the vicar from the rectory land.[1] In the tithe commutation award a modus or customary payment of 6l. 13s. 4d. (ten marks) is stated to be payable to the vicar in lieu of the small tithes of Hall Farm. On the tithe map, fields 58 and 63 of the Hall Farm are described as parsonage 10 acres and parsonage meadow.[2] John Skinner is known to have lived at Brightlingsea Hall.[3]

It may be objected that if this house were called Brightlingsea Hall, how could it be the rectory house? There is evidence that the rectory was a manor, and in such case the rectory house would be called a hall, and was so called in 1458.[4] The change from the name Brightlingsea Rectory Hall to Brightlingsea Hall would be made quite easily. The present hall was built in 1874, replacing the old timbered house, built on an E plan, and evidently not the rectory house of 1458, unless very much altered.

Round the present Hall are some fine specimens of Eucalyptus trees (Eucalyptus Urnigera) grown from seed by the late Mr. J. Bateman, who first introduced them into England.

The Vicarage house stood to the south of the Church facing the Green. The tithe barn stood behind it (see plate ii.). In 1610 it was stated that a stable and garden were attached to it. The house was burnt down in 1816.

78. The situation of the Church away from the Town has caused much discussion. It is usually said that the lord of a manor built a house for himself and a church near by, and that a village grew up round both, and that where the village and church are widely separated, there has been a migration of the people. This explanation has been adopted here, and a suggestion made, which has almost become accepted as a fact, that the change was made as a

result of the Black Death. The concentration of the population in the present place has been one of gradual growth from a condition of houses scattered in small groups or singly over the Island. It is certain that there was no wholesale migration after the Black Death, for we find a large number of properties in the present Town with names which can be traced back beyond that date. Further, the land round the Church was the property of the Dean and Chapter of St. Paul's. The Lord of the manor was not resident until long after the Church was built. Also the Hall has been shown to be not the old Brightlingsea Hall, but Brightlingsea Rectory Hall. The Manor House is the original Brightlingsea Hall.

The Church is placed at a point where the roads from all parts of the island converge. The position was quite accessible from the greater number of houses when they were scattered. It is possible that the Church was once more than a parish church. It may have served the adjoining parishes of Alresford and Thorington. Its position at the junction of the roads from them with the main Brightlingsea road made it accessible from all. Alresford and Thorington Churches are not of early date. Thorington Church was in some way subject to Brightlingsea Church, and the Abbot received 3s. yearly, which was paid to this Church by Thorington Church.[4]

There is another possible explanation. Though there was no resident Lord of the manor, there was in the thirteenth century a resident owner of Moverons, Sir Alexander de Brightlingsea, a man of position and property. And quite likely there was one for years before. He may have built the church mainly for himself, but favoured the parishioners in its situation, because their payments would help the priest. It may be that Alexander de Brightlingsea was the restorer of the church in the thirteenth century. He was probably wealthy enough.

[[1] Fj. [2] Mh. [3] Mb 1718. [4] V. [5] Q 546.]

## NONCONFORMITY.

79. The Wesleyans here date from 1780.[1] It does not appear that John Wesley ever visited Brightlingsea. If Brightlingsea folk came under his magic influence it must have been at Colchester. Brightlingsea does not appear among the places having ministers or chapels named in the Wesleyan Deed of Declaration, dated 1784.[2] Services were first held in a thatched cottage (now in decay) in the present Mill Street.[1] Later they were held in a house in School Yard. A wooden chapel was built in Chapel Road,[1] probably soon

after the trust deed of 1804. In any case it was in existence before 1827. The present brick building was erected on the same site in 1843. A graveyard is attached, but is now closed.

The New Jerusalem Church doctrines were introduced by Dr. Moses Fletcher.[1] The early meetings were held in Mill Street.[1] The congregation had a resident minister in 1813, when it was regularly established, and a chapel was built in Waterside Lane. The building is now 18 and 20 New Street, and may be recognised by the ecclesiastical cut of its windows. The registers of births and baptisms of members of the Congregation exist from 1813 to 1837, and are preserved at Somerset House. The present Church of classical design was completed in 1868, the way being prepared no doubt by the trust deeds of 1861 and 1862; the cost was £1150.[1] The Congregational Church began as a branch of Lion Walk Congregational Church, Colchester.[3] The Congregation had a resident minister before 1848.[4] In a trust deed, dated 1855, relating to a piece of land, they were described as Paedo-Baptist Independents, that is Independents who practised infant baptism. The first building (erected before 1833) was a wooden structure in John Street. When superseded by the present brick building in 1863, it was removed to the Waterside.

The Primitive Methodist church had a building in New Street, now part of Messrs. Seabrooke's brewery. A much larger place of worship was erected in Ladysmith Avenue in 1902.

The Salvation Army has had a corps here several years. The barracks were formerly in the old Temperance Hall on Hurst Green. They are now in Tower Street.

[1 Eh 32.  2 Eo iv. 503.  3 Eh. 33.  4 Aq 452.]

# Chapter IV.

## BRIGHTLINGSEA AS A MEMBER OF THE CINQUE PORTS.

80. A very brief note of the Cinque Ports must be given before dealing with Brightlingsea. The Cinque Ports were Hastings, Sandwich, Dover, Romney, and Hythe. The two ancient towns, Rye and Winchelsea, were added in Henry II.'s reign, and ranked as head ports. All except Winchelsea had members attached to them. Sandwich had a corporate member—Fordwich, and non-corporate members—Brightlingsea, Deal, Ramsgate, Reculver, Sarre, Stonor, and Walmer. Each head port and corporate member was, in the feudal period, subject to a certain amount of control by its lord, and after, each managed its own affairs entirely. Apparently it was not until the fifteenth century that the head ports exercised local jurisdiction in the non-corporate members.

The court of Shepway, presided over by the Lord Warden, and formed of representatives of the head ports and the corporate members, was the chief criminal court, but in time became reserved for dealing with treason, false coining, treasure trove, false judgment, default in service to the king, and neglect of duty by bailiffs.[1]

The court of Brotherhood was formed of representatives of each head port, and had the management of the herring fishery and fair at Yarmouth. The court of Brotherhood and Guestling had in addition representatives of the corporate members. It undertook a variety of matters needing joint action.[2]

The ports and members provided fifty-seven ships for the king's service for fifteen days each year at their own cost.[3] In return the following privileges were confirmed, if not granted:—

(1) Honours at court. The right to carry a canopy over the sovereign at the coronation, and to a place at the coronation banquet. This right was confined to representatives of the head ports.

(2) A lengthy list of exemptions from payment of dues such as wharfage, pontage, etc.

(3) Right to exercise certain franchises, such as infangthef. These could be exercised by Corporations only.

(4) Exemptions from attendance at shire and hundred courts and assizes out of the ports, even when the barons owned land out of the ports. This removed the ports from county jurisdiction.

(5) " Den and Strond " at Yarmouth. The free use of the denes and beach there for drying and mending nets, and beaching vessels.

81. Brightlingsea does not appear in any of the earlier existing documents of the ports. She is not mentioned as a member in the Domesday of the Ports (1229) which details the ship-service given. The fifteenth century was a period in which the connection with the non-corporate members was strengthened. In 1424 a charter was given confirming Margate, Goresend, the parishes of SS. John, Peter, Nicholas, and All Saints, Birchington, Kingsdown, and Ringwould, in their rights as members of the Ports.[4] Deal and Walmer obtained a similar confirmation in 1438.[5] A probable reason for the strengthening of the union between the Ports and the non-corporate members was the decay of the manorial system and the growth of the corporations' power. The manorial lords were losing the old criminal jurisdiction over their tenants (compare the jurisdictions in Brightlingsea granted to the Abbot in the twelfth century and to Cromwell in the sixteenth), while in the Ports' corporations they were ousted. For instance the lord of Sandwich had been the Abbey of Christ Church, Canterbury, which received a rent in herrings from the townspeople.[6] The corporations finally got rid of this overlordship. Edward IV.'s charter of 1465 recognised[7] this increased power and confirmed, if it did not create the jurisdiction of the head ports over the non-corporate members.

Brightlingsea, like the other members, wanted a charter of confirmation, and obtained it in 1442. It was enrolled in the Old Black Book of the Sandwich records, and is somewhat incorrectly quoted in Boys' *History of Sandwich*. It is as follows :—

" Be it remembered that on the 24th day of July in the 20th year 1442 of the reign of King Henry the VIth of England after the Conquest at the Brodhull [Brotherhood] it was agreed, that all the Residents and Inhabitants in the town of Brygthlyngssey in the County of Essex, which town from ancient time has been a member of the Cinque Ports, may have and enjoy all the liberties of the Cinque Ports, and that the town of Sandwich make them a record of the same under the seal of office of mayoralty there, whereof the tenour follows :—

" To all the faithful in Christ, to whom these present letters shall come, the Mayors and Bailiffs of the Cinque Ports, Greeting in the Lord Everlasting. In knowledge and truth to you all by these

Facsimile of the Enrolment of the Letters Patent to Brightlingsea, 1442.—
Sandwich Records.

(Plate v.)

presents we set forth, bear witness to, and make known, that we have seen the records of all the towns and members attached of the Cinque Ports, wherein it is contained and stated that the town of Brythlyngssey in the County of Essex is a town and member of the Cinque Ports, and by cause and virtue of the liberties of the Cinque Ports, all the Residents and Inhabitants of the town of Brithlyngssey aforesaid are free and quit of pontage, segeage, passage, murage, lastage, and of all toll and custom throughout all the land and dominion of our Lord the King of England, which privileges were to the said Barons of the Cinque Ports and their successors by the charters of our Lord the King and by his pro-genitors granted therein. Wherefore we require and friendlily ask you that when the aforesaid Residents and Inhabitants of the town of Brythlyngssey aforesaid with their goods, ships, and merchandise may make journey among you, that, free and quit of all toll and custom aforesaid, you permit them to be and to depart. In testimony of all and singular of these premisses, the testimony of the seal of office of mayoralty of the town of Sandwich in the name of all the Mayors and Bailiffs of the Cinque Ports to the present letters patent is affixed. Given at Sandwich the twenty fifth day of July in the twentieth year of the reign of King Henry the VIth of England after the Conquest." (Plate V. is a facsimile of this charter.)

It should be noted that Brightlingsea is stated to have been a member of the ports from ancient time, and that the main point of the testimonial is that the men of Brightlingsea were each to enjoy exemption from the various tolls named.

82. In 1477 Brightlingsea applied to Sandwich for a record of the freedoms granted by Edward IV. to the ports. This referred to his charter of 1465,[7] which made more definite the old privileges, granted new ones, and mentioned the members for the first time. Sandwich agreed that "they [Brightlingsea's inhabitants] have enjoyment and proof of their freedoms and free customs" on con-dition that they contribute to Sandwich "for the Navy and service of our Lord the King," but no sum was mentioned. The new letters patent are more in detail than the first. The minute and principal parts of the letters are :—

"Be it remembered that on the 18th day of August in the 17th year [1477] of the reign of King Edward IV., came John Cole one of the Jurats of the Town of Sandwich before John Aldy the Mayor and the Jurats there, brethren of the same John Cole, and exhibited [*protulit coram die*] the copy of a certain grant made of old with the

assent and consent of all the Mayors and Bailiffs of the Cinque
Ports, that the Town of Brithlyngsea in the County of Essex is a
member of the Cinque Ports; the tenour of which same copy
remains in this book in the time of Richard Cok Mayor and in the
20th year of the reign of King Henry VI., in fact namely from the
beginning. [This alludes to the loss and regain of the throne by
Henry VI. The words are 'in facto s*cilicet* no*n de* in*choatione,*' sense
only when the *non* is omitted.] Which same John Cole in the
name of the Residents and Inhabitants of the said Town of Brightlingsea sought, that they should possess a Record of the freedoms
now by the Lord King Edward granted to the Barons of the
Cinque Ports and their members, under the seal of office of
Mayoralty. It was conceded to him that they have enjoyment and
proof of their freedoms and free customs to the end that the said
Residents and Inhabitants contribute to the said Town of Sandwich
for the Navy and service of our Lord the King there maintainable,
as the other Combarons of their members in such service and
shipping have been accustomed to do and pay according to their
abilities, which same John Cole then and there promised that they
should so do, and that further he himself should bring this Record
of the said Residents and Inhabitants here for security of the same
to remain. The tenour of which said Writing to the said Residents
and Inhabitants conceded follows :—

"Our Lord Edward . . . conceded that we all and singular of
the Cinque Ports and their members may be free and ought to be,
wheresoever we may have been throughout the lands and dominion
of our Lord King, of all toll, pavage, pontage, quayage, murage,
rivage, sponsage, passage, lastage, stallage, tallage, carriage, prisage,
picage, terrage, hidage, scutage, and of all custom and scot and
geld, and of all wreck, and of all selling purchase and repurchase,
with soc and sac, thol and theam, and that we be wreckfry, witfry,
lastagefry, and lovecopefry, and that we shall have our findings in
sea and on land, and that we be quit of all things and our tradings
as freemen, . . . . Wherefore we signify testify and make known
to you all by these presents that the town of Brichlyngssey in the
County of Essex is and has been from time to which memory
runneth not a town and member of the Cinque Ports, and for that
reason all the Residents and Inhabitants of the same town are our
Combarons free and quit of all toll and custom throughout all the
lands and dominion of our Lord King of England enjoying and
holding all freedoms quittances privileges and free customs of the
Cinque Ports, wherefore we require and friendlily ask you that

when the said Residents and Inhabitants of the said Town of
Brichlyngssey with their goods wares merchandise or ships should
come among you or should approach you or any of them among you
come or approach you that they and theirs whatsoever all the
freedoms quittances privileges and free customs aforesaid be permitted to have and enjoy, and this under the penalty provided in
our charters,.and that they and theirs whatsoever without any
imposition against the provisions of our privileges and without any
toll tax or custom be permitted to go . . . . "

Here Brightlingsea was stated to have been a member of the
Ports from time immemorial, which in its strict legal sense means
going back to 1189.

83. This. however, was not the final settlement. In 1491 there
is this entry in the Sandwich White Book :—.

" *The seventeenth day of May in the seventh year of the reign of King
Henry VII.* By force and strength of a lettere of Advertisement
sent by the Mayor and Jurats of this port unto the inhabitaunts of
the towne of Bryghtlynsey in the County of Essex, which of
auncient tyme out of mind hath bene reported and taken as a
membre of the v. ports deponding and atteyning a membre unto
this their capitall port as more at large may appere in the tyme
of John Aldy Mayor *in the 21st year of Henry VI.* which lettere of
advertisement here upon the ffirst of this yere remayneth in Court.
The hool cominaltie of Bryghtlynsey aforesaid sent here with their
lettere upon the same file hanging, James Turner, William Malyn,
couper, J. ffick [these names are very indistinct in the original]
inhabitants of the same towne suffiseently auctorised for to com-
moune appoynte conclude and establish for euer betwix this town
and them, as betwix the hedport and the membre aforesaid for a
contribucion and aid towards the Kings Navie at this tyme and all
othere when any suche charge of shipping shal happen to this porte
from tyme to tyme when the Kings Navy with his army in his Royall
person entendeth eny viage on the Sea, according to the purport of
oure charter and as also for a yerely pension and recognisaunce as
all othere oure membres do toward [word missing] and other chargs
of parliaments coronacions and otherwise yerely to be contributed
and payed and as whereupon the said persons by the same auctoritie
for and in the name of the hooll cominaltie of Brightlinsea aforesaid
in presence of Thomas pynock Mayor and Jurats in the Councell
Chaumber for and towards a contribucion of our Navie at this
tyme payed and deliuered in ready money vj. pounds sterling, And
for a yerely pension and Recognisaunce yerely about the ffest of

Nativitie of St. John Baptiste to be borne and payed to the use
and behoof of the commonaltie of this towne, the said persons by
the same auctoritie promissed and their comonaltie bounden them
and their successours foreuer to pay yerely for euer henceforth xs.
sterling as above, And thereuppon was graunted that they should
haue letteres certificatoryes under the sealle of office of mayoraltie
here comprising certayn poynts of our Chartere whereof the
tenoure hereafter followeth."

The letrers patent, which follow, begin in the same way as the
others, and give a like list of privileges, and continue :—

"Whereas also in the Court of the Lord the King called the
Brotherhood in the port of Romney, held customarily twice in each
year in that same place, before the Mayors Bailiffs and Jurats of
the said Cinque Ports, the Rolls and Registers of these Cinque
Ports, and of all the Towns and Members to them appertaining,
having been diligently and fully searched, it was ascertained, that
the town of Brightlynsea in the County of Essex, from time to
which the memory of man runneth not to the contrary, was and is
a Member of the Cinque Ports aforesaid, and hence a member of
Sandwich as its headport, because it is the nearest neighbouring to
the Member appropriated, And therefore all the inhabitants and
residents of the same town as the other remaining Combarons of
the other members of the Cinque Ports named, all freedoms
quittances free customs and privileges of the said Cinque Ports
have constantly used and enjoyed as they ought [*deberent*] to use
and enjoy, Therefore all of you we earnestly require and ask that
when our said Combarons the inhabitants of that town of Brightlynsey may come to you or to your places, or any of them may
come, they and theirs whatsoever with all their goods chattels ships
and merchandise be free and they and theirs each of them be
permitted to use and enjoy all and singular of the freedoms
franchises and quittances abovesaid also their free customs and
privileges whatsoever without hindrance interruption or disturbance,
not molesting or oppressing them in anything under the penalty
and punishment laid down . . . ."

It is not clear whether the payment of 6*l.* was to be made whenever the Ports had to supply ships to the king, but it does not look
as though a yearly payment for that purpose was intended. An
interesting point is that the payment was made to Sandwich to
help pay for her ships supplied to the king; Brightlingsea did not
provide ships directly for the king, nor make a money payment to
him instead. Nor is it suggested that Sandwich increased the

number of ships she supplied. Another point is the bargain that
was made. Sandwich did not make Brightlingsea a member of the
ports, nor even recognise her as such. Either was out of her
power. Brightlingsea men wanted a proof of their privileges,
probably because some port was making them pay dues from which
they as portsmen were free. Sandwich gave them this proof in
exchange for financial assistance.

84. Their privileges were denied soon after by the Bailiffs of
Colchester. On the Tuesday after Easter in 1499 the Court of
Brotherhood agreed "that a curteis [courteous] letter may be made
of all the hole howse unto my Lorde of Oxenforde, therin he to be
thankd of his grete kindnesse Schewid [shown] and done unto the
Inhabitants of Brykelyngsey as towchyng the variaunce between
the said inhabitants and Colchester dependyng. And another letter
also to be directyd unto the bailiffs of Colchester requyryng them
to sursese there sute and sofre [suffer] the saide Inhabitants to
enjoy such preuilegis as they heretofore hath enjoyed."[8] The
trouble was not ended then, for on the Tuesday after 20th July,
1499, the Brotherhood decided thus:—

"And for as muche as the inhabitants of Briglensee on of the
membres of Sandwiche by the baileffs of Colchester haue lately
been grately trobled vexed and sued in grete munyssyng [menacing]
of such preuelaces [privileges] as the said Inhabitants theretofore
withoute interrupcion as well of the said Bailiffs and their pre-
decessours as of any other have feasibly occupied and enjoyed, it is
therefore concludid that the Bayleffs as nowe Aymitted [admitted]
to Yermouth schall in ther way titherward schall comen [commune]
with the said Baileffs of Colchestyr to the intent the Baileffs may
sursese of all there said trobles and vexacions and to suffyr the
said Inhabitants to enjoye as well forthon as they have done in
tyme paste." The Earl of Oxford was Lord High Admiral, and a
powerful man in this neighbourhood, and as he intervened, almost
certainly the matter was maritime. It may have been a question
of the fishery, or of tolls in the river or at quays.

85. Henry VIII., in 1510, gave the ports a charter confirming
their privileges.[10] The inhabitants of Brightlingsea asked the
Brotherhood, in 1532, for a copy of this charter. It was ordered
that they have one sealed with the common seals of Romney and
Sandwich "for and in the name of all the Fyve ports."[11] Among
the Holman MSS. is an MS.[12] beginning "Mayors Bayliffes and
Jurors [Jurats] of ye 5 ports ye combarons of ye Towne of Brykylse
*in the county* of Eastsex an antient lymme and member of ye Towne

F

and Capitall port of Sandwich as apperes by ye Records of ye Exchequer at a Brotherhild at ye common house at Romney." The rest is a resumé of the privileges of the Cinque Ports. It must have been written by some one who had access to the copy of the charter soon after it arrived in Brightlingsea, judging from the writing and paper. Evidently only one seal was affixed to the copy, for in 1555 Brightlingsea asked to have the common seal ordered in 1532, and the Brotherhood agreed.[13] This copy would have to be paid for, and probably William Beriffe was referring to it when he made this bequest in his will (1542),[14] " I forgyve the said Towneshipp fourty shillings, which is owing me for such costes and chargies, as I was at at the renewing of the towne charter," or it may have been for Brightlingsea's share of the cost of the original charter. He also gave 20s. to "the maynetenaunce of the fredome of the said towne." These bequests for maintaining the freedom of the town were numerous. The last one known was in 1574.

86. Brightlingsea was often at variance with Newcastle. In 1532 the Brotherhood sent a letter sealed with the seals of office of mayoralty of all the towns of the ports, to the head officers and inhabitants of Newcastle.[15] The contents are not stated, but it had reference probably to interference with their privileges. In 1555 the Brotherhood ordered Sandwich to write a letter on behalf of Brightlingsea "of for and concernyng their molestacion of [by] the people of newecastell which letter shalbe sealed with the seale of office of mayoralty of euery towne of the vij. towns, making relacion that if the seyd people of Newe Castell do not surcease in the troublyng of the seyd Inhabytants of Brythlingessey that then processe shalbe awarded against any of the comminaltie of new castell for theire so troublyng of the seyd Inhabitaunts of Brytty- lingse in every of the seyd townes according vnto the quantytie of the trepasse so commytted by theym by way of wythernam."[18] The Newcastle officials must have been making Brightlingsea men pay tolls on their quays, etc., from which the latter were exempt by charter. Withernam was a means of redressing such wrongs. In this case the goods of any Newcastle man found in any of the Ports would be seized to satisfy the loss occasioned by the Bright- lingsea men in Newcastle.[16] Again, in 1592, "the men of Bright- lingsea which is a member to Sandwich compleyned of some injurye done unto them by the Governors of Newcastle, and do desyre a Lettere or Testimoniall from this House to the men of Newcastle for Reformacion of that enormytie under the seales of the seaven Townes."[17]

The distance between Brightlingsea and her head-port appears to have led to her receiving long credit for contributions. In 1554 Thomas Beryff, John Assheley, and John Webbe of Brightlingsey " solicitors sufficiently auctorized by the commonaltie of Brightlynsey aforesaid" went to Sandwich to pay the contribution money for eight years ending on the next feast of the Nativity of Saint John the Baptist at 10s. a year, and another 4l. towards Sandwich's share of the cost of renewing the Ports' charter, coronation and other charges. They were to have a copy of all records relating to Brightlingsea.

87. In the following year we first hear of a Deputy for Brightlingsea, but the entry does not suggest that it was an innovation. Deputies appear to have been appointed first as a result of the authority given to the head-ports over the non-corporate members in Edward IV.'s charter. Instead of the usual yearly appointment, Sandwich agreed with Brightlingsea "for the electing of their deputie there euery ij. yeres." No hint is given how he was to be chosen; soon after we get a hint.

On 31st May, 1561, Sandwich decided that the Mayor, John Manwood, and Richard Parrot " shoulde Ride unto brightlinsey as well for good order ther to be observed and kepte, and also to take suche further order that the towne of Sandewich may stande in saftie not to be damaged by any actes hereafter to be commytted by the inhabitants of brigtlynsey, and the said maiors and Jurats chardgs to be borne at the Townes coste."

This account of their visit is recorded.

" *Be it remembered that on* [omitted] *day* of June in the third yere of the rayne of our Souerayne Lady Elizabethe by the grace of God Queene [*etc.*] at the visitation there at brightlinsey aforesaid holden before Simon Lynche, gentleman, maior, Richard parrott, and John manwood, of Sandwich, appeyred all the inhabitaunts of brightlynsey aforesaid as well for the election of the deputie there, as for other matters for good order there to be observed, and thes were in elecion—Thomas Beryfe deputie last, Edward Lambard, Stephen Upchurche Senior, Willyam Beryfe, *from whom the said Thomas Beriffe is elected as deputy for the two years following.*

" Also the day and yere aforesaid was an enquest of xii. men of the same inhabitants empayneyled upon thes articles following and they to make certificate at the feaste of St. bartholomew next followynge.

" ffyrst ye shall enquyre of suche persons which refuse to come to ye church at tymes ordayned.

" *Also* to present all suche Typlars [alehouse keepers] as kepe resorte in divine tyme of service.

" *Also* of all suche as lyve in advoutre openly or suspiciously or frequente houses of bawdyre.

" *Also* of all suche as use unlawfull games.

" *Also* of suche ben outlawed in dwellynge within the libertie, and presente theyr names and their goods within the same libertie.

" *Also* of such as obstinately or willinglye dothe refuse or deny any commaundimente of ye maior of Sandwich or deputie of this towne or refuse to paie any cease [tax] for the towne.

" *Also* if any withholde any orphants goods, and to present them.

" *Also* all such as seake to breake the liberties of Sandwich or with any forriners doe joyne themselves in so malicient attempts."

On the same day the said Mayor and Jurats demanded payment of the following sums, and Brightlingsea agreed to pay them by the feast of St. Bartholomew :—

| | |
|---|---|
| Contribution money for four years ended at the Feast of St. John the Baptist last at 10s. a year | 40s. |
| Brightlingsea's share of 20 marks, the cost of renewing the charter by Queen Elizabeth - | 44s. 4d. |
| Payment to two members of Parliament, 6s. a day each, Brightlingsea's share - - - | 5l. |
| Brightlingsea's share of the expenses of the Ports' representatives at Queen Elizabeth's coronation | 20s. |
| A gift was made to Lord Cobham on his being made Lord Warden, Sandwich's share was 11l., of which Brightlingsea paid - - - | 40s. |
| Brightlingsea's share of the expenses incurred at the Brotherhood held at Romney - - | 40s. |
| Brightlingsea's share of 100l., the cost of a *quo warranto* suit (a suit in which the Ports were called on to prove their title to some right) - | 6l. 13s. 4d. |
| | 20l. 17s. 8d. |

88. No hint is given where the meeting was held. Presumably the four men, from whom the Deputy was chosen by the Mayor and two Jurats, were elected by Brightlingsea. On 29th June the Mayor and two Jurats reported " theyr successe of theyr beynge at Brightlinsey."

The contributions were again allowed to accumulate before being paid, as this entry shows :—

" *Be it remembered* that the xxiiijti Daye of January in the yere

aforesaid [1569] before John Tyssar Maiour, John manwood [*etc.*],
Juratts, appeared William Beryfe Deputie of our member of
Brightlingsey Richard Simson and Richard Browne of the same
Towne and made payment unto William Cripps one of the
Treasurers of this Towne of 20*l.* which Mr. William Southwick
late Baylyf to greate yarnemouth demanded at his beinge at
Brightlinzey aforesaid." The 20*l.* was for six years' contributions,
payments to the Ports' members of Parliament, and a share of
Sandwich's expenses at Brotherhoods for six years. A very wordy
and explanatory receipt was given. The reason for the lengthy
explanation appears. later. Brightlingsea was in an aggressive
mood, and wanted answers to several questions as to their privileges
and procedure. These were answered by Sandwich, and the
answers are for convenience given here after each question.

QUESTION: "ffirst whether we may not assesse any newe
Incomer which is not free with [blot] at a resonable fyne for his
freedome, which yf he refuse, how we shall order him."

ANSWER: "They being not corporate cannot assesse any newe
incomer but yf they will obteyne to be corporate then they may, or
yf ther be any manour within there then by consent of byelawes,
they may cesse and fine."

Q.: "yf their being wilful or stoborne person dwelling within our
Towne, which will not do bere and pay towards the maynteninge
of the Liberties of the same as shalbe reasonably assessed by his
honist neighbours, how we may do to recover the same ?"

A.: "by precept from this Towne, beinge their hedd porte corporate to be levied, or ells to be imprisond in the hedd porte."

Q.: "Whether we shall obey a subpena or priue Seale or any
other proces without a letter of attendaunce,· and how the same
lettere Roneth or what the Style thereof is ?"

A.: "Such process as either Sheriffe Bailife or other mynister
ought to serve are not to be obeyed without lettere of attendance,
but other processes must be obeyed." [The king's writs were not
valid in the Ports, unless the Lord Warden added a letter of
attendance to them.]

Q.: "Whether we may not ponishe by fyne or otherwyse such of
our Inhabitance, as do distroy the broods of oysters, or do take and
destroy young fries of ffyshe, which are not market hable ?"

A.: "Ordynaunces and byelawes reasonible beinge made by
them, and confirmed by the hed port, will bind them."

Q.: "Whether we may not also promisse such Strangers, as do
dredge in somer season within our liberties in destruction of our

channell and of the comonwealth, and after what manner we may ponishe them ?"

A.: "The same also by ordynaunce to be made by them, and confirmed by the heddporte."

Q.: "Whether we shall obey any commission comyng to our Towne to presse our masters or mariners, not having a letter of attendance ?"

A.: "As comyssions have heretofore been used, seeinge yt is for the princes service in tymes of necessitie and uppon [blank]."

Q.: "Whether we may not erect and buyld a cage and prison howse for the ponishement and keping such offenders as may happen to be apprehended within our Liberties, and yf we may not, how we shall do with them ?"

A.: "Ye may buylde a cage *namely* stocks for a staye for the tyme, and as the case shall require uppon further examynacion, to send them to the constable of the next hundred or next justice."

Q.: "If ther shall happen any man woman or child to be drowned by any misfortune, where we shall have a crowner to inquire of the death of the same ?"

A.: "They beinge not corporate, the crowner of the Sheere must do yt."

Q.: "Yf there shall happen to be any offendour or breaker of the Kings peace within our Liberties or any other mysruld person, how we shall bynde him to the peace or ponishe the same?"

A.: "The deputie as a constable may promisse the offendour punishment for breach of the peace or take bond by obligacion, but further bond myt be from the hedd porte."

Q.: "Yf there shall happen any man to be outlawed, whether the sheryffe of the shere may come to attach his body or goods, or what we ought to do with the person so outlawed ?"

A.: "That for as myche as they are not corporate, they cannot have yt but the hedd porte."

89. As already hinted, there was a grievance about the payment towards Sandwich's share of the expenses at the Brotherhoods. This is shown in the next entry in the records.

"Also where xls. a yere was demanded of the said Towne of Brightlinsey as a yerely chardge by them of Dute to be paid toward the chardges of this towne of Sandwich ys at bretherhildes gestlings and other metings at Romeney the said Deputie Requyred a lettere by Mr. Maiour of the Towne and his brethren [Jurats] to be dyrected to the Towne of Brightlinsey to let them understande whether of Dutie or of goodwill they paye the same, which was granted under the seale of maioraltie of this Towne in this form following."

"After our right hartie comendacions whereas Mr. William Southwick late Bailife to greate yermouthe appointed from this towne of Sandwich whereunto your Towne of Brightlinzey is a member, amongest other things which he dydd at his late beinge with you demanded of you thes somes followinge as due by you unto our said towne namely [the items follow as already given.]

"And where also we understand by your deputie that ye are greved or ells not fully Satisfied touching the payment of the said xls. yerely towards the purses aforesaid [payments to the expenses at the Brotherhood] Theis shalbe to certifie you that albeyt our Town of Sandwich is greately chardged by purses yerly at brother-helds gestlings and other meetings of the cinque ports, which metings indeed are for the better defence enioynge and mayntenaunce of such pryveleges and Lyberties as to us and our members by charteres do apperteyn, yet we do not nor never dyd meane to clayme or challenge of you the same xls. as a yerely chardge by you of Dutie to be paid unto us, But beinge every yere greatly chardged that waye and many other wayes in Defence of our said Liberties of which ye are partakers with us we trust that as allwayes hetherto we have founde you in suche reasonable causes to be contrybutory with us so amongest the benefits of our Liberties with us ye will not denye reasonably to bere your porcion towards that and such leeke [like] chardges when they shall happen by which expencs both you and we shall contynue in the more quiet and safetie and we shall thankfull accepte and take the same from you and not otherwise as knoweth Allmightie God to whom we commytt you, from Sandwich this xxvth of January,

Your loving friends the Maiour<br>and Juratts of Sandwich."

90. In 1579 Edward Bacon of Brightlingsea, yeoman, was outlawed and his goods and chattels, value 8*l*., became, according to the Ports' charters, the property of Sandwich. James Beryfe and Henry Hubbard, yeomen, were allowed, however, to retain them on condition that they "use Helen Bacon, wife of the said Edward and mother to the said James and Henry, with all curtesye and friendlie consideracion."

It is seen how the Cinque Ports and the Manor shared what may be called the police jurisdiction. But this was not always recognised by others. Lord Darcy of St. Osyth in 1559 had demanded the presence of certain prisoners in Brightlingsea, which had been denied him. No doubt he considered that as a Justice of Peace he

was entitled to deal with offenders in Brightlingsea. He complained
to the Privy Council who ordered that Stannage (or Talnage),
Hickson, Pyper, and Locke were to attend the Council to be examined " touching the denyall of the delyvery of suche prisoners as
the Lord Darcy sent for out of that towne."[19]  Evidently it was
they who had denied the prisoners. In such case they must have
been men of authority, possibly the Deputy and Assistants. In any
case the last three were men of standing. The Privy Council took
no notice of the Deputy, possibly because they did not know of
his existence, for a letter they sent was addressed to the more usual
officers, " the Cunstable and Heddesmen " (capital pledges). They
were " to delyver suche prisoners remayninge in the said town as
the Lord Darcy shall sende for, to those whom he shall sende for
them." They were to bind the four named men to appear before
the Privy Council, or to send them in safe custody. On 10th
February John Talnage, Peter Piper, William Hickson, and John
Locke made their appearance before the Council, and desired that
it might be recorded. The next day they were " for their arrogant
behaviour in denying the delyvery of the prisoners remayning in
that towne to suche as the Lorde Darcy had sent for them, and
taking uppon them to write to the Counsell in this matter, having
no aucthority to do so, were committed to the Flet." On 17th
February Talnage and Piper were bound in the sum of 20*l.* each
to appear before the Council when called upon and on the 23rd
Hickson and Locke were bound in the sum of 100 marks each, to
be " of good abearing and behaviours " till the next Michaelmas.[19]

91.  The Mayor and three Jurats of Sandwich on Saturday, 7th
August, 1601, made one of their two known visits to Brightlingsea.
Single Jurats had visited Brightlingsea when on their way to the
herring fair at Yarmouth, and probably acted as magistrates then.
On this occasion the old Deputy, Thomas Berwick, and his Assistants,
John Beriffe, John Hayes, Barnard ffeuerell, John Chaundeler the
elder, and Ellis Markant, appeared before the Mayor, and John
Hayes was chosen Deputy and sworn.  John Beriffe, Barnard
ffeuerell, John Chaundeler the elder, Ellis Markant, Robert Woodes-
worth, gentleman, and Peter Tompson, were chosen and sworn
Assistants to the Deputy.  Barnard ffeuerell had been appointed
one of the constables, but the Mayor and Jurats thought, as he was
now an Assistant, he should be relieved of his constableship, and
appointed John Harris instead.

A jury of eighteen named inhabitants were impannelled to make
presentments on the following Monday on certain unnamed articles

delivered to them. On the Monday the Mayor and Jurats licensed innholders and gave a warrant for collecting the poor rate. 7*l.* 7*s.* 4*d.* was paid to the Mayor, made of 5*l.* towards the charges of two burgesses for the last two parliaments, 2*l.* towards the charges at the installing of the Lord Warden and 7*s.* 4*d* the balance of 3*l.* 10*s.* for " vii. yeres contribucion money at x*s.* a yere to be ended at Michaelmas next coming." The obnoxious payment to Sandwich's share in the expenses at the Brotherhood was omitted.

This entry shows the result of refusing to act as Deputy :—

1606. " Mr. Maiour and his Brethren assembled in the Counsell Chamber for divers matters concerning the utilitie and tranquilitie of the towne. At the same tyme appeared before them one Barnard ffeuerell of Bricklesey in the Countie of Essex a member of this Towne upon a Subpena served upon the said ffeuerell out of the Chancery of Dover for the Ports and their members to appear before the said Maiour and his brethren upon a contempt, that the said ffeuerell made in refusing to be deputie there, he having been formerly chosen by his neighbours was for the said contempt committed to prison until he had paid five pounds for a fine for the said contempt and so was sworne deputie for the year ensuing."

This entry suggests that the Mayor and two Jurats visited Brightlingsea in 1631 :—" The Deputie and assistants of Brightlingsea beinge the xvijthe daie of Julie 1631 by Mr. Daniel Williams, Maior of Sandwich in the Countie of Kent, Mr. George Willson and Mr. Andrew Gosfirth, Jurats, demanded xxxx*s. a year* for and towardes the expences the corporacion is at in goinge to Romenie to the Brotherhoods and Guestlings, for the benefitt not onlie of the said Corporation, but allso of the members thereunto belonginge. They replyed that yt is nowe sithance [since] the xth yeare of Queen Elizabeth that they did paie the said xxxx*s. a year,* and therefor yt beinge soe longe since they supose they are free from that said charge." This is the charge they made trouble about paying in 1569.

92. A Brightlingsea man was a prisoner in Dover Castle in 1620. He sent a petition asking to be released. His custodian in sending the petition for presentation to the Lord Warden told his secretary, that he hoped the man would be released. He said " I am sure I haue been at charges with him and the Landeres, and must be so longe as they continue, for neither of them hath or hath had, nor no hope hereafter to haue, for ought I know, one penny of money to pay for any part of their charges, And so alwayes it hath been my fortune, yf I haue one prisoner able to pay his charges, I haue had three poore to keep on my owne charge for him."[20]

On 15th January, 1634, " Mr. William Hutt the old Deputy "
was re-elected. Harry Rowse and Thomas Read were elected and
sworn Assistants to the said Deputy. " Mr. ffrancis Wheeler, Mr.
Thomas Goodale, John Nicholson, Robert. Weald, and Josias
Stevens " were chosen Assistants, but being absent their oaths were
deferred. William Hutt on the same day was sworn constable of
Brightlingsea for the ensuing year.

The next part of the minute looks as if there had been a difficulty
about the rates. The Mayor and Jurats decided that six of the
" chiefest Inhabitants " of Brightlingsea chosen by the Deputy and
Assistants were to assist in the " indifferent [impartial] rateing "
of any " taxe or sesse " to be made in Brightlingsea on any warrant
from Sandwich.

93.   Charles I.'s shipmoney became a menace to Brightlingsea.
On 30th December, 1634, Sandwich assessed her members towards
the provision of a ship of 800 tons for the King's service in these
sums—Deal 60l., Walmer 30l., Sarre 20l., Ramsgate 20l., Stonor
6l., and Brightlingsea 25l.   Brightlingsea's assessment was afterwards reduced to 23l.   The Sheriff of Essex also wanted 23l. from
Brightlingsea for the ship Essex was to provide, the Town being
mentioned in his writ.   The people of Brightlingsea complained to
Sandwich, and the Corporation petitioned the Lord Warden to
prevent the Sheriff from proceeding further, but the Sheriff insisted
on Brightlingsea having to pay to the County.   In November,
1635, the inhabitants of Brightlingsea sent a petition to the Privy
Council asking that they should not have to pay twice, and
wanting to know to whom they should pay.[21]   On the 20th
November the petition was presented at the Star Chamber, when
it was decided that Brightlingsea should pay with Sandwich, and
not with Essex.   A copy of the order was evidently given to the
Deputy, who sent a copy certified by him and two Assistants to
Sandwich.   In spite of this order the Sheriff of Essex, for 1635,
complained that Brightlingsea had not paid, and an order of the
King in Council, dated 30th November, 1538, required the Deputy
of Brightlingsea to pay the sum assessed to the Treasurers of the
Navy, or attend the Board the first Sunday in December.   The
Deputy attended that day and produced a receipt dated 12th
October, 1635, from the Mayor of Sandwich for the 23l.   In view
of this receipt and the previous order, the Deputy was discharged.
In future it was ordered that Brightlingsea should pay with Essex.[22]
This soon happened.   In 1638 a writ was issued to the " good men
of Brittlesea," among others in Essex, ordering them to provide a

ship of four hundred and fifty tons and one hundred and eighty mariners, to be ready with double equipment by 15th March next at Portsmouth.[23]

94.  In consequence perhaps of the troublesome times, Sandwich decided in 1642, that instead of making a new election, Bryan Darcy, Deputy, William Hutt senior, John Nicholson senior, William Hutt junior, and William Folkes, Assistants, should continue in their places.  Bryan Darcy continued in office probably until 1644, for 17th July, 1645, it was ordered by the Mayor and Jurats of Sandwich, that if Mr. Darcy, late Deputy of Brightlingsea, do not return within fourteen days, two warrants served by him, at the suit of Thomas Sandford, gentleman, upon William Stone and Barbara his wife, and the other against Richard Ram, he was to be fined 1*l.*  Apparently he did as required, for on 2nd September, 1649, the Mayor and Jurats "did elect and choose him to be their deputy of Brightlingsea a member of Sandwich aforesaid for one whole year there next ensuing, and from thence untill a new deputy was or should be sworne for them, the said maior and Jurats, and in their place and stead to govern and rule the Inhabitantes of the Towne of Brightlingsea in good order peace and tranquility according to the laws of this land and according to the ancient and laudable custom of the said Towne of Brightlingsea.  And at the same time William Hutt the elder, John Nicholson the elder, Thomas Sandford, George Sandford, (all inhabitantes of Bright-lingsea aforesaid) were likewise chosen to be assistants of the said Town of Brightlingsea to assist and advise councell and helpe him the Deputy, for and in the gouerning the said Towne and Inhabi-tants in the same, and for the due and just executing of the said office of Deputy in Brightlingsea aforesaid.  The said Bryan Darcy was then in due and loyall manner sworne, and the said William Hutt the elder, and John Nicholson the elder (being then present) were likewise in due and loyal manner sworne to be assistants to him the said deputy, and in regard the said Thomas Sandford, George Sandford, William Hutt the younger, and William ffolks, were then absent, the said deputy (according to ancient custom) was commissioned to administer to them, as aforesaid by virtue whereof he accordingly administered to the said Thomas Sandford, George Sandford, William Hutt the younger, and William ffolks, the oathe of assistants the 3rd day of November 1649 (but not to the said George Sandford and William ffolks in regard they were both absent)."

In 1655 a Brightlingsea woman, named Goody Taylor, murdered

a boy whom "the Parish had put to her husband to keep." She must have been taken to Sandwich for "she lay in jail there til Tryall" and was condemned. She was hanged the following year after her child was born. Sandwich had by that time given up the old practice of burying her criminals alive in the sand.

95. After this date there is little note (in the eighteenth century none) of Brightlingsea in the Corporation records, but there was some correspondence, for, 1663, the Treasurer's accounts show as paid for a letter from Brightlingsea, on January 14th, 2d.; on April 2nd, 4d.; and on April 30th, 8d. for a double letter.

The contribution money was not forgotten, though there is no note of it being paid. A list was given of the members' contributions (1688) which shows the different rate at which the members paid. Fordwich paid 2l., Deal 13s. 4d., Brightlingsea 10s., Walmer 6s. 8d., Sarre 3s. 4d., and Ramsgate 1s. 8d.

The ports at first were not exempt from paying subsidies, and in the earlier Subsidy Rolls Brightlingsea appears, but later, after exemption was granted to the Ports, rolls for Tendring Hundred are found quite complete, except that Brightlingsea is omitted.[24] Some of the taxes similar to the subsidies were not avoided. The voluntary present to Charles II. in 1661-2[25] and the Hearth tax are instances. To the former Brightlingsea gave 5l. 7s. 6d. In 1666 Brightlingsea paid the Hearth tax with the Ports. The collector of the tax in Tendring Hundred noted that he had seen "an acquitance under the hands of Edward Shelton servant to Sir Nicholas Stroud wherein hee acknowlegeth to haue receiued off Mr. Joseph Hutt Mayor off the Port of Brittlingsey, Lying in this County but a member off Sandwich, one off the Cinque Ports, the summe off seuen pounds seuen shillings and two pence for this half years duty ffor the use off Collonel John Stroude gouernour off Dover Castle."[26] In 1674 Brightlingsea paid with Essex.[27] Though the Sandwich records do not notice the existence of the member again until the nineteenth century, we get hints of it from other sources. We hear of William Pierson, Deputy in 1700, and Martin Skinner, Deputy in 1703 and 1705.[28] One of the Wenlock family was Deputy late in the eighteenth century. John Tabor, who died aged eighty-six in 1799, was described as Deputy-Mayor in the parish register. William Sherlock, in 1773 was described in the same MS. as Mayor. The Deputy and Assistants with the Vicar were entrusted to manage Simpson's Charity in 1632. The Deputy Mayor and Assistants were appointed to assist in the administration of Luck's Charity in 1731.[29]

The Sandwich Records made a brief reference to the Deputy and Assistants in 1803 and 1804. On 22nd August, 1803, " Mr. Samuel Simons " was appointed Deputy for the remainder of that year, and Thomas Jefferies and Thomas Angiers were appointed Assistants. On 8th December, 1803, Samuel Simons was appointed Deputy "for the year ensuing and untill another be appointed in his stead." For some reason the Corporation did not wait until the year expired, but on the 5th July, 1804, decided that he "being now present in Court is continued Deputy of the said parish for the year ensuing, and until another be appointed in his stead, and is sworn." " At the same time appeared Messrs. Orbell Simons, James Harris, Joseph Dawson, John Noble, Abraham Lufkin, and John Jolly, Inhabitants of the said parish of Brightlingsea in the place and stead of Thomas Jefferies and Thomas Angiers, and they the said Orbell Simons [etc.] are severally appointed such assistants to the said Deputy, and are sworn into office accordingly."

It will be noted that the parish and not the town is mentioned ; it is more a question of phraseology than anything else. The old meaning of town was the same as that of the modern civil parish. This is the last entry in the Sandwich Records relating to Bright- lingsea until the revival in 1887.

96. The numerous documents for the Poor Law, which had to be signed by magistrates, who had often also to see the pauper, were a great strain on the union between the Headport and the Member. Some of these papers, dated early in the eighteenth century, were signed by the Mayor, or a Jurat of Sandwich. But after the middle, they were all signed by Essex Magistrates, who had no real authority in Brightlingsea. Probably an Essex Coroner held in- quests in Brightlingsea, when invited to do so, but he had no defined jurisdiction here. This inconvenient state of affairs was ended by an Act of Parliament of 1811, which authorised Essex Magistrates and Coroners to act in Brightlingsea. It also provided that prisoners sent to an Essex gaol would be charged to Brightlingsea. Previously they had gone to Sandwich or Dover. The Mayor and Jurats of Sandwich were still to have the right of levying rates, except for maintenance of prisoners.[91] Brightlingsea did not pay county rates to Essex, except for prisoners in gaol for some years after this date.

When the Tendring Hundred magistrates in 1825 directed Bright- lingsea overseers to prepare a jury list, legal advice was taken, as the parishioners had been previously exempt from serving on juries in the County of Essex, and a special return claiming exemption was made.    Finally the Quarter Sessions decided that Brightlingsea was exempt from jury service in Essex.[52]

97.   Soon after Mr. Pertwee became Vicar in 1872, he interested himself in the Town's membership of the Cinque Ports, and acquired much information all in the right direction for reviving the appointment of the Deputy and the more formal recognition of the union with Sandwich.   At length a visitor to Brightlingsea, who appeared to be an authority on the Cinque Ports and their history, lent his aid.   A scheme was prepared for the revival of the Deputyship, *etc.*, in which unfortunately only a very little of Mr. Pertwee's evidence was included.

The existence of a corporation was assumed.   The details were on the model of Fordwich, except that there was a Deputy Mayor instead of a Mayor, and eleven Jurats instead of twelve, and the election of the Deputy Mayor was by the Jurats, instead of by the inhabitants, as was the ancient custom of Fordwich.   However, the fundamental essentials—the inhabitants being the electors in the first instance, and the " Deputy Mayor " going to Sandwich to be appointed and sworn into office—were preserved.

There was some timidity at first, but the late Mr. John Bateman held the office for five years in succession, and was presented with an illuminated address on their completion.[53]   At the same time he presented a badge and chain of office for the Deputy.   The badge is an opal having a seascape carved on it, and is said to be the largest known opal in the world.   The chain consists of alternate crossed silver sprats and silver gilt oysters.   (Plate VI.)   As there was no corporation in Brightlingsea to hold this badge and chain, a deed of gift was made, in which the Corporation of Sandwich was made a trust to hold it, under certain conditions.   One condition is that should Brightlingsea at any time become a corporation, the badge and chain are to be made over to the corporation to be worn by the Mayor.

A staff, resembling a constable's staff, bearing the Cinque Ports' arms, and the names of Thomas Bundock, Esquire, Mayor (of Sandwich), and Mr. Simons, Deputy (of Brightlingsea), and the date 1804, was presented in 1895.   A staff identical with this one is in the possession of Mrs. Barton, of the Lodge Farm, Alresford. If there had been one only, it might have been the Deputy's staff, in right of his being a constable.   But the existence of two upsets that theory.   Perhaps the Assistants were provided with them.

98.   The history of Brightlingsea up to 1804 shows that Fordwich was not a model for Brightlingsea.   In 1905 some of the facts being brought to light, return was made to the original plan.   The title

THE DEPUTY'S BADGE AND CHAIN.

(Plate vi.)

of Deputy was recognised as the correct one, the eleven Jurats were exchanged for six Assistants, and changes were made in the method of election. The oaths proper to the Deputy and Assistants were made declarations, following the example of the Lord Warden at his installation.

[The Deputy's oath :—

" I shall faith bear to our sovereign Lord the King, his heirs and lawful successors, and the state and liberties of the 5 Ports and especially of the Town of Sandwich and the liberties of Brightlingsea a member of the same, to my power maintain and truly keep ; all lawful commandments and process from the Mayor and Jurats of the said town of Sandwich to me directed and delivered, I shall truly obey and execute, and true and due return thereof make ; and if any harm be pretended against the said Mayor and Jurats of the Port of Sandwich or this member of Brightlingsea, I shall give present knowledge and warning thereof to the Mayor and Jurats there for the time being, and the same to the uttermost of my power shall let and withstand ; not omitting any part of my duty for any reward malice hatred or affection, So help me God."[84]

The Assistant's oath :—

" I shall be, as I ought to be, true and faithful to our Sovereign his heirs and lawful successors, and the state customs and liberties of the Town and Port of Sandwich and the members thereof, shall to my power maintain and truly keep, and shall be ready to the keeping and maintaining of the peace ; and be aiding and assisting to the Deputy of Brightlingsea, and truly to my power advise and counsel him in all things appertaining to the duty and charge of his said office of Deputy ; that disorderly and unruly persons may be punished and reformed, good order and good quiet may be ratified and established among us. So help me God."[85]]

In days gone by the duties of the Deputy and his Assistants were fairly arduous, so it was not surprising that men did not wish for the office, and that severe measures were taken with any one who refused. At the same time these offices were of considerable importance, and the leading men of the place were generally found holding them. Modern ideas of local government have shifted local responsibilities from the Deputy and his Assistants principally to the Urban District Council. The Deputy now "reigns but does not govern."

Sandwich's non-corporate members alone had Deputies and Assistants. Those belonging to the other head-ports had Deputies only. The non-corporate members share with the City of London the distinction of being the only places in England in which the title is now used. The title is an old one. There was a Deputy of Brightlingsea long before there was a Mayor in any of the Essex towns now possessing one. The title of Deputy Mayor, which has often been used instead, is of recent growth comparatively. It was not used in corporations until late in the 17th century, and then the holder exercised powers only temporarily, while the Deputy was in power during the whole of his term of office. As the title came into use in corporations, so it came into use here; the earliest known date being 1731. As the Deputy acted in many ways (but not in all, for he was not a magistrate) as Deputy for the Mayor of Sandwich he might be called Deputy Mayor, but his title should then be Deputy Mayor of Sandwich in Brightlingsea. As has been suggested by Mr. A. A. Jefferies and Mr. T. W. Barnes, he was Deputy of and for Brightlingsea, in relation not only to Sandwich and the Cinque Ports, but to the rest of the country. Every instance found previous to 1805 of the use of the title Deputy Mayor or Mayor of Brightlingsea has been quoted, and although only some of the instances of the use of Deputy are quoted, yet it will be seen that there is an enormous preponderance of evidence in favour of the title Deputy, and, in any case, those who have gone to Sandwich expecting to be made Deputy Mayors have come back Deputies, for it was to that office and by that title they were appointed and sworn in. The title jurat was used for a time instead of assistant, but without any precedent whatever.

The title of Assistant is not as old apparently as that of Deputy. The first Assistant in Brightlingsea of whom a record remains is William Wilkinson in 1586.[36] Before the Municipal Corporations Act of 1835, Colchester had sixteen Assistants, and the City of Oxford eight.[37] At the present time I believe Brightlingsea has the distinction of being the only place in England where the title is now used. The other non-corporate members have allowed the office to lapse, though Deputies are still appointed. It has been claimed that the title of baron or combaron (fellow baron) was not applicable to inhabitants of the non-corporate members, but examples of the application of these titles to Brightlingsea's inhabitants by the Brotherhood and by Sandwich have been quoted already.

The Deputy and his Assistants are now chosen by the Barons of Brightlingsea from among themselves each year on the Monday following St. Andrew's Day. The ceremony takes place in the tower chamber of the Church. The admission of strangers into a village was regulated in the Saxon days by the town moot or town meeting. The manor of Brightlingsea, being an ancient demesne manor, preserved many of the old Saxon customs, of which this regulation was one. When Brightlingsea asked Sandwich in 1569 whether they might make a new comer pay for his freedom, the reply was that they could do so through the manor bye-laws. There is no instance known in which the Manor was made use of in this way, but about the end of the eighteenth century a town meeting was called to consider the advisability of allowing two strangers lately come to Brightlingsea to stay. The meeting at which the election of the Deputy, *etc.* is done, really a town meeting, exercises a nominal jurisdiction over this matter.

99. The existence of a corporation in Brightlingsea has often been assumed, but there is no real evidence of its existence. What confuses the point is the question of the corporation of the Cinque Ports and their members. It is argued that Brightlingsea, being a part of that corporation, must be corporate; then all the members of the Cinque Ports must be corporate, but they are not.

The statement has been made that Brightlingsea received a charter of self-government as a reward for her services to Edward III. at the battle of Sluys in 1340. The statement was quoted from a book of encyclopædia type, probably of about the early part of the eighteenth century, but it has not been identified, so that the quotation and the statement cannot be verified. A charter of self-government would come from the king, in which case it would be enrolled on the Patent or Charter Rolls. There is no such enrolment on the Patent Rolls for twenty-four years after the battle. I have searched the Charter Rolls for six years after this date and found nothing. The Ports were given Letters Patent of protection in 1341 for their services at Sluys,[88] perhaps it was to this that the encyclopædia referred. There is one possible piece of evidence of a corporation here at about this time. Orders were sent in 1346 to the bailiff and good men of Brightlingsea. The bailiffs and good men of Yarmouth, Colchester, Ipswich, Maldon, and Orford were mentioned in the same order. Possibly the Chancery clerk who wrote the order treated all alike, and gave each a bailiff without warrant for doing so. If not, then Brightlingsea had a corporation of which the head was not a Mayor but a Bailiff. If there were a corporation here at this time it soon became extinct, for Brightlingsea appears as a non-corporate member in 1442. In any case a corporation which does not exercise its powers becomes extinct and can only be revived by a fresh charter.

Fortunately Brightlingsea's membership of the Cinque Ports and the existence of the Deputy and his Assistants do not depend for their existence on this elusive charter, nor on an ancient corporation

G

here. Had it been so the revival of 1887 would have been the merest farce. The necessary factors for its success were there, the meeting of the inhabitants (the barons) of Brightlingsea to choose, and the corporation of Sandwich to appoint and swear in. When that corporation ceases to exist the Deputy and his Assistants can no longer be appointed.

[1 Ah, 83.  2 Ab, 177-8.  3 Ab, 88.  4 Ag, 179.  5 Ad, 164.  6 Ab, 36.  7 Ah, 10·  8 Lk, 113.  9 Lk, 114.  10 Ah, 18.  11 Lk, 219.  12 No, 52-3.  13 Lk, 252.  14 If.  15 Lk, 219.  16 Ah, 181.  17 Ll.  18 Ab, 182.  19 P, vi., 262.  20 Ga, cxii., 84.  21 Gb, cccii., 4.  22 Gb, ccccix.  23 Le, 338.  24 Ff, 108/204, 108/206, 109'397, 110/427, 112/638.  25 Ff, 246/7.  26 Ff, 246/20.  27 Ff, 246/22.  28 Bg, 163.  29 Mb.  31 L, li., 120.  32 Mg.  33 Bg, 143.  34 Aj, 831.  35 Le, 375.  36 Fz, cxcviii., 49.  37 Ak, i., 330, Ej, xviii., 19.  38 H, Edw. III., v., 177.]

## THE POSITION OF THE NON-CORPORATE MEMBERS.

100.   Their position has always been a difficulty to Cinque Ports' historians, and none more than Brightlingsea.

As in the case of the other non-corporate members, there has been no satisfactory explanation given of how, why and when, it became a member.   It is necessary before dealing with that point to touch on the origin of the Ports themselves.   One theory is that they are direct descendants of the stations of the Saxon Shore.   Another is that they were made a corporation by Edward the Confessor in return for supplying ships for war service.   The members are considered to have been added to assist in supplying this shipservice, and to have been relatively late additions.[1]   The king's authority would be necessary to admit a town to the Cinque Ports' privileges. With the exception of Tenterden there is no evidence of this authority for any one of the thirty-one members.   In case of one or two the want of it might be understood, but it is difficult for the whole number unless they were very early additions or part of the original.   The way in which they were grouped does not suggest that they were late additions.   The strong ports, Hastings, Sandwich and Dover have the most and best members, Romney and Hythe, which needed them, were badly supplied, while Rye, added in Henry II.'s time, had one member added in 1449 (Tenterden), and Winchelsea, added also in Henry II.'s time, had none, but needed them.   Many of the members were small and feeble when we first hear of them, some stay on the list for a short time only, and others appear to have been no use.   If additions had been made to assist the Headports, flourishing, not decaying villages, would have been chosen.

The aid to the shipservice has been made the test of membership of the Ports. Brightlingsea is not considered to be an early member, because it was not mentioned in the list of members giving shipservice in 1229, yet the Sandwich records most emphatically state that it was a member beyond the memory of man.[8] Boys carries the point of making shipservice a qualification so far, that he dates Brightlingsea's membership from 1492, when the first payment was made to the shipservice, though he quotes a record of fifty years earlier, stating that Brightlingsea was then a member. Burrows evaded the point by implying that 1442 saw the formal adoption of Brightlingsea by Sandwich, and that payment was due then. The record of 1442 does not hint at any adoption by Sandwich then, while that of 1492 contradicts it.[4] Here the theory of shipservice being the first essential of Cinque Ports membership breaks down.

The Cinque Ports' corporation has been accepted as an article of faith. It is based on an opinion expressed in an old customal of Rye, that "all the Cinque Ports intend themselves to be, and are one corporation."[5] There is also a common seal mentioned by Jeake on the strength of a translation of a deed of 1491, which refers to the common seal of the Mayors, Bailiffs and Jurats, in the court of Brotherhood.[6] It is peculiar that before and after the date of this deed, there are no deeds heard of in which it was used, and many are known, which are sealed without it. A deed given by the court of Brotherhood to Brightlingsea was sealed with the common seals of Sandwich and Romney in the name of the others, and two with the seals of office of mayoralty of each of the seven Towns and one with the common seal of each of the seven Towns. It does not seem likely that the inconvenience of using all these seals would have been tolerated if a convenient common one of the court were available. I suggest that the translation was wrong; it should be common seals. These old MSS. were written with many contractions; probably for seals was written the contracted Latin *sig'* or *sigill'*. As no indication would thus be given of the singular or plural, the translator made his choice. Each port and corporate member managed its own affairs, and the only time the ports acted together was in the Court of Brotherhood, and in the Court of Brotherhood and Guestling. The Brotherhood was composed of representatives chosen by each of the seven Headports. The Mayor or Bailiff of each in turn inquired of the others, if a Brotherhood should be held that year. If agreed, notice was sent calling the Court, and each Headport chose representatives to form the Court, the Mayor or Bailiff being one and the rest Jurats and Commoners.[7] The court of Brotherhood and Guestling was similar, but included representatives of the corporate members. When the court had finished its business, it dissolved and further business could only be done in another court called as described. Thus the only time the Ports acted together, they did so in an assembly, which derived its authority, not from the supposed corporation of the Cinque Ports, but from the individual corporations, and moreover the assembly lacked one essential of a corporation, the power of self-reproduction, or, in the legal phrase, perpetual succession. (The essentials of a corporation are the possession of a common seal and perpetual succession.) The meeting not of one corporation, but of representatives of several, explains the reason for the use of their own common seals. The non-corporate members were part of the supposed corporation, yet they did not send representatives to these courts. Burrows suggested that as they had no corporation, they had no power to appoint representatives.[8] But each had its town meeting, and we find Brightlingsea sending representatives to Sandwich authorised to act on her behalf. The non-corporate members had no common seal, and so were unable to give proof of their adherence to any proposal, a sufficient reason for their absence from the courts.

101. There are two sets of charters in the Cinque Ports, the charters of incorporation of which each head-port and corporate member had one or more, and the collective charters given to the ports and members as a whole. These collective charters are printed in Jeake's *Charters of the Cinque Ports*, and though the essence of them is simple enough, the repetition and wordiness are most bewildering. There are only three of present importance, Edward I.'s, Edward IV.'s, and Charles II.'s. Edward I.'s charter (1277), the earliest existing, refers to charters given by Edward the Confessor and later kings. It confirmed certain privileges to the Ports, granted new privileges and did not mention the members at all. Edward IV.'s is referred to in section 82. Charles II.'s contains a list of the Ports and Members. Brightlingsea and all other members, except Tenterden, are said to be and to have been from all time members of their respective head-ports. Then follows a list giving the Ports and Members having Mayors and Jurats or Bailiffs and Jurats. Brightlingsea is not included in this list. There is nothing in these charters creating a corporation for the whole, nor corporations for any of the ports or members. They do not even hint at the existence of one corporation for the whole. No hint is given that some of the privileges can only be exercised by a corporation. It might be argued from this that every port and member was a corporation, but it was not so. Probably it was held that there was no need to differentiate. The corporation would take the

corporate privileges, and the non-corporate members the non-corporate privileges. Even in these advanced days no one sending a parcel of clothes to an orphan school would think it necessary to say that the knickerbockers were for the boys and the skirts for the girls. It might be argued that the mere fact of giving one charter to a group of towns made that group a corporation. It did not. Rye and Winchelsea received a joint charter,[9] but they were two corporations. The difference between the collective charters and a charter creating a corporation may be seen by comparing Charles II.'s charter to the ports (in Jeake) and his to Sandwich (in Boys). Edward I.'s charter does not justify the assumption that the Ports originally obtained their privileges in return for their services, though he confirmed them and granted new privileges as a reward for their services.

It will be seen from the foregoing that there is good ground for believing that there never was a corporation including the whole of the Cinque Ports and their members, and that ship-service for *offensive* warfare was not the origin of the Ports' privileges. Getting rid of a corporation of the whole of the ports and members removes one difficulty of the non-corporate members' position. There is no need to explain the anomaly of an integral part of a corporation not sharing in all the privileges and duties of that corporation.

The following theory of the Ports' origin does not cover every point, but I believe it leaves fewer discrepancies than the others. The Saxons required a coast protection. They could not with their limited localised system of government imitate fully the extensive system, which the Roman highly developed organisation created over the Saxon Shore. They could not manage to control the whole of the Shore, but only the parts most important to them. Yarmouth became their northern limit and their influence there dwindled to control of the Herring Fair. Brightlingsea was the only part of the Essex coast retained. The union of Brightlingsea and Harkstead existing at the Conquest might be due to an old connection through the Saxon Shore. The Saxon Shore was not only the stations but the shore in between. When the Admiralty jurisdiction of the Ports appears on paper it includes not only the coast of each Port and member, but the intervening coast.

The early organisation of the Ports was on the lines of a county. The Lord Warden was lord lieutenant, custos rotulorum, and sheriff. The court of Shepway was the criminal court of the whole, the old county court. The growth of the corporate towns was slow. They had not reached their full growth until the fifteenth century. In Saxon times there was little to distinguish a town from a village or group of villages in essentials. In the Cinque Ports the towns developed in size rapidly, and were relatively much larger than the rest of their 'county.' When they developed in power and organisation, they became markedly the predominant partner, obscuring the county organisation and absorbing it almost completely into their own.

The Saxon inhabitants of this 'county' had to use ships for the protection of their own property as a matter of necessity. The protection of their property was a protection of property inland, and must have been recognised and rewarded as such, perhaps not at first, but eventually. Such ship-service was defensive, not offensive. When the king wanted ships for his fleet, he wanted them for offensive purposes away from their own coasts.

This was an entirely different matter from the Portsmen protecting their own property. The king would obtain them from those ports which had the most and best ships, the larger ports, which would want a substantial return. A grant of privileges was a cheap way. The superior privileges and position of the headports may be thus explained.

As the towns' organisation ousted the county organisation, the smaller places tended to drop out, except when retained by advantages of position or connection with the herring fishery, which was a very powerful force in holding the Ports together. This dropping out still further increased the relative importance of the towns to the rest of the 'county.' When the head-ports began to feel the strain of the ship-service to the king, they remembered the small places, and made them contribute for their share in the privileges. This 'county' theory makes the explanation of the position of the non-corporate members more easy. For one thing it explains their separation from the county in which they were geographically situated. It explains why the town magistrates instead of remaining exclusively town magistrates, acted as county magistrates in the non-corporate members.

Accepting this theory, we may think of Brightlingsea as being part of the Saxon Shore, valuable to the Ports' fishermen as a friendly port of call on the way to and from the herring fishery at Yarmouth, not big enough to get the larger share of privileges, yet too useful to be allowed to drop out, with a loose union to the Ports socially and politically, until the head-ports' development as corporations was such that they were able to exercise jurisdiction over the smaller members.

To-day Dover and Brightlingsea share the distinction of being the only towns which keep the old characteristics of the Ports.

The rest are no longer distinguished as maritime places. They have vanished, become popular and fashionable watering places or golfing centres. Brightlingsea still sends the best of her population to sea, some to serve the King in the Royal Navy or Royal Naval Reserve, some in the North Sea and Channel fishing fleets, and others carrying cargoes of lives or goods in ocean liners, yachts or coasters.

[¹ Ab, 91.  ² Ab, 240.  ³ La, 237, Lb, 20.  ⁴ La, 59, Lb, 20.  ⁵ Ah, 84.  ⁶ Ai, 111-2.  ⁷ Ab, 177.  ⁸ Ab, 178.  ⁹ Ab, 70].

# Chapter V.

## MARITIME AND MILITARY.

102.  The Anglo-Saxon vessels appear to have been large boats, rather than what we consider ships. They were clincher-built and undecked, and some had a burden of as much as fifty tons. The bow was raised and ended in the form of the head and neck of some beast. They were built to be beached easily. The mast carried a single square sail on a yard. Oars were used as well as the sail, which would only be of use with a fair wind. They were steered by a paddle over the stern on the right or steerboard [starboard] side.[1]

Ethelred in 1008 ordered that every three hundreds were to find a ship for war service. Taking one hundred hides to a hundred Brightlingsea would have had to provide a thirtieth part of this ship. As ten hides were to provide a boat, Brightlingsea would find one. Eight hides were to furnish a helm and breast plate.[2] Brightlingsea would find one and a fraction of each.

The very necessary duty in those days of guarding the coast behind the first line of ·defence, the ships, fell on the people of the coast towns. The Anglo-Saxon army was the nation in arms at first. Later the increasing cost of arms and impracticability of withdrawing all able bodied men from the land, led to a smaller number being required.[3] The arrangements in Berkshire, recorded in Domesday, appear to have applied to the rest of the country.[4] In this scheme, Brightlingsea would send two fully equipped men to the fyrd [national army or militia] for a royal expedition for two months, and pay them each 20s. for that time.

It is not until 1233 that we hear anything of Brightlingsea shipping. Not that there was none, but that the records are wanting. In that year Warin, of Colchester, petitioned and satisfied the king, that a Bridlingesea ship carrying his merchandise had got into difficulties, and the merchandise had been thrown to the waves (to lighten the vessel). The men of Cliffe (Clive) took it ashore and held it as wreck. As the men of the ship had escaped alive the merchandise was not wreck, and the sheriff of Kent was ordered to have the merchandise delivered to him (Warin).[5] It was the law, that if a man, dog, or cat escaped alive from a wrecked ship, it and anything it contained should not be held as wreck.[6]

The wars of the Edwards found employment for Brightlingsea ships. Roger de la Walhaghe, master of the Welfare of Bright-lingeseye, in 1299 carried from London to Kingston-on-Hull, and thence to Berwick-on-Tweed, the king's store of salt fish *(duro pisce)* for the use of the hospice and the king's army there. He received 4*l.* for the freight.[7]

The ships now sometimes had two masts, but with the same single square sail on each.[8] A merchant vessel was fitted for war by fixing a box-like structure in the bow, and in the stern, forming the fore and after castles, in which fighting men were placed. A similar structure at the mast head made a fighting top. Bows and arrows, pikes, swords, and other hand weapons were used, together with machines, on the principle of a catapult, to throw stones.[9]

Such a vessel is here copied from the old common seal of Sandwich. The castles, steering paddle, and dinghy are shown. One of the two men reefing the sail is omitted. In the seal the port shrouds are omitted, because of the

FIG. 2.

impossibility of representing them on a high relief seal. They are omitted here for clearness. Vessels entirely propelled by oars were still used. Brightlingsea and St. Osyth were certified to be able to find between them a barge of forty oars and thirty tons burden.[10]

Henry Canon, of Brightlingsea, committed a burglary in the houses of John of Riveshall, in East Mersea. For this he received a pardon in 1313, because of his good services to the king in Scotland.[11] Probably he had been taken from gaol when awaiting trial, or after conviction, and sent to the wars.

103. In 1325, four Brightlingsea ships were employed by the

king, probably for the Scotch war.   They were the " Bocalf,"
William Ecceforthe, master, ten men; "Dene," Henry Pache,
master, twelve men ; "Mylan," Alexander Larch, master, ten men ;
and " James," John Pache, master, eleven men.   The masters were
paid a day, 6*d.* each, and the men 3*d.* each[12]; the usual wages at
that time.

A ship of Whitsand, bound for London, was attacked in the
mouth of the Thames, by certain malefactors, who killed the crew,
seized the goods worth 1000*l.*, and carried off the ship.   The Sheriff
of Essex was, in 1342, ordered to receive this ship and goods, have
them valued and kept till further order.   As a messuage in Bret-
lyngsey was also ordered to be taken, valued, and kept,[13] one or
more Brightlingsea men must have been implicated.

On another occasion in the same year Brightlingsea showed to
better advantage.   Sir Walter Mauny was sent in March, 1342, to
Brittany.   In his fleet were four Brightlingsea ships, the " James,"
John Pacche, master; "seintemaribot," Roger Curtoys, master;
" Johnette," John Pacche, master; "Swallowe," John Estmere,
master.[14].   Owing to contrary winds the ships were sixty days on
the passage.   The Countess of Hennebon besieged in Hennebon
and despairing of relief, was on the point of surrendering when the
fleet was seen off the town.   Sir Walter routed the enemy and " the
Countess coming down from her castle kissed Sir Walter Mauny
and his companions one after the other two or three times; and
truly may it be said that she was a valiant lady."[15]   Some of the
ships of the fleet deserted after a time but none from Brightlingsea.[16]

A Brightlingsea ship, the " Eleyne " of forty-five tons of wine
burden, William Cros, lord and master, was arrested in April,
1344, at London.   The Sheriffs were ordered to de-arrest her, and
Cros was to take her to the port of Colchester, to be ready to set
out in the king's service.   Cros had to find two sureties that he
would do so.[17]   Here we get an example of the origin of tonnage;
the ton burden being a ton of wine.

By this time rudders were used.[18]   Bowsprits had come in, but
were very small and, apparently, were not used for setting sails.
Some ships had a course and a topsail on each mast.[19]

The Bailiff and good men of Brightlingsea were ordered, in 1346,
to send all ships of thirty tons and more to Portsmouth for the
Crecy campaign.[20]

For the siege of Calais (1347) Brightlingsea sent five ships and
sixty-one men, while Maldon sent two ships and thirty-two men.[55]
These are the only known occasions when Brightlingsea supplied
ships to Edward III., but more were supplied.   The total number of

ships and mariners of Brightlingsea that "served King Edward 3rd in these warrs" was the large number of fifty-four ships and two hundred and eighty-three men. Colchester supplied twelve and two hundred and thirty-nine.[21]

There was always the fear of invasion and the coast was guarded. In 1295 Sir Richard de Tany of Elmstead was custodian of the coast of Tendring Hundred. He had command of eight soldiers at Harwich, four at St. Osyth, four at Clacton and Frinton, four at Walton and Kirby, and four at Brightlingsea, which was described as an island. One horse soldier was supervisor of them all.[22] Most likely they would be inhabitants of the places named.

104. The marshes provided feed for numerous sheep, and wool was an important article of commerce. The demand for it abroad, due to its superiority, led to a duty being put on it when exported. The Abbot had, in the three years previous to 1274, sold to three merchants of St. Omer, fifteen sacks of wool, and to Thomas Knyvet, merchant of "Amias," fourteen sacks, and caused this wool to be removed from his manor of Brythlyngeseye to parts of Flanders and other parts beyond the sea.[23] A sack was generally twenty-six stones. Evasion of paying duty led to officials being appointed to prevent it. Seven men were appointed (1341) as deputies of Roger Power, King's Sergeant-at-Arms in parts of the river Colne, namely, Colchester, East Mersey, Brightlingsea, and Haneford. They were to search vessels, and arrest, as forfeit, any wool, wool-fells, etc., liable to pay duty, and on which duty had not been paid, and the vessel too.[24] In the fifteenth century Brightlingsea was one of the wool ports of Essex, and her ships were engaged in carrying wool. In 1478 John Beriffe, master of the "Mary of Bretylsay," and John Pypar, master of the "George of Bredyllsay," were paid 6s. 8d. a sarplar (thirteen stones) for carrying wool, apparently to London. William Recherdlay, master of the "Mary of Brekellyssay," also carried wool to London in 1480.[25]

The civil wars of the fifteenth century do not appear to have affected Brightlingsea, and it is not until the end of the century that her ships were used in the navy. The "Mighall [Michael] of Brekelsey" was in the fleet for the expedition to Britany in 1489.[26]

A rebellion was raised in Scotland on behalf of Perkin Warbeck. A fleet was sent in 1497 to Berwick to quell it. In the fleet was the "Thomas of Brikelsey." She carried two demy curtowes of brass, one "named the libard [leopard], with her old bedd, a pair of newe wheles shodd with hole boxes of brasses [bushing of wheel naves], a pair lymors [shafts for the bed on which the gun was mounted], forlokkes kayes [keys], linces [lynch pins], and her

taillepynne." The other curtowe called the "Ruysbanke" (Ryse-
bank) had a new bed and old wheels. A curtow or curtal was a
short heavy gun weighing about three thousand pounds. They
were used in the field as heavy guns, but were not often used on
board ship. For them were carried three hundred "shot of iren"
and one hundred and fifty "shot of ston." Forty horse harnesses
were taken for them and two "ffare-cartes [travelling or riding
carts] with all apparell." "950 stakes for the feld" were carried
to be used to make a palisade for the protection of the archers in
action.[37]

The "Thomas" returned from Berwick to the Tower of London,
fifty-nine horse harnesses, four charging ladles (used for gunpowder
when loading), four rammers, two demy curtowes of brass, three
hundred "shots of Iren," one hundred "shot of ston," "two ffare-
cartes," two bows, one sheaf of arrows, and one bill.[27]

Ships had become by this time much larger. Usually they had
four masts; the two after masts, the main mizen and the bonaventure mizen, carried lateen sails. Top-gallant masts were fitted,
but could not be lowered.[28] The fore and after castles had become
permanent structures. Bowsprits did not carry fore and aft sails,
but a square sail set beneath, and other square sails on a mast at
the bowsprit end.

105. It appears that the inshore course along this coast sailed
in the fifteenth century, and probably long before, was similar to
the present course. Apparently, about that time, the Spitway was
marked.[29] Show Beacon is mentioned about 1542. It was placed
where the Maplin Light is now.[29] A chart, dated 1584, shows this
beacon and the Whitaker Beacon. Five fathoms are marked in the
Colne from off "Blackstone" to near St. Osyth Point. Off the
Point four are marked, and three in Borefleet. The Bench Head,
Knowle, Buxey, Swin, and Gunfleet, are shown.[30] The name
Gunfleet then applied to the water, not to the sandbank as is the
modern use.

A chart, dated 1590, gives Brightlingsea Church as a mark. In
addition to the Show and Whitaker Beacons, one unnamed is shown
about six miles north of the Whitaker Beacon. Three fathoms is
marked through the Spitway, then called the "Spittes." The
passage is shown to be about three miles across.[46]

The appliances used in navigation at the end of the fifteenth
century were a compass, a cross staff or astrolabe, a moderately good
table of the sun's declination, a correction for the altitude of the
Pole star and, occasionally, a very incorrect chart.[47] A Brightlingsea mariner's widow, in 1537, bequeathed a ship's chest containing

a ship card[48]; a card meant either compass or chart.[49]  Henry Frost
(1571) spoke of his small danske chest with a double lock and his
"austrolabie."[50]  The astrolabe was used for taking altitudes.[47]  In
the same year John Weoulde left a " sea carde of Appletons makinge
with a quadren of brasse."[51]  The quadrant appears to have been
introduced in the sixteenth century.  It was used for taking altitudes
and zenith distances.  As made then it required an inconvenient
plumb line for its use.[47]  Richard Browne, in 1584, spoke of his
books, cards, and compasses.[52].  Thomas Bullivant, in 1608, left
the books, nets, and instruments " which commonly I do use and
practise in my trade."  He also left his barber's latten warming
pan.[53].  Perhaps he combined both trades.

Henry VIII.'s French and Scotch wars needed large fleets.  The
most famous addition was the " Henry Grace Dieu."  Shipwrights
and caulkers were taken from Brightlingsea to assist in building
her.  They received ½d. a mile for food and lodging on their
journey to Deptford.  They were paid from 1d. to 6d. a day, and
fed at an average cost of 2½d. a day.  They were given bread, beef,
ling, cod, hake, herring, peas, and oatmeal.[81]  James Goldacre, of
Brekellsey received 46s. 8d. for the freight, from Hull to London,
of six great cables for this ship.[82]

In building the barque " Kateryn Plesaunce " (1519) for the
navy, five hundred planks were used, bought from John Sargeant
of Brykyese and carried by water by William Beriffe, who received
4s. for the freight.[83]  Among the expenses of the " Swallow, Row-
barge," is 3l. 4s. 8d. paid to " John Brylle of Brykellsey for a bote
that master [blank] toke fro hym " and for twelve oars.[84]

106.  Mariners were pressed for service in the navy.  In
1512-13 (war with France), for the " Anne of Greenwich," four
men were taken from Brightlingsea, receiving each ½d. a mile as
conduct money for forty-eight miles.  Two men were taken also
for the " Jerrett of Purwyn " and two for the Christopher Davy.[85]

A ship of one hundred and sixty tons, sometimes called the
" Barbara of Brykelsey[86] " and sometimes the " lesser Barbara," to
distinguish her from the " Great Barbara," a royal vessel of four
hundred tons, appears several times in the navy lists.  She was
not a hired merchant ship, but was actually described as a king's
ship.  Apparently she was bought in 1512,[87] and must have belonged to a Brightlingsea man or been built here, perhaps both.
She was one of the eighteen ships forming the fleet under Sir
Edward Howard called together in 1512, " in consequence of the
wars threatening the holy Roman Church."  The admiral's pay
was 10s. a day, each captain's 1s. 6d. a day.  The mariners, soldiers

and gunners received 5s. a month wages each and 5s. a month for victuals.[38]  In April, 1514, she was in commission with seventy mariners, forty-five soldiers and ten gunners on board.[39]  In the same year seventeen tons of beer were delivered to her purser as six weeks' supply for one hundred and thirty-five men (? one hundred and twenty-five).[40]

The "Anne," forty-five tons, carrying twenty-four soldiers and ten mariners; "Julyan," forty tons, twenty soldiers and ten mariners; "Maryflower," forty tons, nineteen soldiers, ten mariners —all of Bryklesey—were serving the king in the retinue of Sir William FitzWilliam, vice-admiral (1513) as transports except the "Anthony," which apparently was a victualler.  The soldiers and mariners had the usual 5s. a month wages.  There were dead-shares also, four of 5s. each a month to each ship, which were divided among the crew.[41]

Among "the hoyes and shipps waged and hyred to sette ouer into England the King's grace and his Arme Royall from the parties beyond see," in 1513, were "The Trinitie of Brickylsey," seventy tons, John Beriffe, master; "Peter and poll (Paul) of Brykkylsey," sixty-five tons, William Smith; and "Elleyn of Brykilsey," fifty tons, William Beriffe, master.  Each master received for a month for tonnage, victual and men's wages, 8l. 3s. 4d., 5l. 10s., and 7l. 10s. respectively.[42]

To bring the king's army back from Calais, the following Brightlingsea ships were hired from 12th October, 1513, "Edward," forty tons, John fferiar, master; "Mary Galant," forty tons, John Walgraue, master; "Grete Mary," fifty-six tons, William Harrys, master; "Antony," thirty-two tons, John Haukyn, master; and "John a Baptist," thirty tons, John Kele, master.[43]

Henry began another war with France in 1522.  In July the "Mary of Brekelsee," William Alyson, master, was carrying dried cod for the army.[44]  War with France in those days generally meant with Scotland too.  In 1524, "Henry Browne, master of the Mare Galant of Brykesey," carried two hundred and forty-four quarters of malt from Barrow to Berwick for the army.[45]

A number of men were bound by obligation to convey victual to Calais and other places for the king's use, according to an order dated April, 1531.  Among them were Thomas Turnbull of London, fishmonger, and Henry Smyth of Brekelsey, mariner, who had conveyed to Berwick "xxvi. wayes baysalt [a way = forty to fifty-four bushels], ii. last pitche and Tarre [a last = fourteen bushels], one last Soope, iiij. tonnes Iron, and viij. tonnes wynes."  Apparently a bond of 200l. had been taken for the due performance of the above. Henry Smith no doubt carried the goods, and Turnbull was his joint guarantee.[46] In 1528 Brightlingsea joined with Colchester and Wyvenhoe in sending twenty crayers (cargo boats of moderate size) to the North Seas.

[[1] Cv, i., 11. [2] Cf, 399. [3] Ci, i., 210. [4] By, 31. [5] I, Hen. III., ii., 211. [6] Ai, 28. [7] W. [8] Cv, 138. [9] Ct, ii., 174. [10] Fe, 2/46. [11] I, 6 Edw. II., pt. ii., m21. [12] Hd, 26891. [13] I, Edw. III., vi., 404. [14] Fe, 2/35. [15] Ct, ii., 72-3. [16] H, Edw. III., vi., 108. [17] I, 18 Edw. III., pt. i., m19d. [18] Ct, i., 370. [19] Cv, i., 145. [20] Fc, 19 Edw. III., pt. ii., m8d. [21] Ha, 246, 16b. [22] Fe, 2/12. [23] E, i., 163. [24] H, Edw. III., v., 256. [25] Dp, 10, 43, 194-6. [26] Fp. [27] Cy, 4, 82, 90, 92, 116. [28] Cx, 53. [29] Au, 268. [30] Hc, Aug., vol. i., no. 44. [31] Cx, 72-3. [32] Fr, v., 301. [33] Fr, xi , f. 87d. [34] Fr, xii., 16. [35] Fr, ii , 17, 24, 27. [36] Fw, i., 4745. [37] Cv, i., 26. [38] J, i., p. 344. [39] J, i., p. 812. [40] Fr, ii., 279. [41] Hb, 14, B, xxv. [42] Fr, ii., 396, 413, 415. [43] Fr, ii., 425, 429, 431. [44] J, iii., p. 863. [45] J, iv, p. 281. [46] Fw, v., 381. [47] Cs. [48] Ej, xvii., 250-4. [49] Jg, 7. [50] Co. [51] Ik, 24. [52] Ik, 17. [53] Io, 37. [54] Ju. [55] Cu, i., xlii.]

## THE ADMIRALTY JURISDICTION.

107. One of the Earls of Oxford bought from the Abbot a piece of land about four perches square, in the common outmarsh in Brightlingsea, and banked up from the rest of the marsh. It abutted on " the Ladys Bridge." The Earl, who was Lord High Admiral, "bought it to the intent to hold his Admirallty Court there."[1] Admiralty Courts were usually held on or near the sea-shore, and dealt with a variety of maritime offences. This land had ceased, apparently, to be so used before 1556.

Ordinarily all wreck belonged to the king, but he made grants to lords of manors on the coasts, and to towns of the right to take wreck on their own coasts. The Abbot in 1274 claimed this right in Brightlingsea,[2] though no definite grant of it is in his charters. One of the privileges of the inhabitants of the Ports was that of being " wreckfree," that is their ships and goods were not forfeited when they were wrecked. By Edward IV.'s charter (1465) the Ports were to have wreck of the sea " howsoever happening in whatsoever coasts and arms of the sea adjacent to the ports and members aforesaid, and all and singular things to such wreck appertaining or belonging."[3] It seems that the right to wreck was an old prescriptive right of the Ports. The Lord Warden soon obtained part at least of this privilege for himself, as he did some other valuable privileges. Brightlingsea shore, Borefleet, Alresford Creek, and part at least of the Colne were clearly included in Edward IV.'s grant or confirmation. In 1525, the Lord Warden's jurisdiction was declared to extend as far as St. Osyth, though in the following year the Horseshoe, in Essex, was stated to be the northern limit.[4]  There were three claimants to wreck and Admiralty jurisdiction in the Colne,—the Cinque Ports, the Burgesses of Colchester, and the Lord of the Manor of Brightlingsea, each supported by a grant by Royal Charter.

Pirates infested the North Sea and took their toll of Brightlingsea ships.   Thomas Laws writing from Elsinore to a merchant in London (9th Sept. 1535) said " here is the false thief who took the crayer of Brekellsay."   " He is a great captain here, and boasts he will be in England shortly and fetch as many more as four or five ships."[5]   Soon after the Mary Flower of Brycklesey fell into the hands of pirates.[6]  A case was tried in the Admiralty Court about 1538, between Thomas Spysall of " Brellsay," owner of the "Gabriel," and Thomas Watters of Lynn, owner of the " Barque of Lynn." The barque collided with the Gabriel at anchor and struck her " with a great and heavy blow so that by reason of such blow and stroke the said Thomas Spysall was damaged in the sum of 16l." Thomas Watters was ordered to pay the 16l. and the costs.[7]

There was no marine insurance then.  It appears that a system of having shares in several vessels rather than having the entire ownership was used as a substitute.   John Piper in his will (1539) bequeaths these shares,—Mary Fortune, three quarters;  Mary Mighell, one half ;  the Mighell Bonaventure, one quarter ;  Martin, one third ;  and Mary Gallande, one quarter.[8]  The smallest share found was John Ayre's " half quarter of the Mighell Bonaventure " (1537)[9]  The ships belonging to Brightlingsea in the 16th century were numerous.   Those mentioned in wills for that time are Advantage; Anne, Anthony, Anne Gallante, Barbara, Clement, Elen, boat Elen, George, Gregorye Fortune, crayer Lyon, Lytyll Michaell, Martin, Mary Anne, crayer Mary Anne, Mary Edward, Maryflower, Mary Fortune, Mary George, Mary Grace, Mary and John, Mary Martin, Mary Swepestake, Mighell, Mighell Bonaventure, and Trinity.

108.  Brightlingsea ships were sometimes employed on peaceful errands for the king.  Peter Bodell of Brykkylseie in 1539 took in his ship a freight of Newcastle coal to Calais for the works there. He was paid for the freight, 7s. 6d. a chalder[10] (a chalder = 36 bushels heaped up).   Brightlingsea was one of the five ports in Essex in 1552 whence provisions might be exported.  A Brightlingsea crayer, the Mary Galant, laden with salmon was in 1553, ordered to be stayed as one last and three hundred barrels of salmon were the Queen's property.  The rest was for a London merchant. The master was to be paid for the freight "so that the poere man have no aggrevaunce."[11]

John Lylly, mariner, in 1542, left 10s. to the maintenance of Scarborough pier. Perhaps he felt that from a Cinque Portsman, relieved from paying dues, some recompense was required. In another will we get a hint of the difficulties of sea life. In 1571, John Girdler, of Brickesley, mariner on the seas between Spain and England, aboard the bark Chapman, made his will. He left his house to Sarah Sympson "his betrothed wiffe" also four old angels, and a variety of clothes, including a jerkin and pair of breeches "skye color." His godson was to have 30s., and 25s. were to be given to the poor by the hands of Mr. William Berry[f] Deputie. 12s. were to be distributed among "such as taketh parte with me in the shipp." The will was evidently drawn up by one unskilled in such matters, no doubt one of the crew, as no executors were named.[12]

109. All males between sixteen and sixty had to be prepared to defend the country, and arms and armour for them had to be provided. It appears that each township provided one or more horsemen. Brightlingsea in 1538 contributed to the horsemen of Tendring Hundred, Thomas Keye, yeoman, " well horsed harnyssed armoured and ordyred." He was paid by the town apparently, as his wages were 18s. 8d., " the whyche money is redy in the hands of Jaukyn Beryff, constable of the same town."[13] Encouragement was to be given to shooting with bows and arrows, and in 1541-42 butts were ordered to be put up in every village. Possibly the field here called " Shooting Field" was used in which to practise. Inhabitants of the sea coasts were allowed to have firearms such as hand-guns, hagbuts, and demyhakes, on account of their liability to attack.[14]

In 1539 war seemed likely with France and Flanders, and orders were sent that on the Essex coast vigilant watch was to be kept, and the beacons tended.[15] Beacon Hill (where the second Martello Tower stands in St. Osyth) no doubt was so called from one of these beacons. The site was most suitable for warning Brightlingsea and the neighbouring places of an enemy approaching by sea. A fort was built at East Mersea some time before 1547, and another before 1543 at St. Osyth.[16] This would most likely have been on Beacon Hill, though it might have been on St. Osyth Stone. In this connection there is this curious order of the Privy Council, dated 21st July, 1553: " Lord Darcy's House. John Claare John Locke and Thomas Locke [all] of Bryckelseye stand charged with the safe custodye of the Lord Darcye's goodes and stuffe in his house at Sayncte Ooses, being charged cheyflye with the ordenaunce munycione [ammunition] and artillerye and all other things comynge into their hands there, and that no spoyle be made therof as they wyll

H

answer to the contrarye."[17]    Lord Darcy owned the Priory and if
this were the house meant it seems extraordinary that three Brightlingsea men should have charge of it.  Again, why should the Priory
require artillery ? or was it merely stored there ?  If the artillery
were in a fort on or near the Stone, it would be quite easy to understand Brightlingsea men having charge of it.

Henry VIII. was at war with Scotland and France in 1544, and
Brightlingsea mariners and ships were pressed for service to help
in taking the army to Scotland.  The "Margaret" of Brickelsye
was arrested in the Port of Lynn.[18]  Thirty-seven mariners from
Bryeckelseye, Alresford and East Mersea, and thereabout, were sent
to Deptfordstrand to serve in the "Mynyone" and the "Primrose"
"for the wafting [conveying] of his graces leade from benorthe into
fflaunders."  The voyage was given up, and the mariners allowed
to return home.[19]  The "Mary fortone," Brykkylsey, 120 tons, and
the "Mary Edwardes," 95 tons, were employed, and the former was
reported to have had this ordnance remaining in her—four port
pieces, three slings, one fowler, three great slings, nine basses (for
sponging out the guns), and the latter two great slings.[20]  Twenty-
three ships are mentioned in this list, only two (from London) were
larger than the "Mary Fortune," and by 20 tons only.  Other
mariners from here had been employed, for eight were paid conduct
money on 5th November, 1544, from Deptfordstrand home.[21]  As
a means of harassing the enemy, two "showe beacons" on the
Essex side, indicating the "Swynne," were ordered in July, 1545, to
be taken down to hinder the passage of strangers coming from the
Naze or the North Sea.[22]  Five hundred soldiers were quartered in
Brightlingsea for ten days in 1545, and were paid land wages at the
rate of 6d. a day each.[23]  Probably they were waiting for a transport.  Tranports were in the Colne that year,[24] and Brightlingsea
was an embarking place for troops, for in 1546, one hundred and
forty soldiers were ordered to be sent there to serve in the "Greate
Barke,"[25] and Colchester was in 1554 ordered to find eighteen
armed men to be ready to embark at Brightlingsea at an hour's
warning, for the service of Queen Mary.[26]  She was engaged in a
war with France in 1557.  The "Marie Fortune," 66 tons, and the
"Marie Martyn," 60 tons, both of Brekelsey, were employed in the
fleet.[27]  In 1559 a return of the vessels of 100 tons and over in the
various ports was called for, and Bricklingsey had the distinction of
being the only port mentioned in Essex as having vessels of that
tonnage.  They were two—"The Barke," 140, and the "Mary
fflower," 100 tons.[28]  Henry VIII. had in 1543 "perused two notable
havens, but liked Coln Water best."[29]  The Colne became a royal

naval station, for in 1545 orders were given to an official to make an estimate of the King's marine charges there. We have the accounts of these charges for 1562.[30] Among the ordinary charges are :—

"To Edward Lambart, the Last daie of March for his wagis dailly attending and serving hur highnes in saif keping of her graces storehowses and Tymber yeard contayning iiij[xx] [90] dais. Begun the ffirst daie of Januari last and this daie ended, at xij*d. a day*."

" To Thomas Richardson, marynner, the same daie for his wages daylly attending and serving hur highnes in saif keping of hur graces shippe named the Trinitie Henry by the space of iiij[xxx] daies, Begun and ended as aforesaid at vj*d. a day*."

William Abraham, tiler, and his man were paid for repairing the store house eight days at 12*d.* a day. Lime cost 2*d.* a seam, and a load of sand 12*d.* Jasper Smyth was paid for four small dogs of iron for mending the storehouse, at the rate of 4*d.* a pound. Robert Consent and three other labourers were paid 9*s.* 4*d.* for lading water out of the " Trinity Henry," and other services. William Beriffe was paid 13*s.* 4*d.*, one quarter's rent of a storehouse and ground of him hired " whearin lyeth hur hignes store of prouisions of all kindes for the use of hur shippes," and Thomas Beriffe received 6*s.* 8*d.* for one quarter's rent of another storehouse. Robert Consent and three other labourers were paid on 30th June 8*s.* " for ther wagis in labouring about the clensinge scowinge and having out of the water in the Docke theare whearin Lyethe hur highnes shippe the "Trinitie Henry." John Paige and divers other mariners were paid 12*s.* 6*d.* on 30th June, " for there paynes taken with their Boattis at soundrie tymes in scearching for one of hur gracis greate Ankers which was lett faulle in Barflet [Borefleet] water between a hoye and the greate barke at the greate barkes last being theare as yet not founde."

For 1563, in addition to similar payments for the care of storehouses, yards and dock, and rent of stores, there was paid to John Deathe, shipwright, 5*s.* " for mendinge of ye Pompe standing in the Docke their, and for the makinge of a newe Boxe for the use of the same Pompe." William Bewicke, smith, was paid " for pryce of viij. lb. weight of his own newe Iron and for the newe makinge of the Iron worke belonginge to the same pompe iiij*s.* viij*d.* ; more for a pompe staff, one pompe hoofe, with the stroppes and scoopernoivillis to the same, iij*s.* viij*d.*, and more to him for vjli. weight of spykes and smalle nayells at iij*d.* euery pounde xxj*d.*" The pump hoof was probably the bucket ; the stroppes, the iron fastening the rod to the bucket ; and the scoopernoivillis the suckers of the bucket.

The storehouse and yards were in Brightlingsea, as may be seen
by the fact that provisions for ships were removed from Brightlingsea.  The King's storehouse here was mentioned in 1552, when the
confiscated Church goods were removed to it.[31]  Edwarde Lambarde
was stated to be a Brightlingsea man and Robert Consent belonged
here.  It is not likely that Brightlingsea men would be employed to
work in another part of the Colne.  For them to get to Wivenhoe
or Mersea would have been very troublesome, so it is more than
probable that the dock was in Brightlingsea.  Lambarde appears
to have taken an important part in local naval affairs.  Besides his
duties above mentioned, he and his man rode three times from
Brightlingsea to Harwich, to deliver divers provisions to the
" Swallow " and the " Willobye," at their being in the North seas.
In 1562 and 1563 he pressed mariners here, in the latter year they
were sent to Chatham, and received conduct money for twenty-four
miles.[32]  It was a very long twenty-four miles, even by water.

110.  In a survey of the Port of Ipswich and its creeks in 1565
we get this description of Brightlingsea :—

" A ladinge place at Brightlingsea which is the Queens towne
[she owned the Manor] parcell of the Cinque Portes, which at all
tymes hath bene a ladinge place as well to transport merchaundizes
into the partes beyonde the Sea, as from porte to porte within the
Realme, and so ys mete to be contynued, And the same ys a place
mete for the buildinge of the Quenes Majesties Shipps, and ys
dystant from Ippswich, xj myles xxij myles, ffrom Harwich x myles
xvj. myles, ffrom Colchester vj. miles vj. myles."  One distance
must represent the distance as the crow flies, and the other that of
the sea route.  Two creeks are mentioned as being " within the
lybertyes of Brightlingsea,"—Borefleete mill and Alresford ford.
Creek here means a landing place.  Ipswich, Harwich, Colchester,
Maldon, Brightlingsea, and Leigh had been and then were " moste
frequented and haunted with the trafique of marchauntis and
merchaundizes, And ar mete so to be contynued for that purpose."[33]
The landing places at Bricklingse are given in greater detail in 1577.
They were at the ford, obviously in Alresford Creek, the common
key (quay), no doubt the present Hard with a small quay on it, the
bridge (see section 146) and two " other crekes by the haven of Coln
Water," that is between West Marsh Point and Alresford Creek.
In St. Osyth were lading places called Black Stone, and Borefleet
lading, the latter being no doubt the present St. Osyth Stone.
Borefleet Mill is this time said to be in Great Bentley.[34]  In 1565-66
Brightlingsea had thirteen vessels, twenty-one masters and owners,
and fifty-nine mariners and fishermen.[35]

111. Piracy was prevalent at this time. The offenders were Englishmen, of whom it was said that they were good sailors and better pirates.[36] They were aided by persons ashore receiving the stolen goods, and supplying them with provisions. Commissioners were appointed to prevent this assistance, and to help them they had deputies, "honeste discrete and trustye persons" in each port.[37] There were three such deputies in Brightlingsea.[35]

In 1558 a list was issued of the armour, which holders of various yearly values in land and goods should provide. Land worth one hundred marks had to provide the equipment necessary for one lighthorseman, two archers and one soldier with firearms. Land worth 6*l.* was to find one longbow, a sheaf of arrows (twenty-four to a sheaf) and a steel-cap. 10*l.* in goods found the same as 5*l.* in land with the addition of a black bill or halberd.[38] Lists of the armour and arms in each place were ordered to be kept, and the arms and armour were inspected regularly. The constable of each place kept a list of the men liable to serve.[39] In 1580 two Brightlingsea yeomen were required to find one light horseman each. A little later Humphrey Hastler, rated at finding one lighthorse, refused as being resident "within the Cinke Portis in the Towne of Brickelseye."[40] "A" is placed before his name on the list, meaning probably that his refusal was allowed.

A list of arms and armour provided in Brightlingsea for about the second half of the sixteenth century has survived.[41] An exact year cannot be given to it because it had been corrected from time to time, showing that it was in use for a number of years. The date of death of most of the men whose names it contains are known, pointing to it being drawn up in the latter half of the sixteenth century. The list is headed "Brightlingsea a member of the Cinque Ports The names of all those that fynde armoure in the same Towne." Those finding armour numbered sixty-two. There were provided six "corseletts furninshed *namely* with pyke sword and dagger," seven "muskets furninshed, twenty-six colliuers furninshed *namely* with moryan sword and dagger," ten "longe bowes furninshed *namely* with one sheffe of arrowes, steel cappe sword and dagger," and eleven "Halberdes or black bylles with a steel cappe." A column for "the name of all those that are appointed to serve with the said armoure" is left blank.

A corselet was a piece of armour covering the body, the term generally included the head-piece, gorget (neckpiece), and the tasses[42] (plates covering the thighs). A pike, which here as usual, went with a corselet, was like a lance, and often as long as sixteen feet. Muskets were heavy firearms, which needed a rest to

take the weight when fired.   For this a forked rod was used.
Colliuers or calivers were lighter firearms.   A morion was a steel
helmet introduced early in the sixteenth century.   A halberd was
a pole with a head combining the point of a pike and a cutting
edge like a hatchet's but lighter.   A black or brown bill was like a
modern bill fastened to the end of a pole.[42]   They were not kept
bright, and hence were
called black.   Some men
left their armour by will.
Thomas Beriff left " An
Almayne Rivet,"[43] a
corselet made of plates so
rivetted together as to
be flexible.   They were
a German invention.[42]
William Beriffe, the
Deputy, left two daggs
(pistols) and a target
(shield).[44]   A sword, a
bow and a sheaf of arrows
were left in 1608,[45] and a
back sword and belt in
1637.[46]

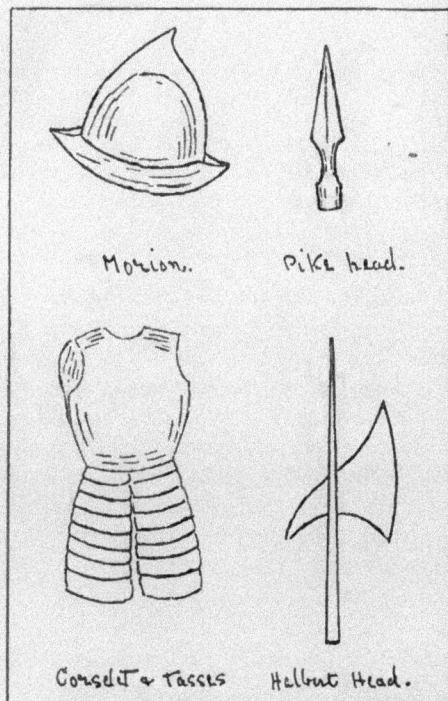

Morion.     Pike head.

Corselet & Tassels    Halbert Head.

FIG. 3.

A law passed in 1562-3
made it compulsory for
people to eat fish on
Wednesdays and Fridays
to encourage the fishing
trade.[47]   In 1580 an
enquiry was made to
ascertain the increase of
fishing boats.   In Colne
water there were thirty
fishing vessels, an increase of ten of from sixteen to thirty tons each
since the last Parliament.[48]

These vessels were arrested in 1570 at Brightlingsea for the Queen's
service:—Anne Galant, fifty tons; Mary Anne, thirty-six; Marye
Grace, fifty-six; Mary James, forty-two; Marye Edward, fifty;
Lyon, thirty; and Martyn, thirty-six.   Edward Bokking, of Stanway
Hall, who was ordered to arrest ships in Essex, when reporting his
work to the Council, said "There is within this Countie a Towne
called Brightlingsey, beinge a membre of the Cinque portis havinge
good shippinge belonginge to the same, which I have stayed and
certified as the rest, untill yours honours pleasure be further knowen

therein."[49] No doubt Brightlingsea folk objected to him, though authorised to deal with Essex, arresting ships within the jurisdiction of the Cinque Ports. Large ships were dying out hereabouts, for in December, 1582, neither Colchester nor Brightlingsea had a vessel of one hundred tons or more.[50]

[[1] Nb, 169. [2] E, 163. [3] Ah, 112. [4] Fw, iv., 1820, 2250. [5] I, ix., p. 108. [6] Fw, xx., 1202. [7] Ep. [8] Ie. [9] Jg, 10. [10] J, xiv., w. 250. [11] P, iv. 298. [12] Jk, 3. [13] Fb, 59/8. [14] A iii., 835, 838. [15] J, xiv., pt. i., xxxv. [16] Au, 271. [17] P, iv., 300 [18] Fw, xix , no. 355. [19] Hd, 7968, f. 8, 9b. [20] Fw, xix. no. 502. [22] J, xx., p. 573. [23] P, i , 174-5. [24] J, xx., p. 268. [25] P, i., 420. [26] Y, i. 80-1. [27] Fy, xi. 2. [28] Fx, xi., 27. [29] Fw, xviii., 740. [30] Ka, 113, seq. [31] Fk. [32] Ka, 315. [33] Fi. [34] Fz, cxviii., 31. [35] Fz, xxxix., 22. [36] Cx, i., 187. [37] P, 8, Nov, 1565, [38] Fy, xiii., i. [39] M, Addenda, 1601-3, 488. [40] Fz, 11, 39. [41] Ma. [42] Eg [43] Ih. [44] In. [45] Ju, Thos. Bullivant. [46] Ju, Josias Stevens. [47] A, iv., 424. [48] Fz, cxlvii. [49] Fz, lxxi., 64. [50] Fz, clvi., 45.]

## THE ARMADA.

112. The trouble which led to the Armada was brewing in 1586. In February of that year, surveys of shipping were made, and these vessels were certified to belong to Brightlingsea :—The William, barque, eighty tons; Marie Flowre, eighty; Pernelle, barque, eighty; "The Hooye," fifty-two; Anne Galante, fifty-two; Pelycane, thirty-eight; Dove, thirty-four; Mathewe, crayer, twenty; John, monger (fishing-vessel), six; and William, monger, six. The Pelican and Swallow were "not at home nor when they wylbe is uncertene." The names of sixteen able masters belonging to Brightlingsea were given, of whom five were then abroad. Twenty-nine able mariners, who were householders, and eighteen able mariners "Bachilers or single mene" were named. One of the latter had no surname, he was "George at Chaundlers."[1] Ships were hired at this time at 2s. a month,[2] and wages a year were, master 26l. 1s. 3d., boatswain 10l. 17s. 3d., purser 8l. 13s. 9d., cook 7l. 12s. 1d., carpenter 10l. 8s. 7d., and mariners 10l.[3]

Of Brightlingsea's land preparations for resisting the Armada we have no special knowledge. No doubt beacons were watched, the sixty sets of arms and armour would be worn by those appointed, and the latter were ready prepared for action. The Vicar would share with the rest of the clergy of the Archdeaconry of Col- chester, in finding the arms and armour for twenty-one horsemen and ninty-one foot, which were ready in August, 1558.[4], There are many lists of the ships, which opposed the Armada. In some, among the coasters with Lord Henry Seymour, is the "William" of Brickelsey, one hundred [or eighty] tons, Thomas Lambert, captain.[5] In others there is the "William" of Colchester, Thomas Lamberte, captain, fifty men.[6] Colchester in another is named, as the town finding the William of Bricklesey.[7]   The ship probably was not a Colchester one, but was hired no doubt from Brightlingsea by Colchester, and probably was the "William" mentioned in Brightlingsea's list of shipping in 1586.   Lamberte or Lambarde was known as a seafaring name in Brightlingsea a little before this time.   It is hardly likely that a town, Brightlingsea's size, would be able to fit out a ship at her own cost.   In any case, as Sandwich and her Members sent the "Reuben," Brightlingsea had done her share already.[8]   The "William" was "attached to Lord Henry Seymour's division, watching the Flemish Ports, which joined the main fleet off Calais on 27 July, and they were no doubt in the subsequent battle of Gravelines, but like the rest of the merchantmen did no particular service."[9]   On 1st August he writes to the Queen, saying that he " has returned to guard the English coasts, to withstand any attempt of the Duke of Parma."[10] The next year a fleet was sent to Portugal to place Don Antonio on the throne "and dismember the Spanish empire, and end the war." Ships were sent from Brightlingsea in this fleet.[11]

Harwich was ordered to find four ships, and the other Essex Ports three for the Cadiz expedition in 1596.  We may expect that Brightlingsea had to share in finding the latter, unless she joined with the Cinque Ports in finding the five ships required of them.[12]

FIG. 4.

SMALL VESSELS, LATE SIXTEENTH CENTURY.

Here ended Brightlingsea's many years' connection with the Royal Navy in supplying ships. The reason is not far to seek. The man-of-war had become specialised. It was now impossible to make a man-of-war of a merchant vessel by putting up temporary fore and after castles, and arming her men. Also merchant vessels were not large enough in most cases.

The end of the sixteenth century saw Brightlingsea men cease to be merchant traders.  The formation of numerous trading companies, such as the Levant Company in 1581, and the Baltic

Company in 1579, hindered private enterprise.[13] Brightlingsea's barks and crayers gave place to smacks and dredging boats.

The Lord Warden had been thinking of disposing of his privileges in Brightlingsea, judging from the beginning of this letter to him from Thomas Berwicke (probably the Deputy).

"Right honorable, these are the Royalties and benefitts which your honor haue and which your honour shall loose if you gyue awaye the Royaltyes of Brickelsea in the County of Essex, a member of the Cinques Portes. 12 Februari, 1597.

"The Admyraltie in which your honour hath all—

"The benefitts of wreckes and findals at sea wherin your honor hathe a thirde parte as wee firmly holde. The benefitts of the goodes of Pirates and Rouers which come into the harboroughe [harbour] and of all comyttinge murther or any felonye within the high water marke. The ferryage whereof Sir Thomas Heneage once made a lease, it beinge a dutye of your honours, if the towne cannott otherwise by custome clayme it, as also the election of the sommer dregger. The Anchorage [payment for anchoring] and measurage [tonnage] of all straungers comynge into the harboroughe, and the searchinge and takinge of all goodes oncustomed. The fines amerciaments and other benefitts of the Admiraltye Courte.

"The Clarke of the markett for weights and measures—

"In which your honour hath the jurisdiction by acte of parliament of assessing the quantytye of all weights and measures. The fines for offences comytted contrarye to your honors order herein.

"The Captayneshippe where in your honor hath—

"The commaundinge of all the inhabitauntes as well seamen as lande men for all servyces mylytarye, whiche your honor shall appointe. The stayinge and commaunde of all the shippes of the thatt place, or which lye in thatt harboroughe for the Queenes Maiestyes seruyce.

Your humble and obedient Servaunte,

Thomas Berwicke."[14]

The benefit of wrecks has been already described. Findal means treasure trove.[15] Brightlingsea evidently wished it to be understood that it was only a third part that the Lord Warden was to take. "Within high water marke" means the sea side of high water mark. The ferry would most likely mean to East Mersea as well as to St. Osyth Stone. Payments would be demanded for license to ferry, and the right to the ferrying could be let for a payment, as Sir Thomas Heneage had done. He must have claimed it as Lord of the Manor, though his grant did not mention it. It might have been an old prescriptive privilege of the Abbot's,

and so transferred to Heneage by the clause confirming him in all
privileges held by the Abbot.

The town apparently had some claim to it by custom.  It is not ·
clear whether the town could not claim the election of the summer
dredger by custom too.  The Admiralty Court mentioned was the
Lord Warden's.  The Clerkship of the Market does not mean that
there was necessarily a market in Brightlingsea.  It was generally
speaking the counterpart of the modern weights and measures.  In
the last paragraph the Lord Warden appears as Lord Lieutenant
and as Admiral.  The Lord Lieutenant and Vice-Admiral of Essex
had no jurisdiction in Brightlingsea, which explains her objection to
obeying orders from them.  Sometimes when orders were given,
Brightlingsea escaped, the Ports left the matter to Essex, and Essex
left it to the Ports.

114.  People hostile to the government appear to have entered
and left the Kingdom by the Ports.  Commissioners were appointed
by the Lord Warden in 1608, before whom all suspected persons
were to be taken.  None was to embark but at Dover, Rye, and
Sandwich, where passports were issued, and registers of passengers
kept.[16]  Naturally persons attempted to leave or enter anywhere
but at those three ports.  The Lord Warden, Lord Northampton,
sent a letter addressed to " My verie louvinge worthy Friendes, the
Deputy of Brightlesey for the time beinge, The Minister there for
the time beinge, John Uuedale, Robert Bridgeman, Edward Clare,
Thomas Gill, Barnard Feuerell, and Humphrey Hastler," ap-
pointing them or any two or more of them " commissioners for the
passage at Brightlesey otherwise Brightlingsey in Essex to doe
execute and perfourme in this behalf what in your discrecions shal
be thought meete and expedient, And as occasion shall serve, to
minister the oathe of allegiance prescribed in the Instrucions to
such as you shall hould in any sorte suspicious."  The letter ends
" and so leavinge the burden of this charge to your care industrie
and trauell, I rest

Your verie louinge Friend<br>
H. Northampton.

Northampton House,
xxj. Januraij 1608."[16]

The Lord Warden had here an official called a droitgatherer, to
look after his interests, and to collect the dues coming from his
various rights.  He had difficulties at times.  John King, who held
the office in 1620, wrote to Lord Zouch, then Lord Warden, that
he had " demanded ankeredge [anchorage] of Henrye Nelson of
Saint toosei [Osyth], and he said he would paye nonne, and said he

would spoyle me if I came aborde for aney, and said I must come with my Lordes Cullicanc [badge or cognisance] one my sleue and a white Rod in my hand, and so by the Reason of him no other of that Towne will paye, but do agre all together not to paye anye deuties."[17]

A notice issued to the Ports in 1619 by the Lord Warden stated, that he found it needful to hold courts of Admiralty within the Ports, but that his officers going to each town to hold a court "would draw very great and excessive charges uppon the inhabitants." To ease them of such charges one general court was to be held in Dover "at the publique place called the Mount uppon the shore of the sea there" on the following 19th August, at 8 o'clock in the morning. Brightlingsea was required to send two delegates to this court.[18] This was a breach of the Portsmen's privileges. They were not to be required to attend enquiries outside their own towns.[19]

Piracy, this time by foreigners, was such a menace to shipping that contributions from coast towns were called for to enable it to be suppressed. The Cinque Ports in 1619 were requested to pay 200*l.* a year for two years, but objected. Apparently the amount was reduced, for on 28th June, 1620, it was reported that all the 100*l.* required from the Cinque Ports was paid in, except Winchelsea's share.[20]

Fear of invasion led to military activity in Essex in 1624-5. The Deputy Lieutenants rated William Hudd (Hutt), of Bricklesey, to send a light horse to Sir John Mead's troop. He did not do so, and was returned as a defaulter, 31st July, 1624. The Lords Lieutenant of Essex, the Earls of Sussex and Warwick, were instructed on 24th January, 1625, to arrange for the billetting of certain companies of the Earl of Essex's regiment in the maritime towns of the county. The troops were to "keep a military watch as well for exercise as for the preventinge of any suddaine surprise," and were to be provided with sufficient fire, when on their guards during the winter. The charges whereof were to be repaid, "itt being his Majestyes gratious pleasure that the Countrie should not bee burthened with any expence in that kind." The townspeople were to find free lodging for the billetted soldiers, but were to have 2*s.* 6*d.* a week for each soldier's food. A company of one hundred men of this regiment was ordered to be sent to Brightlingsea.[21] This did not please the people, who sent this petition to the Duke of Buckingham, the Lord Warden :—

"The humble Peticion of the Inhabitants of the Towne of Brightlingsea in the County of Essex a member of the Towne of Sandwich, one of ye Cinque Ports.

" Humbly showing that all the Inhabitants of Brightlingsea (four or five persons excepted) rely on theire small means and hard labours for their maytenance, and yet are to prouide fifty soldiers which are ready upon any occasion at an howers warning to defend the Towne ; and of late they haue byn and are charged by the Leiutenants deputy of Essex with the finding Light Horse and billeting 100 soldiours (albeit theire acustomed and extraordinary Taxes and payments to Sandwich).

" Pleaseth your Grace; your Graces said Peticioners (as members of Sandwich under your Graces protecion were neuer questioned to doe seruice in this kind to the County of Essex) by reason of which undue course the liberties and immunities of Brightlingsea (in case the Peticioners be not releued by your Grace on whom they all depend) will be infringed, and your Grace thereby much damaged and the Peticioners ouer burthened.

" The Peticioners therefore humbly pray your Grace of your gratious and accustomed goodnes to defend and protect them against the Leiutenants deputy of Essex ; and that they may (as allwaies they haue byn) be under your Graces Lieutenant of Dover Castle or his deputy or the Maior of Sandwich and to be pleased to signify your Gracious pleasure herein to the Lieutenant of the County of Essex, that the Peticioners may be noe further charged and opressed and They (as in duty bound) will euer pray for your Graces health and eternal happiness."[22]

The Duke of Buckingham on 9th March wrote to the Lords Lieutenant of Essex, stating that he had received this petition. As the Cinque Ports and their members have never been liable to tax or service for this kind to the county, he prayed the Lords Lieutenant " to give presente order to your Deputy Lieutenants and such other your officers whom itt may concern, not only to free whatsoever taxes and charges have beene by them layd upon the saide towne, but alsoe henceforth to forbeare to meddle with the government or orderinge of anythinge belonginge to the Inhabitants of that place, itt beinge a peculier libertie out of the Jurisdiction of the County."[23] The regiment was not sent however, because of the great expense the County had been put to in keeping troops at Harwich.[23]

The mariners between Berwick and London petitioned for ships to guard the coast, and the Bailiffs of Colchester in 1630 asked the Council for some protection for mariners, as five or six pirates from Dunkirk had been cruising on the coast for two months, and had taken divers ships.[24]

Corn was very scarce, and in consequence of its high price in

1631 its export was prohibited. The Justices of the Peace on November 30th reported that they had "belayed" the Port of Bricklesea among others to prevent transportation. They found that only brank (buck-wheat) was exported, which they said was only eaten in England in times of extreme dearth.[25]

In three instances only is Brightlingsea known to appear in the disturbances of the Civil War. The well-known Countess of Rivers, of St. Osyth Priory, was a Royalist and a Roman Catholic, and an Essex mob, after pillaging Sir John Lucas' house at Colchester, sacked the Priory. Goods and furniture of various kinds were removed.[26] Some Brightlingsea men were implicated in this, either as thieves or receivers. The Countess obtained an order of Parliament allowing search to be made for the goods, and directing them to be restored to her when found. As some of the goods were in Brightlingsea, and so within the jurisdiction of the Ports, a warrant to search had to be obtained from the Mayor of Sandwich, and was given on 2nd October, 1642.[27]

In 1642 the Counties of Essex, Suffolk, Norfolk, and Hertford, were associated by an ordinance of Parliament. Brightlingsea was requested to pay towards the 40,000*l*. required to find arms and men for their defence. The Deputy and Assistants wrote to the Mayor and Jurats of Sandwich asking if they should pay. They replied that Brightlingsea must pay if an assessment were made for it, but "as for the voluntary contribucion required toward findinge of armes men and monys for the officers fees, they advised them to deale very wisely therein, lest they should be doubly charged or fall into trouble or prejudice theire Liberties."[28]

When the Royalists were besieged in Colchester, an attempt was made to run two ships laden with provisions and stores through the blockade in the Colne. The officer in command of the Parliamentary ships concealed his forces in Brightlingsea Creek, and attacked the Royalist ships as they came up. They all got into shallow water off East Mersea, and the Parliamentary dragoons, garrisoning the Blockhouse, rode into the water, and joined in the fight.[29]

The naval warfare with the Dutch in Charles II.'s time must have been an anxiety to Brightlingsea, though as far as is known no part was taken in it. In 1666 the Essex Militia was called up, and the coast watched and defended. On 7th June, 1667, the Dutch fleet of fifty or sixty sail anchored in the Gunfleet.[31] On June 11th the Dutch landed at St. Osyth and attempted to steal sheep, but retired when the people appeared. On the 18th two or three Dutch ships were reported to be aground near St. Osyth.[32]

"In 1620 Captain John Seaman sailed from Brightlingsea in his own ship for the New World and took possession of a great part of Long Island which had been granted to him by Charles I."[33]   In 1666 John Seaman, senior, obtained a grant of two tracts of land in Long Island, one near Oyster Bay and one of 400 acres called Jerusalem.  More land was confirmed to him in 1686.  In 1667 he, with others, obtained a confirmation of the town of Hamstead in Long Island.[34]   Probably this is the John Seaman from Brightlingsea, and, if so, a mistake was made in the above statement between Charles I. and Charles II., and in the date.

[¹ Fz, cxcviii., 49.  ² M, i , 242.  ³ Hc, Otho, E, ix., 304d.  ⁴ Fz, ccxv., 14.
⁵ Hb, 14, B, xiii.  ⁶ Fz, ccxv., 76.  ⁷ Fz, ccx., 34.  ⁸ Ab, 199.  ⁹ Au, 278.  ¹⁰ M, i., 520.
¹¹ Au, 278.  ¹² Ha, 51, 51d.  ¹³ Ej, xxi., 827.  ¹⁴ Fz, cclxvi., 53.  ¹⁵ Ah, 42.
¹⁶ Ga, xliii., 34-5.  ¹⁷ Ga, cxvi., 110(a).  ¹⁸ K, Rye, MSS., 156.  ¹⁹ Ae, i., 277.
²⁰ M, x., 12, 25, 26.  ²¹ Nn, iii., 205-6.  ²² Gb, xxi., 7.  ²³ Nn, 209.  ²⁴ N, ii.,
107, N, iv., 207.  ²⁵ N, v., 191.  ²⁶ Al, 227-8.  ²⁷ Le, 227-8.  ²⁸ Lf, 10.  ²⁹ Bd,
23 May, 1908.  ³⁰ O, v, 219, 231, 500.  ³¹ O, vii., p. xiv.  ³² O, vii., 171, 206.
³³ Bg, 191, quoting *Essex Standard*.  ³⁴ Gc.]

## THE EIGHTEENTH CENTURY.

116.  Oyster dredging, salving, and smuggling, were the chief maritime occupations of Brightlingsea men during the eighteenth century.  Smuggling does not appear to have been done on a large scale in Essex, but good profits were made.[1]  Laws were made to prevent the building and use of fast rowing and sailing boats.  Vessels caught smuggling were ordered in 1795 to have ballast, masts, pumps, and bulkheads removed, decks ripped up, beams sawn through, bottom planks ripped off, keels cut into four pieces, and the stemposts into three.[2]  An instance is remembered of a Brightlingsea vessel being so treated on the Hard.  Convicted smugglers were at times made to serve in the Navy.  A Brightlingsea man so sentenced was serving on a frigate.  The ship was anchored in the Downs, when it came on to blow, and the cable parted.  Nothing could be done but set sail and get clear, but there was the difficulty of getting through the treacherous sandbanks of the Thames estuary, the only refuge.  Word was passed round if any one on board knew the locality.  Our neighbour came forward, took the ship safely through, and brought her back when the gale moderated.  He received a considerable rise in rank as a reward.  In 1831 another convicted smuggler, serving as an ordinary seaman on H.M.S. "Shannon," left a wife and three children behind, and it was ordered that 14s. a month be deducted from his pay for their benefit.[3]  Smuggling went on here well into the nineteenth century.  There are many tales told of the expedients adopted to evade the Customs Officers. Perhaps the most ingenious was the pair of metal cases made to fit

inside a pair of water boots (which come well above the knee), in which were conveyed to a safe place the contents of a cask of brandy.

The country was in 1797 getting ready for war with Napoleon. Part of the scheme of defence was the Sea Fencibles, drawn from the local fishermen and seamen.[4] They were to be volunteers and were not liable to impressment while enrolled. They were trained in the use of the pike, and in gunnery when possible. The rank and file were paid 1s. a day when on service and the sergeants 1s. 6d. The Brightlingsea company in April, 1799, had twenty-one men and two sergeants—John Fieldgate, senior and junior. By November there were sixty-three men and three sergeants. Drills were held every fortnight. The number of men was one-hundred-and-one in 1801.[5] The officers writing to Lord Nelson, Commander-in-Chief from Orfordness to Beachy Head, made many complaints. One trouble was that many of the men were engaged in small fishing boats carrying two men or a man and a boy. To take them away meant stopping the fishing.[6] Many of them also refused to serve afloat. It seems they were afraid that they were to be retained. One of their officers writing to Lord Nelson gave a different reason. He said " The People who are Smugglers and Wreckers object to go on broad the Revenue Cutter, I imagine owing to her Commander having been very rigid in his Duty." " There are two owners at Brightlingsea . . . and one at Mersea Island . . . who have done much mischief by their endeavouring to persuade the men not to embark."[7] The difficulty was overcome. On 29th August, 1801, twenty Sea Fencibles from Brightlingsea embarked in the smack " Friendly " for H.M.S. " Alliance," at the Nore, and were re-landed at Brightlingsea by the gunbarge "Ceres" on 12th September. They had 9d. a day each for provisions while on the smack.[5] On 13th September twenty-seven went on the " Alliance " for a like period.[5] Brightlingsea's company volunteered for service afloat very much better in proportion to their numbers than did the rest.[8]

In 1801, "two floating batteries were anchored behind the Gunfleet, closing the three passages through the sands," and a river barge carrying four guns was placed in the mouth of the Colne.[9] These were to be manned by the Sea Fencibles, who were also to man a flotilla of small craft.[10] A Martello Tower (built 1808-9), and a battery of five 24-pounder guns on St. Osyth Stone, and another 24-pounder battery placed near West Marsh Point, protected the Colne and Borefleet.[9] The armament of a Martello Tower was a swivel gun and two howitzers.[11] Ashore each parish was to provide arms (to be kept in the Church) for the men, who were to be exercised two hours every Sunday.[12]  The highways, except the turnpike roads, were to be broken up as soon as the French landed.[13]  Arrangements were made to remove inland people and provisions from the coast.

Matthew Warren, who owned the shipyard here, was employed by the Government to build ships for the. Navy.[14]

He built in 1804[15]—

The "Sparkler," gunbrig, one hundred and seventy-seven tons, twelve guns.  Her services were in the Channel and North Sea, 1805-8.  Wrecked 12th January, 1808, on the Dutch coast.[16]

"Thrasher," gunbrig, one hundred and fifty tons, twelve guns. Service, the North Sea, 1806-14.[16]

"Tickler," gunbrig.[15]

In 1805—

"Sharpshooter," gunbrig,[15] one hundred and seventy-eight tons, twelve guns.  Services, Channel and North Sea, 1805-13.[16]

"Protector," gunbrig,[15] one hundred and seventy-eight tons, twelve guns.  Services, Cape, 1806; Brazil, 1807; Blockade of Texel, 1809; West Coast of Africa, 1810-12, etc.  Employed for many years on survey of the East coast.[16]

"Raven," brig,[15] two hundred and eighty-two tons, sixteen guns. Services, Mediterranean, 1806-7, etc.[16]

"Kite," brig,[15] two hundred and eighty-two tons, sixteen guns. Services, North Sea, 1805-6.[16]

In 1806, "Redwing," brig,[15] three hundred and eighty-three tons, eighteen guns.  Services, Mediterranean, 1807-13.  On 7th May, 1808, off Cape Trafalgar she destroyed six out of seven gunboats, and took seven and destroyed four merchantmen under their convoy.[16]

"Ringdove," brig,[15] three hundred and eighty-five tons, eighteen guns.  Services, Reduction of Martinique, 1809, etc.[16]

In 1807—

"Sparrowhawk," brigandine,[15] three hundred and eighty-four tons, eighteen guns.  Services, Mediterranean, 1810-14, etc.[16]

"Eclair," brig,[15] three hundred and eighty-seven tons, eighteen guns.  Services, Mediterranean, 1809-14, etc.[16]

The vessels were to be finished in a specified time.  He was over the time with most of them, but the "Eclair," "Redwing," and "Kite," were within.[15]  The penalty was not inflicted in the case of the "Tickler," because a supply of copper bolts had been delayed.  There was an excess of eighteen days in delivering the "Sparrowhawk," but the fine of 600l. was not inflicted, because the delay was due to the workmen attending the General Election at Ipswich and Yarmouth.[15] Evidently workmen had been imported.

A pass for protection from the Press-gang, given by Warren to one of his employés, is in the possession of Mr. R. L. Jefferies (of Colchester). The man was employed in bringing timber from Manningtree for the construction of these vessels.

During the American War (1812-4), the Lord Warden raised a corps of Volunteers in the Ports for general service. The men were to be under the General of the district, and were to be marched wherever he directed in case of invasion, thus cancelling their ancient privilege that they should not be marched out of their own towns.[17] Brightlingsea was not included in this Corps, no doubt, because of her isolation from the rest, nor in the surrender of the old exemption from service in the Militia, made in 1816 to the Lord Warden by the Mayors of the Ports.[18] This privilege still remains to Brightlingsea.

The Lord Warden was declared at an Admiralty Court held at Dover, in 1682, to have taken wreck at Brightlingsea, during the preceding forty years apparently.[19] In 1808, an Act defined his jurisdiction as extending to Brightlingsea.[20] It was confirmed by another in 1820.[21] There was a Cinque Ports wreck-house here. It was the building at the Waterside now used by Messrs. Bridges and Son. A later one was built in Sydney Street; the name over the door "Cinque Port Board of Trade Wreck House" was painted out when it became the Customs Office.

The Ports had their own system of pilots. Brightlingsea, Wivenhoe, and Rowhedge formed in matters of pilotage a member of Sandwich.[22] In 1853, the Ports system was absorbed by the Trinity House,[23] but the Admiralty jurisdiction continued to include Brightlingsea and Wivenhoe. In 1861, the Cinque Ports agent resided at Wivenhoe.[24]

Before the days of steam, when the Thames estuary was not lighted as it is now, the sandbanks were very destructive to shipping. Brightlingsea men made a fine art of salving ships and bringing in wreckage. The work was of a very hazardous nature, whether lives or goods were to be saved, and very speculative from a commercial point of view. The best known wreck in which Brightlingsea men figured was the "Knock John ship," a richly laden vessel. The salving of her freight led to wild scenes afloat, and rioting ashore. In a diary for 1849[25] we get a glimpse of the frequency of wrecks near here. Twelve dates are given on which wreckage was brought in. A shipwrecked crew was landed and a

I

foreign schooner brought in.  A schooner was lost on February 28th, and a Government ship and a hundred and seventy lives were lost on the Long Sand the same day.   On 7th December, five vessels were stranded on the Gunfleet.

The manning and laying up of yachts, Brightlingsea's staple industry, began about 1840.  Lord Wharncliffe's schooner "Romulus" is believed to have been the first yacht to sail from here.[26]  In 1849, only four yachts are mentioned by our diarist, "Pearl," "Daring," "Romulus," and Mr. J. R. Kirby's yacht, which was launched on 20th September.[25]  This could not be the "Fawn," a ten ton cutter, as she was built for him in 1846,[26] but must have been one of his numerous later vessels.  The yachting season of 1849 was closed by a yachts' sailing match in the Colne on 30th October.[25]  To trace adequately the development of the industry from the four yachts of 1849 to the present one hundred and twenty (approximately), employing about eight hundred men, would require a volume to itself.

[¹ Au, 298.   ² Dt, 329, 386, 399.   ³ Mg.   ⁴ Au, 302.   ⁵ Gd.   ⁶ Hd, 34918, f., 79.   ⁷ Hd, 34918, f, 150.   ⁸ Dv, i., 187,   ⁹ Au, 303.   ¹⁰ Dv, i., 185.   ¹¹ Dv, ii., 150.   ¹² Dv, ii. 57.   ¹³ Dv, ii., 129.   ¹⁴ Au, 301.   ¹⁵ Ge.   ¹⁶ Au, 311.   ¹⁷ Ae, xxxvi.-vii.   ¹⁸ Af, 41.   ¹⁹ Aj.   ²⁰ L, xlviii., 439.   ²¹ L, 1819-22, p. 453.   ²² Aq, 129.   ²³ Ej, xix., 98.   ²⁴ Am, 568.   ²⁵ Nq.   ²⁶ Br, 21st Dec., 1905.]

# Chapter VI.

## INDUSTRIES.

### THE OYSTER FISHERY.

119.  The earliest notice of Brightlingsea's share in the Colne
Fishery is in 1362, when the Patent Rolls tell that the men of the
commons of the towns of Colchester, Alresford, Brightlingsea, *etc.*,
and their ancestors from time immemorial had been accustomed to
have common of fishing in the arms of the sea called "la Swyn,"
"Geden," and "la Parrok," of Colne Water.' The Swyn was
probably the main channel.   Nothing was said about the rest
of the river, because it does not come into the case, the trouble
being that Lionel de Bradenham of Langenhoe claimed these waters
as his own, and had obstructed them with stakes.   No doubt the
fishery had been common to the men living on the banks from the
earliest times, not from any royal grant, but from natural use.
Richard I.'s charter to Colchester, which confirmed her right to the
fishery,² does not even hint that it is exclusively hers.   That it
should become hers was inevitable.   A large and wealthy corporation
with its prescriptive rights in the fishery confirmed by royal charter
had an enormous advantage over the unorganised body of scattered
fishermen, who had no charter to back up their prescriptive right.
Edward IV.'s charter granted to the Corporation exclusive fishing
rights in the river (1462).³   The fishermen's old right has been
recognised by the fact that licenses to fish were not granted to any
one, but only to those living on the shores of the River.   The
fishermen certainly gained in the end.   Without that continuity of
purpose which a corporation had, they would have almost certainly
allowed their rights to be lost, and some powerful landowner would
have obtained the fishery.   As it was, the Earl of Oxford obtained
it, and would have kept it but for Colchester.   The Corporation's
control never seems to have been accepted cheerfully by the fishermen.   Fishing without license seems to have been common judging
by the number of convictions for that offence.   In 1556-57 the men
appealed to the Privy Council against the Corporation as regards

their fishing rights.[4]  In 1630 "the poor fishermen" in Essex
petitioned the Lords of the Admiralty, that they had time out of
mind the liberty of dredging oysters in Colne water, but that the
Bailiffs of Colchester prevent them, and ask that the Corporation
be required to show their title.[5]  The result of these requests is not
known.

The Customary Court and Court of Admiralty for the fishery was
"held by prescription at a Place called the Block House in East
Mersea . . . Time out of mind used and approved and by Virtue of
divers Letters Patents and Verdicts confirmed, and now held at the
Moot Hall in the Year 1766 . . . in Pursuance of an Act of
Parliament made and passed in the Thirty first year of George II."
[1757-58].  Rules and orders had been made by a jury of twenty
licensed dredgermen at a Court held 24th July, 1758, and are now
[1766] ordered to be reprinted."  From them, these are extracted:—

I.  That the fishery of the River Colne with the waters and
Creeks thereto belonging shall be shut up on 1st March until 15th
August (formerly 9th October).  Penalty for dredging in closed
time 40s.

II.  No dredgerman was to take more than the quantity or stint
of five bushels of oysters "in one Day for each dredge he is licensed
to use."

III.  The size of oysters to be dredged and taken "shall contain two inches and a Quarter in Length on the flat part."  In
Pyefleet and Bracefleet to be two and three quarter inches.  Under-
sized oysters were not to be sold as Colne, Colchester, or Pyefleet
oysters.  Licenses were given only to persons apprenticed to an
oyster dredger in St. Osyth, Brightlingsea, Alresford, Wivenhoe,
East Mersea, Langenhoe, Fingringhoe, and East Doniland.  "No
one person" was "to work in more than one Boat at one Time,"
nor to work more than four dredges at a time.

On the subject of Borefleet or Brightlingsea Creek, being outside
the Colne Fishery, it has been said " For some unexplained reason
the Borough of Colchester claims no exclusive fishery rights in
Brightlingsea Creek and its tributaries, though these are within the
bounds of the fishery as defined by the wording of the ancient
charters of the borough under which it holds."[6]  The translated
words of the charter bearing on this point are "and all places called
the creeks to the same water within the precincts aforesaid adjoining
and belonging."[7]  To prove the Corporation's claim to Borefleet, it
must be shown, that it was called a creek of the Colne, and that it
belonged to the "water."  If geographical creeks had been meant,

the words "called" and "belonging" would not have been used.
There is no evidence that Borefleet was ever considered a creek of
the Colne.

120.  Most probably the oyster fishery in Borefleet was, until the
beginning of the seventeenth century, common to the people of
Brightlingsea.  Before that date, none of the Brightlingsea wills
examined mention oyster layings at all, while after, bequests of
them were frequently made.  The questions which Brightlingsea
asked Sandwich in 1569 as to how the former should deal with
strangers, who destroyed the oyster brood or dredged in summer,
"within our Liberties in destruction of our channell and of the
commonwealth" corroborate this idea.  The change to private
oyster beds was probably due to the increased interest in oysters,
when the carrying trade decayed.  The change could have been
made by an agreement between all the commoners.

The Lord Warden owned some beds in Borefleet, and they were
a trouble to his Droitgatherer.  These letters were written by the
latter to Lord Zouch, when Lord Warden.

"Right Honourable,

"My humble duetye Remembered, may yt please your good
Lordshippe to bee advertized, that ther was a fisherman dwellinge
in Barkinge neere London, whose name is Attewell, who at the
Staboote [stowboat] Season was 12 moneth [12 months ago] came
into our haven of Balflete [Borefleet] and threwe out a greate
quantitye of unsavoury stale fish which hath soe tainted the oshters
there that they dyed and weare lost, soe as I could never since untyll
nowe that I haue newe stored them, haue any good of your
Lordshipps laine [laying] there, wherfore my humble suite ys that
your honour wilbe pleased, not only to make him an example in
this case that others may take warninge therby not to comyt the
lyke, but also to sett doune such paines and penalties and gyve
warrants to the Deputie and assistants for levinge [levying] of them,
as your Lordshippe shall thinke fitt to be levied of such offenders or
of any other our inhabitants, that shall offer to dredge oshters in
Balfleete at vnseasonable tymes in the year, or be bould to meddle
with your Lordshipp's laine there soe they may haue punishment
within our towne because the tounesmen are loth and unwillinge to
carry them to Dover or Sandwich, yt beinge a greate charge and
hardly to be levied amongst us, And then your Lordshipp's good
pleasure made knowen to the inhabitants, I maye the more peaceably
having their assistance, performe to your honour some acceptable
service in that and other business, which nowe without daunger to

myselfe I cannot doe.   And soe most humbly take my leave restinge
ever

Your Honours humble Servant

Bricklingsea this 23                         I. K.

of April 1620.                              John King his mark."⁸

Evidently warrant was sent as requested, for a little later he sent
this letter :—

" My humble duetye remembered, may yt please your Honour to
gyve me leave to signifie, that accordinge to your Honours Com-
maundement and warrant directed vnto me, I haue laboured to
suppresse the unlawfull Takers of oshters in the Sumier season, and
more especially by name one John Bens, Thomas Cornish, [blank]
Wade and Elliot of Chich Saint Osyth, who in the exicution of my
office haue vyolently sett upon me with weapons and stones,
greviously hurtinge me, and not therewith contente made complaint
vnto the right Honourable Lord Darcye [he owned St. Osyth
Priory] who directed his Lordshipp's letter vnto our Deputie to
bringe me before his Honour.   Whereuppon I doubting my Lords
displeasure refused to goe, but wrote to my Lord howe his townes-
men had wronged me, and therewithall sent a coppie of your
Honours warrante directed vnto me, prayinge his honors ayde to
take order with those men that had so wronged me, that they would
not hereafter doe the lyke, neverthelesse one of the same men this
present daye, whos name was Wade, came and landed at our Towne,
and their rayled against me most disdainfully, as I shall further
acquaint your Honour at my Cominge to London, not doubtinge but
your Lordshipp will right my wronge in these abuses offered vnto
me in the due execution of my office, and in the meane tyme I haue
sent your Honour two firkins of Oshters by the Colchester Carryers,
one greene and another greate Oshters, and soe weekely will doe yf
I may knowe your Lordshipps good pleasure to be such, for though
that way they wilbe much more chargeable, yet soe they shall surely
be delyvered.   Wherein cravinge to knowe your Honours good
pleasure, I commend your Honour to the protection of the most
high, restinge

Bricklingsea this 26                    Your Honours humble servant

of 7r [September] 1620                    John J. K. Kinge."⁹

Further details of the iniquities of the St. Osyth men apparently
were required, for he made this statement dated 27th October, 1620.

" John Benes of Sainte toosie ded kech osters a fore mihellmus
[Michaelmas] last in Barflet against Brightlingsey, and I went to
him for to se what oyesters he and Thomas Ellet and [blank] Wade

and Thomas Cornish of Sainte toosei ded kech, and they would not let me come nye them but ded throwe greate stones at me, and did hit me and hurt me verye sore and they called out one to another for to kill me, and say they would dredg ther for it was ther Lord Darcyes, and so I was faint for to gooe awaye from them for feare of my lyfe."[9]

It used to be the custom of the Corporation of Colchester to grant a license for a summer's dredging in the Colne to a poor man of each of the eight parishes, on the banks of the River, on the recommendation of the inhabitants.[10] Among the privileges of the Lord Warden, enumerated in 1597, is the election of the "sommer dregger."[11] This was not choosing the Brightlingsea man who was to have the Corporation's license, but was for dredging in the Liberty of Brightlingsea, as a letter of Lord Northampton's to the Deputy shows :—

"Whereas I did by a late Warrant vndder my hand and seale appointe one John Wolphe to be a Somer Dredger of Oysters within ye libertie of Brightlesea with express inhibicion to all others to forbeare dredging yeare [there] ye Monethes prohibited, to ye end both ye Brood, which was muche decayed by ye greatnes of ye froste in ye winter before might be againe restoared, and that my prouision to be made theare out of priviledge and ancient prescription might be more serviceable, and whereas I did yen [then] likewise giue direction vnto you ye Deputy both to make choice and assign some convenient places wherein ye said Wolphe might lay his oysters to be safely kept and to be uttered from time to time as occasion should require, ffor, as much as I am informed, you have notwithstanding in all duety performed what you receaued in charge from me, that certain lewd and unruly persons inhabitants of that towne whose names are underwritten in contempt of authority and to the great destruction of ye Broode which for ye publique service I desire [illegible] to preserve, verie disorderly dredged up ye place allotted for ye proper use of ye said Wolphe, which offence must not suffer to escape unpunished to ye ill example of others. Theis are therefore to will and commaund you to call theis persons before you and if upon examinacion you finde ye complaint to be true to inflicte some suche punishment vpon them for yeir [their] contempe and Disobedience as ye quality of ye offence in your discrecion and judgement shall diserue. Wherof I require you not to faile and withall to advertise me of your proceedings therein.

[Date 1613 ?]                    Northampton House."[12]

The names of the offenders are not underwritten, probably this was a draft only.

122.   When the Duke of York (afterwards James II.) was Lord Warden, the Lord of the Manor interfered with his oysterlayings. The matter was raised in the House of Lords.   On 23rd January, 1670, William Foakes of Brightlingsea, gentleman, stated on oath at the Bar of the House, that Abraham Bradway servant to one [blank] Lucas of Colchester, an attorney, did in December last deliver a Declaration of Ejectment to him (William Foakes) for certain oyster layings belonging to his Royal Highness James Duke of York, in which action Charles Aston, lessee of George Thompson, [Lord of the Manor] is plaintiff, who was warned of his said Royal Highness's interest as aforesaid ; and also that Vincent Hawdler of Lexton Bailiff did, at the suit of the said George Thompson, arrest the said William Foakes in December in an action for trepass for taking oysters from these layings.   All these proceedings "being contrary to the privilege of Parliament," the arrest of Abraham Bradway, (blank) Lucas, Vincent Hawdler, and George Thompson, was ordered and they were to attend the House to answer for their offences.   On 27th January, it was reported, that his Royal Highness had received "satisfaction upon further information concerning this Matter," and the order for arrest was countermanded.[13]

It was reported in 1634, that oysters usually sold at $4^d.$ a bushel were at $2^s.$ $8^d.$, and the larger oysters which had sold at $1^s.$ a bushel then cost $8^s.$, and orders were given that none were to be exported by foreigners or in foreign vessels.[14]   In that year Robert, Earl of Warwick, Vice-Admiral of Essex, was requested to see that the above order was carried out in the County.[14]   Apparently it was no use for in 1638, an inquiry was made into the great scarcity of oysters.   It was reported that in Essex the scarcity was due to taking brood and spat, and culch from the common grounds to private grounds, and to the increased practice of sending them barrelled to London.   The Corporations of Colchester and Maldon "pretending jurisdiction of Admirality doe challenge ye Waters of Pont and Colne which are ye best and cheefest places for ye brooding of Oysters to belong to them," and allowed dredging in prohibited times.   Sending oysters abroad and to the North had added to the scarcity.

As a remedy it was ordered that no oysters be taken from the common grounds until they became "wear and half wear."   No oysters were to be barrelled except from Colchester, Brightlingsea, Colne, and Ponte, and other places, where the best green oysters were bred. No oysters were to be exported, except for the Queen of Bohemia (Elizabeth, eldest daughter of James I.) and the Prince of Orange. No dredging was to be allowed in Ponte, Colne, or elsewhere in Essex, Kent, or the Cinque Ports, or their members during prohibited times. The Lord Warden was to see these orders obeyed in the Ports.[15] A special message was sent to Colchester ordering the Corporation to cease licensing persons to dredge in the close season.[16] Evidently summer dredger licenses had been given profusely.

123. Fuller says that Essex oysters, "the best in England, fat, greenfinned, are bred near Colchester where they have an excellent art to feed them in pits made for that purpose."[17] Green oysters were artificially coloured. They were kept in shallow pits filled by spring tides only. A green scum grew on the water and was absorbed by the oyster. These green oysters were highly prized by people away from the neighbourhood. The Brightlingsea pits would green winter and summer, others in the summer only. Greening was discontinued on the Colne about 1825.[18]

From the Oyster Dredgers' Petition, of 1736, it appears that the Essex dredgermen went to the Western Channel to take oyster brood and lay it to fatten in their own grounds. They complained of the unfair competition of foreign oysters being imported into the Kingdom from Cancale, especially as the importers, to avoid duty, rated the value very low. The oyster fishery was much injured they said, and thus good seamen were not trained, who were very useful people in His Majesty's ships of war. The Customs Commissioners reported that oysters were imported into Rochester, Faversham, Colchester, and Maldon only. 213897 bushels had been entered between 1718 and Christmas, 1735. The oysters had been considerably under-valued, sometimes as low as a farthing and under a bushel. Finally foreign oysters were rated for import duty by the bushel instead of by value.[19]

Oyster edges were mentioned in the Manor Court Rolls as well as layings and pits. Possibly they were what we now call ledgings, small accessible pits, in which oysters may be kept convenient for sale. Oyster pits were used before 1612. Borefleet and St. Osyth Channel were and are the chief cultivating grounds. It appears that the smaller creeks, such as Cockfleet, were used for oyster laying in and before 1709. In a law suit about tithes 2s. in the pound of the rent of the layings was claimed as tithe of oysters. It was pleaded that Cockfleet and Borefleet had been or could be used as arable or pasture land, but without success.[20]

124.   The oyster fishery was undoubtedly the main industry of
Brightlingsea during the eighteenth century.   Whenever Brightlingsea men's occupations are mentioned then, oyster dredger is the
most frequent by far.   Morant, writing in 1768, said it drove a
great trade in oysters.[21]    Arthur Young, in 1806, stated that
dredged oysters were sold at 2s. to 3s a bushel.   According to him,
a dredging boat was from fourteen to forty tons: some were built
at Brightlingsea.   The cost was 10l. a ton for the hull only ; one of
twenty tons would cost 180l. to fit out.   Each carried from two to
four men, who were paid by shares of the profits.   The owner had
for a vessel carrying two men one and a half share, for a larger one
two shares.   The vessels would last with care from thirty to forty
years.   The men and boats had increased by one half in the thirty
years preceding 1806.   In the spring they went dredging off the
coasts of Hampshire and Dorset.   As many as one hundred and
thirty vessels had been seen at work at one time off Mersea.[22]   In
1836 oyster dredging was considered the mainstay of Brightlingsea.[23]
The industry was thus described in 1848 :—" Brightlingsea Creek
has on each side of it innumerable oyster layings where the fishermen lay the spat and young brood [which they gather in the Colne.
Blackwater, etc.] till they grow to the size of oysters," when they
are nearly all sold to be laid in Kentish beds, where they fatten, and
are ultimately sent to London as the finest native oysters.   About
this time about sixty smacks went annually in February or March
to Jersey, Falmouth, etc., where they continued two or three months
dredging for oysters.   About one hundred and sixty smacks of from
fifteen to forty tons belonged to Brightlingsea then.[24]   In 1861
there were as many as two hundred smacks.[25]   Brightlingsea smacks,
because of their speed, were employed in carrying fish from the
North Sea fleets, before the days of the steam carriers.

The oyster would not be expected to have a demoralising
influence, but judging from the war-like exploits of Brightlingsea
men when dredging, the dredgerman, peaceful as he is ashore, often
became a bandit afloat.   As early as Edward III.'s reign an enquiry
was made at Fingringhoe into the death of a fisherman, who had
been killed in a fight between men of Mersea and Tollesbury and
men from Brightlingsea, Wivenhoe and Alresford.[26]   The fishery
was apparently the cause of the dispute.   Dredging without license
was all in the day's work, and convictions for it were very common.
Thirty-five smacks from Brightlingsea and other Ports of the Colne
on 25th January, 1808, sailed to the Crouch to strip the oyster
layings of Sir Henry Mildmay's "from which they had a few days

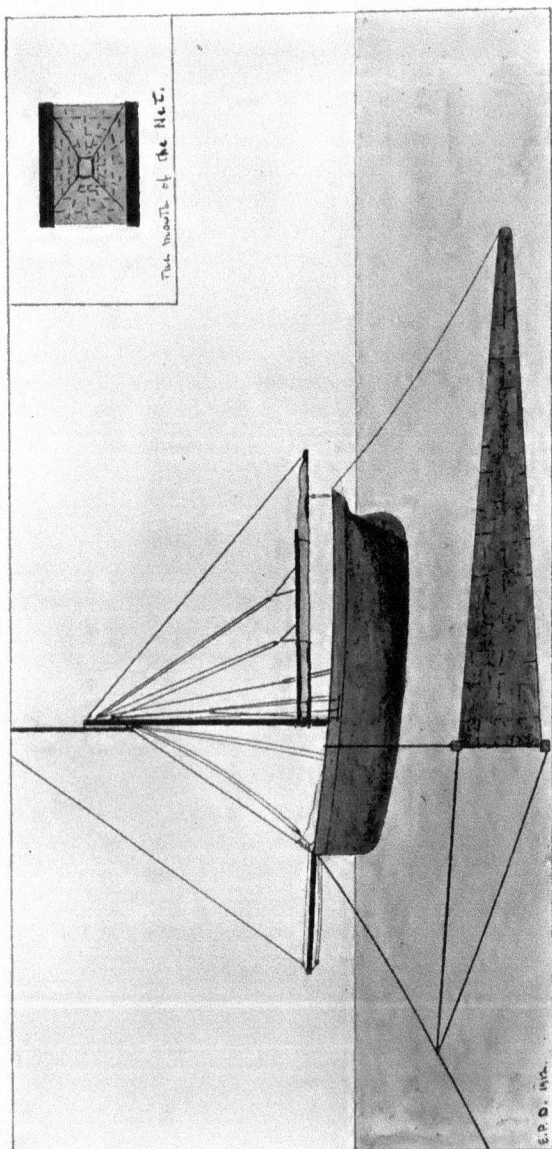

The mouth of the Net.

E.P.D. 1912.

A Smack "Stowboating."

(Plate vii.)

before carried off oysters to the amount of some hundred pounds."
Despite warnings and entreaties to desist, they proceeded with their
work, which the Burnham men prevented by cutting away the
dredges. Some of the ringleaders went to Chelmsford gaol, and
some of the rest, when sailing home, were intercepted by a man-of-
war, and pressed for service afloat.[37]

In the Channel they often dredged within the French three mile
limit, reliance being placed on their superior sailing powers to get
away if chased. Once the Government was petitioned to protect the
Brightlingsea smacks from the French vessels. The reply was to
the effect that no action be taken, as they deserved all they got.[38]
The Government knew more than was suspected. The deep sea
oyster fishery was always a gamble, catches being very uncertain.
The danger is well shown by the number of lives lost. A heavy toll
was taken in 1883, when four smacks and twenty-six men were lost
in the North Sea.

## STOWBOATING.

Sprats are caught in the Thames estuary by 'Stowboats.' The
boat is anchored, a long bag net, the mouth kept open by two balks
of timber at its top and bottom, is slung beneath and the sprats are
carried into it by the tide. The net is closed by hauling the balks
together ; the net and catch then are hauled on deck. The popular
derivation of the name stowboat is, that it is so called, because the
sails are stowed. The older form is 'stall boat,' that is fixed,
evidently alluding to the boat being anchored. Most likely 'stow'
is but 'stall' lazily pronounced. The fishery is an ancient one.
In 1488-89 the use of "stall botes fastened with ankres havyng
wyth theym suche maner of unresonable nettes and engynes" was
prohibited in Orford Haven as destructive of fry and brood of fish
there.[39] In this is suggested the idea that sprats are young herrings,
which was believed for a long time. Tobias Gentleman, a mariner
of Gt. Yarmouth, writing in 1614, had this belief. He says of the
Colne, "I can scarce afford the men of that water the name of
fishermen, for that their chiefest trade is dredging for oysters ; yet
have they, in the summer some eight or ten boats in the North
Seas for cod ; which if they happen to spend all their salt and to
speed well, they may get some twenty pounds in a summer clear.
But here by the way I will make known a great abuse that is
offered to the commonwealth, and especially to all the herring
fishermen of England, only by these men of Colchester Water.

For these men from St. Andrew [October 24th] until Candlemas [February 2nd] and sometimes longer do set forth stale boats amongst the sands in the Thames mouth for to take sprats, with great stale nets with a great poke bag, and they standing in the Swinne or the King's channel on the back of the Gunfleet, they do there take instead of sprats infinite thousands of young herrings, smaller than sprats, and not good to be eaten, for one sprat is better worth than twenty of those Bleakes or young herrings. But because they do fill the bushel at Billingsgate, where they do sell them for sprats; the which, if that they were let live, would all be, at Mid-summer a fat summer full herring and a Peck is sometimes there sold for twopence; which number of herrings at Midsummer would make a barrel of summer herrings, worth twenty or thirty shillings."[31]

For all this the sprat harvest continued. Fuller called them the weavers' beef of Colchester in 1662, and said of them: "These are sprats caught hereabouts and brought hither in incredible abundance, whereon the poor weavers (numerous in the city) make much of their repast, cutting rands rumps sirloins chines and all joints of beef out of them as lasting in season well nigh a quarter of a year. They are the minims of the sea; and their cheapness is the worst thing (well considered thé best) which can be said of them. Were they as dear they would be as toothsome (being altogether as wholesome) as anchovies; for then their price would give a gust unto them in the judgment of palate men."[32]  Brightlingsea is still the most important sprat port. In 1911, over 1430 tons were landed here; forty-five per cent. of the catch on the East Coast.[33]

## WEIRS.

Fishing by weirs was anciently practised here. Domesday does not mention such a fishery here, though there were stated to be some in neighbouring places. In 1274 the Abbot and John de Moveron and others had weirs in the river.[34]  Colchester complained in 1284 that these weirs (the Abbot had one, and John de Moveron six) were a hindrance to navigation. The holders pleaded that they and their ancestors had held these weirs from time immemorial and that they injured none. It was decided that they were to remain.[35]  These weirs were most likely formed of rows of stakes driven into the river bed, and on which nets were set. They would be placed between high and low water, so that they could be got at

to remove the fish. There are no remains of them on the Brightlingsea bank, but rows of stakes, possibly remains of such a weir,
are found off St. Osyth beach and on the " West Edge."

[¹ Fb, 36, Edw. III., pt. ii., m43d. ² Au, 428. ³ Au, 429. ⁴ Au, 431. ⁵ Au,
431. ⁶ Au, 428. ⁷ Au, 429. ⁸ Ga, cxiii., 85. ⁹ Ga, cxvi., 110. ¹⁰ Au, 431
¹¹ Ga, cclxvi., 53 ¹² Ga, lxxv., 83. ¹³ Dz. ¹⁴ N, vii., 359, 462. ¹⁵ Gb,
cxcix., 22. ¹⁶ Gb, xiii., 38. ¹⁷ Bo, 493. ¹⁸ Au, 438-9. ¹⁹ Db. ²⁰ Fh,
²¹ An, 454. ²² Dc, ii., 387. ²³ Ak, ii., 769. ²⁴ Aq, 450. ²⁵ Am, 569. ²⁶ Bd,
25 July, 1908. ²⁷ Bd, 13 June, 1908. ²⁸ Me. ²⁹ Au, 427. ³⁰ A, ii., 544.
³¹ Bt, ii., 57. ³² Bo, i., 498. ³³ Bd, 17 Aug., 1912. ³⁴ E, i., 163. ³⁵ R, 24].

## COPPERAS MAKING.

The raw material for copperas making was collected by dredging.
The raw copperas was found in the London Clay, from which it
was washed, where the Clay was exposed to the waves. It is a
bisulphide of iron. In the process of treatment it was converted
into green copperas or Sulphate of iron. It was used, mixed with
verdegris, as a cure for scab in sheep,¹ but its chief use was to
make a black dye, for which there was a demand when cloth was
made in Essex.² Brightlingsea was one of the three chief places,
where it was made.³ The manufacture was known here before
1674,⁴ though probably it was made here long before. John Beriffe,
in 1542, bequeathed some "copperys" to his wife.⁵ Ray described
the process thus—"They lay the stones on a large Bed or Floor,
prepared in the open air, underneath which there are gutters or
troughs disposed to receive and carry away the liquor impregnated
with the mineral to a cistern, where it is received (for the Sun and
weather dissolving the stones, the Rain falling upon them carryes
away with it the vitrioline juice or Salt dissolved). This liquor
they Boil in large leaden Pans putting in a good quantity of old
iron. When it is sufficiently evaporated, they pour it out into large
troughs wherin it cools, the vitriol crystallizing to the sides of the
Troughs, and to cross pieces put into them. The liquor that
remains after the vitriol is crystallized they call the Mother, and
restore it again to be evaporated by boyling."⁶ There was a house
called the Copperite House here in 1685,⁷ and the Copperas House
and grounds appear many times in the Manor Court Rolls. In
1770, it was said that the works at Brightlingsea kept a large
number of smacks employed dredging for copperas.⁸ In a map of
1772, Copperas House is shown on the site of what is still called
the Copperas ground.⁹ Here were the works until about 1840.
The remains of the troughs sunk in the ground may still be seen.

The Copperas used to be taken in barrels to London in smacks, and the smacks came back loaded with old iron, which was consumed in the works.

## ROMAN CEMENT MANUFACTURE.

The process of making Roman Cement was patented in 1796.[10] The "stones" are septaria, nodules of argillaceous limestone, washed out of the London Clay.[11] A cement factory was started in Brightlingsea in 1826.[12] The stone was first taken from the cliffs along the Coast, and afterwards dredged up. For some years before 1848, about thirty smacks from Brightlingsea were engaged in dredging for it.[13] Most of it came from off Harwich, but some was got off Brightlingsea.[14]

[[1] Bz, i., 31, [2] Au, 411. [3] Bn, ii., Coprose. [4] Bb, vi. [5] Ju. [6] Bl, 17. [7] Np, cxl., 3. [8] Au, 411. [9] Ax. [10] Au, 408. [11] Au, 9. [12] Au, 408. [13] Aq, 450. [14] Au, 411].

## SALT MANUFACTURE.

Saltpans are not mentioned here in Domesday, though there were some in Great Bentley. The salt could be abstracted by the heat of the sun, or in pans artificially heated. When the manufacture began here cannot be said. John Beriffe mentioned a packet of salt in his will dated 1496. He also bequeathed one hundred wey of salt. Joan Benet ordered in her will (1537) that 20*l*. was to be paid out of the salt in her house.[2] John Pyper in 1539 left to his wife "all my Salte that lyeth in the salte house."[3] The last notice of this kind known to me is John Walker's salt, which he bequeathed in 1589.[4] The name Salcotts and its variant, Silcotts, suggests salt houses, but the name is that of property belonging to a man named Salcott.[5] The industry appears to have died out by 1600. From the wording of an entry in the Manor Court Rolls, it was considered possible to revive it in 1730.[6]

## AGRICULTURE.

The chief points of the agriculture here were dealt with in the description of the Manor. The Extent of 1300 speaks of cheese being made on the Demesne farm.[5] This was no doubt the cheese made from ewes' milk, of which Mr. J. Horace Round has traced the manufacture back to Domesday times.[7] It was still made from the milk of ewes on the Essex marshes, when Norden wrote in 1594.[8]

In the thirteenth century (and much earlier) nearly every man was a small holder. In the sixteenth century the practice was still wide spread. Mariners as frequently as any kept oxen, sheep, pigs, and poultry. Horses were very rarely mentioned. Either oxen were used for ploughing or most of the land was pasture. Sheep were far more numerous than any other stock. When there was plenty of free pasture on the Commons, every tenant would keep some. The yeomen, however, held large areas of land. In 1546 Edward Lamb, John Locke, and John Clare, each held land worth 20*l.* a year, an equivalent of £240 now. Thomas Beriff held 10*l.* worth, John Beriff 5*l.*, and William Hykson 3*l.*[9] In addition to the usual corns, rye was then grown here,[10] and well into the seventeenth century. In that century agriculture became more specialized. It was yeomen and husbandmen who kept stock then; the mariners did not. We hear of a " Northern Coowe " in a will of 1603, apparently of special value, as it is mentioned apart from the rest.[11] Saddle-horses were kept; a " Paceing Bay Nagg " in 1665,[12] and a riding horse in 1676 were bequeathed by will.[13]

[[1] Bz, iii., 335. [2] Jg, 7. [3] Ie. [4] Ir. [5] Na. [6] Nd, 280. [7] Vt, 369, 371. [8] Aa. [9] Ff 110/320. [10] Ju, John Edwards, 1574. Robt. Hubarde, 1587. [11] Ju Hugh Nevell. [12] Jo, 119. [13] Jp, 42.]

## INNS.

128. The monasteries and clergy found shelter for travellers nearly up to the Reformation, except in large towns. Also brewing at home meant little need for alehouses. Beer (ale with the addition of hops to flavour and keep it) was introduced into England in the fifteenth century.[1] John Beriff of Jacobs left his " tenement called le Berehowse " to his son in 1496.[2] Possibly the Swan was this beerhouse ; the building was old enough. As a badge a swan has no known connection with Brightlingsea; it is not found in any known local coat of arms. Possibly the sign may have been taken from the white swan ducally gorged, the badge of Henry IV., and used as an inn sign in the fifteenth century.[3] John Beriff in 1521 left 6*l.* 13*s.* 4*d.* a year out of the profits of his beerhouse to provide masses for the repose of his soul.[4]

Seven men and one woman were licensed as victuallers here in 1601.[5] Probably most were for beerhouses. John Taylor, the Water Poet, in 1635 mentioned one tavern at " Bricksley " out of one hundred and seven in the county, From his dedication it appears that he meant hostelries rather than beerhouses.[6] This is corroborated by the fact that there were five licensed victuallers here in that year.[7]

The first inn mentioned by name is the Swan in 1663.[8] In 1668, depositions in a case about tithe were taken at the "common inne called the Swanne."[9] It was let at a rent of 10*l.* a year in 1779.[10] The Ship appeared on the Court Rolls in 1698, and the Anchor in John Scarlett's will in 1695.[11] This is not the "old Anchor," which stood on the Hard where the present Anchor Hotel now is, but was the ancient house at the west upper corner of Queen Street. The King's Head was first heard of late in the eighteenth century,[12] and the Duke of Wellington naturally does not appear until the nineteenth century. These with the White Lion and two beerhouses were the licensed houses in 1834[13] and 1848.[14] Hops were grown here, for a piece of land was called Hopyard in 1842.

The sale of ale has been long the subject of legislation. The Assize of ale (date uncertain but early) fixed the price at which it should be sold. When a quarter of barley was sold for 20*d.* or 2*s.*, the brewers out of cities were to sell three or four gallons for a penny.[16] The Manor Court was entrusted with the regulation of the price and quality.

In 1561, enquiry was to be made if any tipplers [beerhouses] were kept open during divine service.[17] The Mayor and Jurats of Sandwich, being Brightlingsea's magistrates, licensed the victuallers here. There are records remaining of licenses being given in 1601, 1635, 1638, and 1639. Each victualler was bound in his own bond for 10*l.*, and two sureties of 5*l.* each for his good behaviour. In 1639, the entry was headed "Bunn pence,"[18] bunn meaning bound.[19] The Manor Court had cognisance of not only the old Assize of ale, but of offences under later licensing laws; of these there are some instances in the Court Rolls. In 1661, the jury presented John Pinner, husbandman "because he kept a common alehouse one whole month last part, and further is used commonly to sell beer and drink obstinately by his own authority without license of two Justices of the Peace against the form of the Statute, and in bad example of other subjects of our Lord now King." He was fined 20*s.* Thomas Andrews was presented in 1664 for receiving and entertaining "lazy and evil persons in his house, and for permitting them to drink, and to be drunk on the Lord's Day against the form of the Statute" *etc.* He was fined 10*s.*

[[1] K, iv., appendix, 431. [2] Ib. [3] Cb, i, 502. [4] Jc. [5] Ld, 318. [6] Dy. [7] Ljj. [8] Nb, 38. [9] Fg. [10] Mc. [11] Ji, 285. [12] Mg. [13] As. [14] Aq, 452. [16] Mf. [16] A, i., 200. [17] Lc, clxxix. [18] Li, [19] Co].

## MILLS.

129. The importance of a mill in a manor was due to the fact, that the tenants had to take their corn to the Lord's mill to be ground, and to pay for it being ground. Private mills and querns were prohibited. There was a mill here in 1086, and it is mentioned in section 19. The Abbot had another mill called Brightlingsea Mill, but situated on Thorington Marsh. Near the mill was a landing place called Killers hith probably on the Thorington side, and from which a road was made to join the main road to St. Osyth, probably near Saltwater Brook. In 1291 the value of the Abbot's temporalities in lands mills and store beasts (? fetis animalibus) was 6l. 13s. 7½d.[1] This must represent the value of the demesne lands, and the profits of the mills and cattle. The rents of the tenants' lands cannot be included as they alone were worth more than this. The Beriffes owned a windmill here in 1521.[2] Its site is not easy to locate, but it seems to have lain a little west of Hurst Green[3] Querns had not gone out of use by 1549, for John Beriffe mentioned two for grinding malt in his will of that year.[4]

The present windmill was brought here by water on two oyster skiffs from Fingringhoe some few years ago. As may be guessed from this, oyster skiffs are beamy boats of very substantial build, and not of the slenderness usually associated with the name skiff.

[¹ Ha, 60, f. 87.   ² Ja.   ³ Ju, John Beriffe, 1542.   ⁴ Ig.]

## THE SCRIVENER.

130. When learning was scarce, the Scrivener was an important person. He wrote accounts and letters, but it was in wills that his work is most seen. Thomas Boysse "scriptour" was a witness to Thomas Beriffe's will in 1563.[1] (William Beriffe's will (1527) was witnessed by a "Notary Publik").[2] "Mr. Atkinson" so described himself throughout a will (1587) of which he was the "writer," though every one else was named without any title.[3]

Henry Collins, Scrivener, received 20s. in 1637 for making a will of short length.[4] Thomas Drury, mariner, in 1697, "did on his death-bed (having neither wife nor child at that time), and desiring to make his last will and Testament and sending for the Scrivener of the said Town, for that purpose, who happened then not to be at home therefore he . . . . did make his last will noncupative."[5] A nuncupative will was made by word of mouth, and reduced to writing either before or after the testator's death.

[¹ Ih.   ² Jd.   ³ Ju, Robt. Hubarde, 1587.   Ja,   ⁵J   469.]

K

# Chapter VII.

## DOMESTIC LIFE.

### SAXON TO TUDOR TIMES.

131.   The Saxon house of importance was a long large room,
the hall, which the owner, his family, and retinue occupied by day
and night.   The hearth was in the centre of the floor, and there
was a hole in the centre of the roof, through which the smoke
could escape.   The floor was of beaten earth, sometimes covered
with rushes.   Tables, made of boards on trestles, forms, and chests,
which made beds for the night, were the chief furniture.   A room
for the owner and his family at the end of the hall was the next
development.   This plan of a hall being the main part of the house,
continued in use till the fifteenth century.   The Saxon peasant
lived in a mean thatched one-roomed hut.   The only known
reminder of Saxon dress and ornament relating to Brightlingsea
is a gold bracelet found here, and now in the collection of the late
Sir John Evans.   It is made of two strands of gold wire twisted
together and gradually tapering.[1]

We get in Domesday (1086) the first hint of the population.
There were forty landholders, ten bordars who held no land, and
five serfs.   There would be a bailiff and possibly other residents as
well, so there would be not less than fifty-six heads of families.
Allowing four to each family, a modest number, when a villein's family
probably included grown up sons and their families, we get a
population of two hundred and twenty-four.   This was a large
population for a village then.   Under the Normans the people
lived much as they had done in Saxon days.   An iron tripod with
a brass dish was the cooking apparatus ordinarily found in labourers'
cottages in the thirteenth century.   The labourer ate his food from
wooden bowls, with wooden spoons, and from wooden trenchers.[2]

In the Extent of the manor of about 1300, there were mentioned,
ninety-two messuages and thirty-six cottages.   Four to each dwelling
give a population of four hundred and ninety-two.   Brightlingsea
must have been a relatively large and prosperous place then, for

prosperous towns are considered to have had populations of from
five hundred to one thousand about this time.[3]   A little later (1327),
a return for a subsidy (a tax of one twentieth of the value of
moveable goods) contains thirty-two Brightlingsea names. The
total tax paid was 70s. 2¾d. The goods, on which the tax was
assessed, averaged in value 2l. 3s. 10d. each person, at present
value, equal to 32l. 18s. 8d.   The lowest assessable value was
13s. 4d. or 10l. present value, the highest, 8l. 7s. 6d. or 125l.
12s. 6d. present value.[4]   About one third of the house holders were
wealthy enough to be taxed.   As an equivalent of 10l. modern
value was the apparent limit below which none was taxed, this
represents a fair amount of wealth considering the modest furniture
of the period.   Master (Magister) Moueron, probably John de
Moveron, who held Moverons, paid on 54l. 1s. 3d. present value.

Brightlingsea had not recovered from the effects of the Black
Death by 1394-95, judging from the subsidy payments.   In that
year, Brightlingsea's total for a fifteenth was 53s. 3¼d.,[5] a drop in
value compared with the payment in 1327, in the proportion of
seven to two.   Men of the working class, of this period, were
simply dressed in tunics gathered in at the waist by a belt, which
carried a knife; the legs and feet were covered by hose and shoes.
The head was as a rule bare.   Mariners were similarly dressed, as
may be seen on the Sandwich ship (Fig. 2).

132.   We get an account of the Rectory Hall in 1458.[6]   It was
timber built and tiled.   There was a large central hall, with a
chamber at one end, and another chamber and two outhouses
(aomus) at the other.   There is no suggestion of a second storey.
So it must have belonged to an earlier period than the timber
houses now remaining in Brightlingsea.

Judging from the number of old timber built houses still remaining,
almost all of the old houses were so built.   When were they built?
It is not likely, that they were built before Edward III.'s reign.
The external staircase of the house called Jacobs, in High Street,
might be held to show an earlier origin, but these early external
staircases were open and like a flight of steps, and not a spiral
contained in a turret as is this.   As the overhang of the upper storey
is slight, they were built before Elizabethan times.   If they were
not built before the Black Death, they would not be likely to be
built until sometime after, as the prosperity of the country was
injured by that disaster, and took some time to recover.   Most
likely they were built in the fifteenth century, when there were
prosperous men of the middle class in plenty.   The foundations of

these houses were often septaria, and the framework of beams and uprights mortized together was strengthened by diagonal braces. The intervals between the timbers were filled in with oak laths

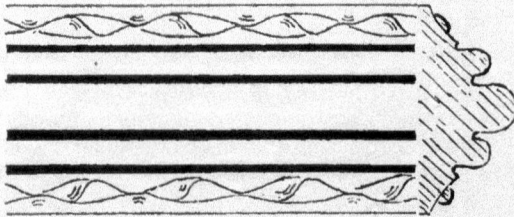

FIG. 5.

PLAN AND CROSS SECTION OF BEAM AT "JACOBS."

bound together with spun-yarn and plastered over.[7] The dark timber contrasting with the light plaster was their distinctive outward feature. Each storey overhung the one below. A

fine example was "Jacobs." It has been so much altered that most of its features are hidden. The fact that the second storey overhung the first and the gable the second storey, is concealed by the lower walls having been brought out in a line with that of the gable. The first floor level has been altered, and the old second storey made into two by the addition of another floor. Some of the beams are handsomely carved (fig. 5). When the old floors were removed a few years ago they were found to be of oak two inches thick. The curious hexagonal tower containing a spiral staircase is now hidden largely by modern additions. Fig. 6 is a representation of it with the additions removed.

FIG. 6. "JACOB'S TURRET."

The Swan, before it was renovated, was a good example of this style (fig. 7). The least altered example is 13 Victoria Place, but in it the "magpie" effect is hidden by the timberwork being covered with plaster.

133. Well into Elizabethan times the hall and parlour were the chief rooms in this class of house. The parlour was used as a bedroom,

apparently for the head of the house. The second storey was one
large dormitory at first, to be divided into bedrooms later. Houses
were comfortless until the fifteenth century, but in the sixteenth,
the well-to-do mariner and yeoman lived in quite comfortable
surroundings.

In this century we get details of the actual furniture used here.
The walls of the hall, and sometimes of the bedrooms, were covered
with hangings in the better houses.[8] The hangings were usually
described as being stained or painted cloth.[9] The painting in the
case of some took the form of pictures; one is described as
illustrating the story of Noah's Flood.[10]

FIG. 7.        THE OLD SWAN (RESTORED).

Candles and candlesticks, made of silver, brass, latten, or pewter,
were used.[11] One house had in 1546 two pairs of silver torches,[12]
these were probably small oil lamps.

The large open fireplace with the fire on the hearth was furnished
with a pair of andirons or cobirons (firedogs), a pair of tongs, and
sometimes with a "fyrepan" or shovel.[13] Chafing dishes were also
used as a source of heat.[13] Pot hooks and a trammell[14] (a notched
bar) were used to hang over the fire, by which pots could be placed
at the right distance above the fire.

For seats there were forms, chairs, occasionally stools, settles,
and transoms.[15] The stools were sometimes described as joined
stools,[16] these were made of pieces of wood joined together distinguishing them from those made of a single block of wood.
Comfort was provided by cushions, which were plentiful. Some

were described as being stuffed with feathers, and others as
"Spanish."[17]  For storing things, there were cupboards, hutches,
chests, and coffers.[18]  Cupboards were originally boards on which
cups stood.  As in one instance a cupboard cloth is mentioned, some
were still probably in this primitive form.  Hutches were what we
call cupboards now.  Chests and coffers had the same box form ; the
distinction appears to be in size, and in the value of the things stored.
The coffer was smaller and used for more valuable goods.  There
were coffers and chests of spruce (deal), cypress (cedar), or walnut.[19]
Among mariners Danske (Danish) chests were popular.[20]  One
Danske chest was described as painted.[21]  Another chest was
called a "borde chest."[22]  This may mean that it was used to hold
food, or that it was made of boards put together, instead of being
cut out of the solid, as chests had been.

Some of the tables used had advanced beyond the board and
trestle form.  There were joined tables,[21] that is framed and joined
together, and counter tables,[23] of which the name is self-explan-
atory.  Tablecloths were used.  Some were described as diaper.[24]
To one belonged "a bering semyd [seamed] with blacke silke and
white" whatever it might be.[10]  Table napkins also appeared ; some
were of diaper.[24]  Knives and forks are not named in any will
examined, the former, no doubt, because each diner brought his
own, the latter because they had not come into general use.  Silver
spoons were numerous.  John Piper in 1539 mentioned twenty-four
in his will.[26]  Bequests of half-dozens were common.  A silver
spoon left in 1549 was said to have "a Joynte."[14]  Six silver
spoons in another will were called "slippe spoons."[21]  Two silver
spoons were in 1556 priced at 10s. ; whether each or the pair is not
indicated.[29]

For plates, wooden platters, called trenchers, and pewter platters
were used.[30]  Dishes were of pewter ; some had "ears" or
handles.[31]  "Troye dishes" were mentioned in 1551,[32] possibly
troye means trow or trough.  Porringers or porridge bowls were
numerous,[14] and were made probably of wood or pewter.

The salt cellar was an important piece of plate.  Sometimes it
was made of pewter.[33]  Silver ones were frequent.  William Beriffe,
the Deputy left three silver salt cellars, double or parcel gilt.[34]
Masers, bowls of turned wood, generally maple, were highly prized
and generally ornamented with silver.  Thomas Beriffe, who lived
on East End Green, had a "great maser bole with a band and boss
silver gilt."[28]  For drinking there were also goblets, cups and pots.
The pots were generally of pewter.[36]  Thomas Beriff had a silver
goblet with a cover parcel gilt, a silver goblet parcel gilt, and two

silver bowls.[34]  William Beriffe, the Deputy, had two silver pots parcel gilt, two silver bowls parcel gilt, and a pot covered and footed with silver.[34]  A stone pot covered, lipped, and footed with silver was bequeathed in 1585.[37]

Brass pots were the most numerous cooking utensils.  There were also cauldrons (sometimes of brass), boilers, kettles (sometimes copper), latten chafers (saucepans), iron pots, posnets (little pots), kettles of brass as large as two gallons, dripping pans, spits, ladles, scomers (skimmers), and latten pestles and mortars.[38]

The bedrooms apparently had not much furniture besides the bed and bedding.  In one case there was a joined table.[39]  A close bedstead (covered in with wooden sides and doors) was bequeathed in 1537.[10]  Another was described as carved.[41]  The four poster was not mentioned, but five white curtains for a bed left in 1580 suggest it.[42]  The bed and bolsters were usually feathers or down, but some were flock.[41]  The pillows apparently were usually feathers.  Two were specified as being down lined with fustian.[14]  Pillow cases, then called pillow bears, were provided.  Two were described as seamed with black silk.[10]  Canvoys (canvas) sheets are mentioned once,[46] and sheets of "ye brishettis whete" were bequeathed in 1531.[47]  This may mean brightest white.  Coverlets for the beds were usual; once a quilt was mentioned.[10]  The cost of bedding is given in 1542, when 33s. 4d. was left to buy bedding.[49]  The warming pan was not forgotten, for a "panne for a bed" was left in 1549.[14]  Washing utensils do not appear often.  A basin and ewer were bequeathed once.[51]  Towels were mentioned.[14]

Thomas Beriffe had a clock in his house on East End Green in 1563.[28]  Books were rare.  Some were mentioned without being named.[54]  Thomas Beriffe left Erasmus's "Periphrasis,"[53] and a small Bible was bequeathed in 1571.[55]  Thomas Beriffe bequeathed the glass in his houses.[53]  This suggests glass in removeable frames fitting into the windows, a method used when glass was first used for glazing windows.

The only musical instrument appearing is a virginal in 1585.[37]  It had strings struck with hammers, worked by keys after the manner of a piano.  The instrument was small and placed on a table when played.

[1 At, 327.  2 Ed, i., 104.  3 Cd, 414.  4 Ff, 107/12.  5 Ff, 107/73.  6 V. 7 Bc, xiii., 220.  8 Ig, Ii.  9 Jf.  10 Jg., 7.  11 Jg, 7, Ju, Edw., Duke, 1572, Wm. Folkes, 1597.  12 Ju, Rob. Ientry.  13 Jg, 7, Ju, John Edwards, 1574, Co, firepan. 14 Ig.  15 Jg, 7, Jf, Ig, Ju, John Edwards, 1574.  16 Ju, Edw., Duke, 1572.  17 Jg, 7, Ii.  18 Jg, 7, 27, Ie.  19 Jg, 7, Ie, Ju, John Harvey, 1582.  20 Ik, 3.  21 Ju, Thos. Keble, 1588.  22 Jg, 28.  23 Ig, Ju, John Edwards, 1574.  26 Ie.  28 Ih.  29 Ju,

John Assheley, 1556. [30] Ig, 28, Ju, Agnes Martin, 1551. [31] Jg, 7, 28. [32] Ju,
Agnes Martin. [34] In. [36] Jg, 7, Ju. Edw. Duke, 1572. [37] Ju. John Ayers. [38] Jg,
7, 28, Ig, Io, 7, Ik, 24, Ju, Wm. Osman, 1580, Wm. Folkes, 1597, Anne Smythe,
1539, John Edwards, 1574. [39] Ju, Wm. Folkes, 1547. [41] Ju, Edw Bulvan, 1584.
[42] Ju, Wm. Osmann. [43] Ju, Agnes Martin, 1551. [46] Ju, Anne Smythe, 1539.
[47] Ju, John Chaunceler, 1531. [49] If [51] Ju, Edw. Duke, 1572. [54] Ir. [55] Ik, 24.]

## SIXTEENTH CENTURY DRESS.

134. The Beriffe Brasses give a good idea of the dress of the
wealthier class here in the late fifteenth and sixteenth centuries.
John Beriffe (died 1496) wears a plain gown reaching to his feet,
his under dress, probably a tunic, shows on the arms through the
wide loose sleeves of his gown. His girdle carries a gipciere on
the right side and a rosary on the left. The gipciere was a large
purse, and the distinguishing badge of a merchant.[1] It had a
D-shaped frame of silver or brass with a rim pierced with holes
through which the bag was laced to it.[2] The brass of one of his
three wives, the only one remaining, shows her wearing a long gown
with a square cut neck. The tight sleeves are turned back to form
cuffs. As the cuffs are furred and fur also shows at the neck, the
gown was presumably fur-lined. She wears a girdle and the
'butterfly' headdress. The children are dressed like their parents,
except that the sons have neither gipciere nor rosary. (Plate viii.)

Mary Beriffe (died 1505) wears a similar overgown, which allows
the undergarment to show at the neck. Her girdle has a long end
hanging loose. Her headdress is of the pedimental type. Her sons
wear plain loose sleeved gowns, and her daughter is dressed like
her, but has no headdress, and her hair hangs loose down her back.

Margaret Beriffe (died 1514) is similarly dressed. Her girdle has
a long embroidered pendant end.

William Beriffe's (died 1527) tunic does not reach to his knees.
It is confined by a belt, which carries a gipciere. He wears hose
and broad-toed shoes. Over all he wears a long furlined gown
with large cuffs. His wife's gown is like Mary Beriffe's. Her
girdle is very loose, and is fastened by three rosettes, from one a
ball-shaped ornament is suspended by a chain.

Alice Beriffe (died 1536) was a widow, and wears the conventional
nun-like widow's dress. Her outer garment is a long cloak,
fastened across the chest by cords. These are shown of enormous
thickness, probably due to bad drawing. The pendant cords are
knotted at the waist level, and end at her ankles in unproportional
tassels. Under the chin covering the neck is a linen wimple. Her
head is covered by a kerchief, of which the ends fall on her shoulders.
(Plate viii.).

JOHN BERIFFE,
1496.

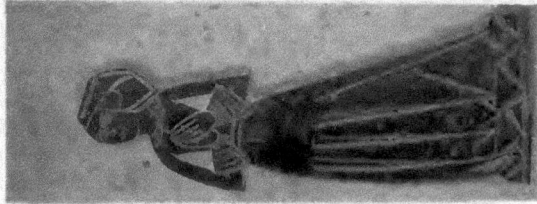

AMY BERIFFE,
1496.

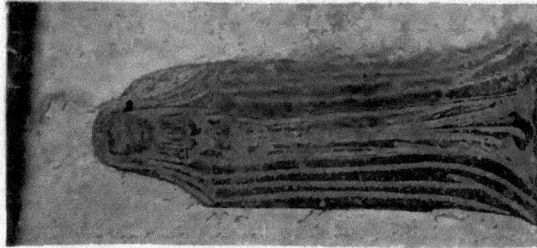

ALICE BERIFFE,
1536.

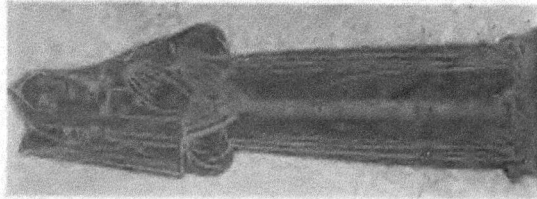

MARY BERIFFE,
1521.

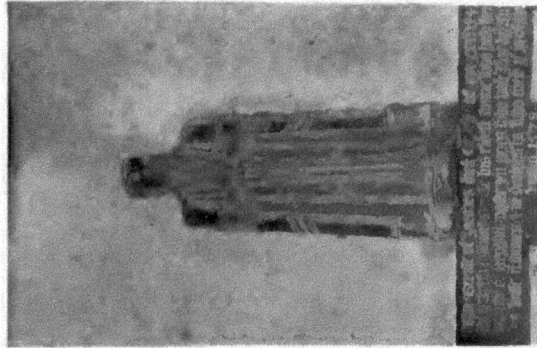

WILLIAM BERIFFE,
1578.

BRASSES.

(Plate viii.)

Margaret Beriffe's girdle carries a chain; at its end is what looks like a pomander, the old equivalent of a smelling salts bottle.

William Beriffe (1578) shows a change in fashion. His hair is short, and he wears a beard and moustache. Over all he wears a furlined robe with short sleeves having long pendants, embroidered across the middle, and fringed at the ends. " If not the ordinary gentleman's overgown of the period, it is probably his official robe as 'Deputy of Brightlingsea.' In any case it very much resembles the robes now worn by aldermen on occasions of civic state."[27] His under garment is a doublet with small frills at the neck and wrists. If it could be seen in its entirety, it would be found no doubt to have full sleeves puffed and slashed to show the lining of contrasting colour. The hose had now become divided into two parts, the upper, the hose proper, the counterpart of the later breeches, and the lower, the stockings. His hose are concealed, or they would be found no doubt to be of similar make to his doublet. His shoes are low and broad-toed. (Plate viii.).

135. The wills of this period give many details of dress and ornament. Joan Benet (1537) left a worsted kyrtell, two gowns lined with "satten of Sypers" (Cyprus), and one gown lined with black shanks (fur from the legs of kids or sheep), five silver pins, two pairs of silver hooks, a black dymisent (girdle), two pairs of silver aigletts (tags fastened to ends of laces or " points " used to lace different parts of dresses together), some beads, three silver gilt rings, and six of her best kerchiefs.[3] Dymisents were common. One was described as garnished with silver.[4] Sleeves were some-times detachable, and made of different material from the rest of the dress. Ann Smythe had in 1539 a black kirtle "with ye chamlett upper bodye and a pair of worsted sleeves." Gowns of grogram and black mourning gowns were bequeathed.[5] Corduroy, or what appears very like it in the indistinct writing of the will, was the material of a black gown in 1531.[6] Kerchiefs were the only headdress mentioned. Coral beads sometimes "gawdyd" (ornamented) with silver were worn by women.[7] A " bearing " bequeathed in 1580[8] was probably a bearing cloth, in which children were wrapped when baptised.

Men's gowns were mentioned as being lined with black fur, white fur, fox fur, or unlined.[9] Coats were occasionally named. William Beriffe left a black coat, his best tawny coat but one, and his worst tawny coat.[10] John Beriffe had a black frieze coat and a green one.[11] Frieze was a coarse woollen cloth, in favour because of its warmth.[1] A coat of " marvell " was left in 1534.[13] Was it the same as the modern material 'merveilleux' ? Men's jackets were often mentioned.

John Ayre had one of "unwatered chamlet,"[14] and John Beriffe's was black garded (trimmed) with velvet.[11]   Chamlet was a mixture of wool and silk, expensive but good wearing.[16]   Doublets were also made of chamlet, fustian (a strong cotton cloth), sackcloth, black satin, canvas, buck's leather, and "grogreyne" (grogram, a coarse woollen cloth).[17]   John Beriffe, who appears to have gone in for rich effects, had one of green unwatered chamlet.[11]   A "taylleyd" (tailed) doublet was bequeathed in 1545.[19]

A jerkin was like a jacket.   One man had one and a pair of breeches of "skye collor."[20]   Others were made of leather or frieze.[21]   Hose are of course often mentioned.   Nether stockings were mentioned once.[22]   They were worn under the hose or outer stockings.   Breeches only appear late in the century.   Robert Hubarde, husbandman, in 1587 left three pairs of wearing breeches.[22] Another pair was described as being "of black pewke laid with lace."[23]   "Pewke" probably meant puce, though black puce sounds contradictory, unless a dark shade was meant.   These lace trimmed breeches belonged to a Brightlingsea dandy; he also had a sky-blue jerkin and breeches.

The most common men's head-dress mentioned was the cap. These were no doubt flat and round in shape, and sometimes ornamented with feathers.   Hats were occasionally bequeathed.   They were usually worn by the wealthier classes, and made of velvet with wide brims and high crowns.   One was described as a "stitched Hatt."[20]   Rings of gold and silver were fairly frequent.[11]   A signet of silver was bequeathed in 1538.[25]   William Beriffe, the Deputy, left a ring of gold with three stones, a ring of gold "with my marke uppon yt," a ring of gold with a "deathes head uppon yt," and a gold ring with a white stone.[26]   Silver whistles and chains were very common,[13] especially among mariners, probably because they could be used for giving orders at sea.

The general impression left is that life in the sixteenth century in Brightlingsea was certainly comfortable, and for the period luxurious to some.

Taking evidence from wills, a mariners' roll, and the armour schedule, there would be about one hundred and ten householders in Brightlingsea at the end of the sixteenth century.   Four to each house gives a population of four hundred and forty.

[¹ Eg.   ² Do, cciii.   ³ Jg, 7.   ⁴ Ju, Hen. Benet, 1534.   ⁵ Ju, Ann Smythe, 1539. ⁶ Ju, John Chaunceler, 1531.   ⁷ Ju, Robert Ientry, 1546.   ⁸ Ju, Wm Osmann, 1580. ⁹ Jg, 28, Ir.   ¹⁰ If.   ¹¹ Ig.   ¹³ Ju, Hen. Benet.   ¹⁴ Jg, 25.   ¹⁶ Eg. Camlet.   ¹⁷ Jg, 25, Ig, Ik, 3.   ¹⁹ Ju, Ric. Myllys.   ²⁰ Ik, 3.   ²¹ Ju, Hen. Benet, 1534, Rob. Hubarde, 1587.   ²² Ju, Robt. Hubarde, 1587.   ²⁵ Jg, 28.   ²⁶ In.   ²⁷ Eq, 30].

## The Seventeenth Century.

136. Barnard Feuerell, a yeoman, who had been Deputy, gave a list of household goods, which he bequeathed in 1609. He mentioned his best feather bed and bolster, two pairs of good blankets, three pairs of good sheets, two best coverings, two pairs of good pillows and pillow bears, a holland table cloth, six good napkins, a new "cubboard cloth," six of the "midle sorte of pewter platters," six of the "midle sorte of porringers," two pewter dishes, one pewter salt cellar, two saucers, the best brass pot, the biggest new kettle, a spit, a dripping pan, two "needlework quishions" (cushions), a wicker chair, a new painted cloth in the hall, a silver salt cellar, the biggest silver spoon, six best silver spoons, the best down bed and bolsters, a bedstead and bedding, a best silver cup, and a silver wine cup.[1]

" Posted " bedsteads (four posters) were mentioned.[2] Another was called a " fayned bedstead,"[3] probably one with curtains to it. Beds were still used in the parlour. In some houses there were two parlours, as a little parlour is mentioned.[2] A bed is mentioned as being in a " buttry chamber."[4] This was more likely a room over the buttery than the buttery itself. A solar (a principal room usually facing south) was named in 1608 as containing a bedstead.[5] A trunk bedstead (probably the same as a close bedstead) was bequeathed in 1608.[6]

Among the household goods of this century were mentioned a desk, a trunk chest, a high chair, a leather chair, a turned chair (the legs or parts forming the back were turned), and a latten frying pan.[7]

There was not much plate mentioned, perhaps because some of the wealthier men like Francis Wheeler bequeathed their goods without giving details.[8] A silver beer bowl, a silver salt cellar with a silver cover parcel gilt " of the old fashion," a pot lipped with silver, a " best silver salt," a silver tankard, and some silver spoons were bequeathed by various persons.[9] John Beriffe, of Jacobs, in 1624 mentioned five pieces of silver plate, but did not specify their nature. His grandson was to have 5l. to buy a silver tankard parcel gilt.[10]

The dress of the first part of this century was similar to that of the end of the sixteenth. There were the same enormous ruffs, puffed and slashed doublets and breeches, and hats with extravagant feathers worn by the wealthier class of men. Women of the same position wore similar dresses with the skirts held out to an enormous extent by farthingales, large ruffs and " Mary Queen of Scots " caps.

Extravagance in dress grew until the Puritans introduced their well known sombre attire, in turn replaced by the equally well known and extravagant dress fashionable in Charles II.'s reign. A yeoman in 1684 bequeathed his best red petticoat "with the small silver galloon."[11] Petticoat here is used in the original sense of a short coat. Galloon was originally a lace made of worsted, but afterwards sometimes made of silver. The owner evidently favoured the gay clothing of the period. The only other part of men's attire mentioned are cloaks. A woman's hat and red petticoat were bequeathed in 1609,[6] the latter was probably a coat. A flannel petticoat in 1662 was no doubt of the ordinary type.[13]

Jewellery was specified a little more frequently. A small gold ring with " Moyses Tables in it," a great gold ring, a dial ring, and a seal were left by Nicholas Swallowes, mercer, in 1602.[14] A dial ring had possibly a small compass in it.

137. The Plague was raging in Colchester in 1666. Among the regulations issued at this time was one requiring every place to provide a "pest house" for the isolation of cases.[15] There was here until a few years ago a house lying on the west side of East End Green, which was called the Pest house, a name no doubt handed down from 1666.

Charles II.'s hearth taxes give an idea of the number of the houses. In 1674, forty-four persons paid the tax on one hundred and eighty hearths, and nineteen were excused ; their hearths numbered twenty-two. Some are entered as having more than one house, and the total number of houses amounts to seventy-one.[16] This at four persons to a house gives a population of two hundred and eighty-four. This is probably an under-estimate. Probably the practice of using one house as two or more tenements, which was certainly done in the eighteenth century had begun by this date. The fifteenth and sixteenth century mariners' houses were too big for the less wealthy dredgermen of the seventeenth and eighteenth. Seven houses had five or more hearths, which fact lends colour to this idea. The available details of the household goods of the period do not suggest that there was any increase in the material comforts in the seventeenth century compared with the sixteenth.

[[1] Ju. [2] Ju, John Standinot, 1603. [8] Ju, Josias Stevens, 1637. [4] Ji, 108. [5] Ju, Thos. Bullivant. [6] Ju Ric, Ambler, 1609. [7] Ju, John Sallowes 1602, John Standinot 1603, John Harlow 1605 ; Jl, 196. [8] Jb. [9] Ju, Wm. Parker 1600, John Standinot 1603, Humphrey Hastler 1614, Saml. Wilton 1641 ; Ji, 225. [10] Ju. [11] Jr, 31. [13] Jm, 174. [14] Ju. [15] O, v., p, xv. [16] Ff, 246/22].]

## The Eighteenth Century.

138. There is not much information available about the social life in the eighteenth century. Only a few wills have been transcribed, and only one gives any information. In 1703, three pewter dishes, a great brass kettle, and a brass pottage pot were bequeathed,[1] showing that some at least of the old style of utensils were not out of use.

Among the Parish papers is a "neurytority" (inventory) dated 1737 of a parishioner's furniture. It does not suggest wealth nor comfort. Probably the owner required relief. In the chamber were a bed and table. In the house, a hutch, a box, a cupboard, two tables, a "joynt" stool, a long form, a half hogshead, a "nedden trofe" (kneading trough) a washen keler (shallow washing tub), a "cole racks" (firedogs),[2] "a porrage pot," a firepan, a pair of tongs, and a gridiron.[3]

From the Parish Registers a little information is obtainable. Shipwrecks show their results in the burials. In 1698, was buried "Arabella ye Daughter of William Whitehouse, shipwreckt people bound for Ireland." In 1766, Moses Brown was drowned by accident, and in 1769 Edward Keble was drowned in the Creek. Among the entries relating to strangers are 1700, "a Traveller [blank] was buried;" 1709, "The son of a stranger yt [that] came into ye creek was buried;" 1717, "Edward Rowland from little Bentley strayed in ye rage of his fever and dieing in a field was buried." Possibly he had small pox. The dread of it was so great that those affected were sometimes left unattended. Probably this was the reason for his having been allowed to stray not less than six miles.

To encourage the wool trade it was made compulsory in 1666 for bodies to be buried in woollen material.[4] The Act was not repealed until 1815. There are many notes in the Parish Register of the oaths made, that the Act was carried out. Generally the person making the oath was described as "Mother," evidently the title given to the nurses of the period. The baptism of a daughter of "Mr. Bayley, Surgeon," entered in 1772 is the first notice of a medical practitioner here I have found. Baptisms in the Church were not the rule apparently, for in 1774 it is noted that the Vicar's son "was brought into the church" for that purpose. The same remark was made of another child in the same year.

Entries of suicides were not common. In 1710 one was "then buried but without ye solemnitie of christian bureing by permission in a remote corner of ye churchyard." Another was in 1742

" buried behind ye church. Fee for it was 5s." No doubt this refers
to the custom of burying suicides on the north side of the church ;
the south side being reserved for those having Christian burial.
The usual explanation given is that of the sheep and the goats
(Matthew xxv. 31-3). The practice, however, is older than Christianity. The place of torment among the northern heathens was a
cold place, hence the sunny side was preferred in pre-Christian
burial places.[16] Suicides were often buried by night, at cross roads.
Samson's corner got its name from a suicide so called, who was
buried there.

The Parish Registers show a heavy mortality. Plague appeared
in England in 1727-30. Here the deaths reached thirty-seven in
1728. Several of the same name died at dates close together,
corroborating the idea that it was an infectious disease which
was rife.

By multiplying the average of the baptisms from 1711 to 1750 by
thirty, a population of four hundred and forty-five is obtained. This
should be correct within ten per cent.,[5] but is almost certainly an
under-estimate, because the Register was not well kept at times, and
there were some children who were not baptised. An allowance
for ten per cent. error gives a population of four hundred and
eighty-nine, a more likely number. The figure (four hundred and
eighty) obtained by multiplying the one hundred and twenty houses
here in 1763 by four, corroborates the corrected estimate.

The yearly birth rate must have exceeded thirty-six per thousand
of the population. Yet the population increased very slowly. The
yearly average of burials for the period 1711-50 was 24·5, giving a
death rate of fifty-one per thousand, a figure which makes a poor
contrast with the average Brightlingsea death rate of 10·9 for
1906-10, even if a very liberal margin is allowed for error.

The yearly average number of baptisms from 1765 to 1800 mul-
tiplied by thirty gives an estimated population of nine hundred and
forty-one. This does not agree with the census figures of 1801,
which gives the population as eight hundred and seven, but the
latter is an estimate too.[6] As the population in 1811 was 1020, and
as there were one hundred and thirty-nine deaths in 1803-04, suggesting an epidemic, probably of influenza, which was raging in
England at that time,[7] it is probable again that eight hundred and
seven is too low an estimate. Since then the population has made
great strides ; there was a drop of two hundred in 1851, but this was
more than made up by an increase of over seven hundred in 1861.

139. There was a marked increase in prosperity here in the
beginning of the nineteenth century. The timbered houses were

altered probably about this time, and some others of brick were built. The old style timber apparently was not good enough, so brick fronts had to be added, or the lower storeys had walls put flush with the walls of the overhanging storey, and the remaining timber work was hidden by plaster. A number of wooden doorways in the Adams style were artistic additions. Many still remain. Good examples are at 85 High Street, and 40 Queen Street.

As there were no insurance companies in early days, people were licensed by brief from at least as early as 1518, to make collections to compensate them for heavy loss occasioned by fire or other calamity.[8] Later briefs were issued on the recommendation of the Quarter Sessions. Such a brief was granted to a Brightlingsea man. It states that on 25th September, 1798 " a terrible fire broke out upon the premises belonging to the said resident, whereby his dwelling house was considerably damaged and the barns, stables, grainary, and other outbuildings with several stacks of hay and corn were entierely consumed, by which dreadful calamity the said poor sufferer is reduced from comfortable circumstances to great difficulty and distress." Nathaniel Wenlock and Joseph Stammers, "credible and experienced persons" estimated on a moderate computation that his loss amounted to 1205$l$. 14$s$. 6$d$. to be reduced by 535$l$. covered by insurance. He was licensed to collect contributions throughout England, Berwick-on-Tweed, Flint, Denbigh, and Radnor, and from house to house in Essex, Herts, Kent, Suffolk, and Middlesex.[9]

In the list of furniture, *etc.*, in a bill of sale dated 1794, given by a resident, appear a " fly cupboard," an anker (cask holding ten wine gallons), a pair of racks (firedogs), a flour kid (small tub) and a child's cart. The books consisted of a Bible, three Prayer Books, " Family Instructions," " The Poorman's Family Book," " Compassion for the Aged," " The Christian's Monitor," " Considerations upon Eternity," " The Judge in his own Cause," and " Prayer and Meditations."[10]

Brightlingsea does not appear to have had a regularly constituted market. In 1476, Colchester complained of markets being held here to the injury of the market at the Hythe.[11] These must have been unauthorised, or Colchester could have had no just cause for complaint. There was a fair here on 1st August, but it was obsolete when Holman wrote his notes in 1710.[12] The fairs, which have survived, are those held in July and October. The latter was for horses, but became a toy and merchandise fair like the other. A Brightlingsea woman was in the "fair" business. In her will, dated 1631, she speaks of the "tiltes [canvas covers] and timbers

of her boothes."[13]   Notice for the suppression of the fair was
prepared in 1843.[3]   It has been threatened since, but still survives.

140.   The Post Office arrangements were not always so extensive
as they are now.   In 1834, letters arrived at 4 p.m. by foot post
from Thorpe,[15] and were dispatched at 8 a.m.   In 1848, letters
went by foot post to Colchester at 5 p.m.[16]   There were three
carriers to Colchester in 1834, going every day between them.[15]
In 1848, a cart and van carried daily to Colchester, and an omnibus
went on Mondays, Wednesdays, and Saturdays.[16]

A diary for 1849 gives some details of life here then.   A great
deal of visiting went on.   Nearly every day someone was break-
fasting, dining, teaing, or supping at the diarist's house.   He and
his family also visited frequently.   There were many public
entertainments.   The year began and ended with a tea party at the
Temperance Hall.   On January 23rd there was a " grand Procession
in the street."   A theatrical performance took place in the Temperance
Hall on February 9th.   On the 12th there was another tea party
there.   The next day " there was a great bait of Frumenty," and a
lecture on vegetarianism in the hall.   The lecture was continued
the next evening.   On 31st March, there was a donkey race from
the well (? in Hoglane) to the King's Head.   In April there was an
examination of the children and a temperance lecture in the hall.
There was a grand dinner party at the Swan, and a Jury dinner at
the King's Head   Was the latter a Colne Fishery Jury ?

In May there was a "Grand Fete of picking stones, running, *etc*."
Summer's Bazaar was on the Green from 22nd May to 23rd July.
In June there was a tea party at the Swan, a cricket match at
Great Bentley, and a lecture and tea party at the hall.   In July
there were two " Gipsy Parties " on Beacon Hill (picnics at the
second Martello Tower), and hornpipe dancing on the Green.   In
August a regatta was held at East Mersea, and there was another
jury dinner at the King's Head.   The children had another tea
party at the hall in September.   A largess party dined and tea'd at
the diarist's house.   This was probably a harvest home feast.   A
general fast on account of Cholera was ordered on 26th September.
This stopped the festivities to a large extent.   Brightlingsea did
not escape the visitation, for two deaths were recorded.   A tea
party and a lecture on Natural History at the Hall, a Court (manor
court probably) and tithe dinner at the Swan were held in October.

November 15th was a general " Thanksgiving Day on account of
Cholera."   A " raised treat " (probably a subscription party) was
held at the Ship on 21st November.   On 14th December, they had
their " first mess of sprats."[17]

Brightlingsea could not be considered dull in those days; there was plenty of amusement, and none the worse for being the home-made type.

[1 Jl, 196.  2 Co.  3 Mg.  4 L, iii., 300.  5 Bp.  6 Au, 351.  7 Ea, 374.  8 J, ii., 1269.  9 Hd, charters, B, xxxix., 6.  10 Nr.  11 Z, ii., 25.  12 No, 45.  13 Ix.  15 As.  16 Aq. 451.  17 Nq.  18 Bc., i , 228].

# Chapter VIII.

## MISCELLANEOUS.

### THE RELIEF OF POVERTY AND DISTRESS.

141.   In the ancient village community there would be no pauperism.   The family would provide for the aged and sick, while the able man who would not work, would be turned out to live as best he could in the wilds.

Under the early manorial system the lord would for his own sake see that his tenants were cared for.   If a man, through misfortune, were unable to pay his debts or keep himself, he sold himself and became the property, the slave, of the man who kept him.   As the manorial system decayed, responsibility for the poor increased, and a greater burden fell upon private charity.

The Pre-Reformation faith provided much relief for the poor in many of its ceremonies.   Bequests were also made apart from ceremonies.   John Street ordered a dole of 6s. 8d. to be distributed to the poor of Brightlingsea every Good Friday for ten years.[1] Stephen Smythe (1538) made a similar bequest to be given on Good Friday and Easter Eve.[2]   Joan Benet (1537) ordered 3l. 6s. 8d. "to be distributed unto poor people in thingis most necesarie and nedfull"; the money was to be paid out of a certain ship, the "Mighell" (Michael) "and God send it well home in saue gard."[3]   The Reformation and the dissolution of the Monasteries dried up the main sources of charity, and the provision of relief became urgent.   Something had been done by law for relief previously.   In 1530 Justices of the peace were allowed to license poor persons to beg within a definite area.   Vicars and Curates were ordered in 1547 to exhort the people every Sunday and holiday to charitable relief for the poor.[4]   John Beriffe left in 1549 half the proceeds of the sale of a house and garden "to go to the poore mens box to be dystrybuted accordynge to the Kyngs Iniunctions."[5]

By a statute of 12 Richard II. poor persons unable to work were to be sent back to the hundred to which they belonged.   By a law passed in 1556, their parish, when they had returned to it, was to maintain them.   Alms were collected in boxes every Sunday, holiday or other festival.[6]   Thomas Berif in 1563 left 40s. yearly for five

years for " the boxe of the poore."[6]   As time went on bequests of
direct payments to the poor became more numerous, and indirect
benefits were ordered, such as payments to poor men to carry the
deceased to the Churchyard.   The Deputy had a hand at times in
the distribution, for in 1571 he was entrusted to give 25s. to the
poor.[7]   The bequests were generally in sums of from 10s. to 40s.
John Gardenere in 1546 left 1s. to each of twelve poor households.[8]
Another bequest was 3d. "unto euery pore houssold within
the towne."[9]   Sometimes goods were given instead of money ; a
seam of malt and half a seam of rye were left in 1568 for the poor.[10]
20s. was left in 1584 to provide smocks for the poor.[11]   There was
an almshouse here in 1598, for in that year 20s. was left to the
children of the almshouse of Brightlingsea.[12]

142.   The Churchwardens had the principal part of managing
the affairs of the poor, and in the only old Churchwardens' account
existing are some details.[13]   The account apparently dealt with the
money raised by the sale of the church goods, since it was audited
by the Commissioners in 1552.   It appears to cover three years,
probably 1550-1-2.   A reference to the loss sustained by the
reduction in the face value of money was struck out by the
Commissioners.   A Royal proclamation in 1551 had reduced the
value of the coinage by a half.[14]

The Churchwardens had paid 20s. to a poor lame man called
Thomas King, and 5s. to Widow Baryngton for a "cote" (coat)
cloth due to her husband.   One item was for 4l. given to " Henry
[blank] to gyve unto sertayne of the parysyoners where thought
nedefull and to helpe their necessytye in consyderacion they shall
have no occasion to rayle upon the parishe, and slander the same in
raylyng and tellyng of lyes, which thyngs yf they hayd done, might
have turnyd and put the parish at that tyme to forther dyspleasure."
It looks as if the Churchwardens had been too lavish, and had
made elaborate excuses.   Apparently they protested too much in
the Commissioners opinion, for the item was disallowed.

In the years 1548-52 there had been bad harvests ; wheat was
very dear.   In 1550, it was at 20s. a quarter (about 10l. modern
value), and in the next year it reached 26s. 8d. in London.[15]   There
was an extensive epidemic of sweating sickness. in 1551.[16]   Brightlingsea did not escape the prevalent distress.   Three men rode into
Lincolnshire to buy corn for the poor; their expenses were
2l. 16s. 1d.   No doubt they went to Lincolnshire for it, because it
was too dear anywhere nearer, and there is also the possibility,
that the removal of corn from other counties was prohibited.
" Hylyre Balet" was paid 3s. 4d. for fetching twelve seams (a

seam = eight bushels) of rye from Colchester (probably brought there from Lincolnshire) to Brightlingsea for the use of the poor, and for carrying it from the Waterside up into the town. For carrying another four seams of rye he was paid 12*d*., and George Hope carried another four at the same price. There is this curious entry, "lost in bying of the rye aboue named, x*s*. viij*d*."[16] Possibly this meant the loss resulting from the reduction in the value of money.

143. Various other laws were made in Elizabeth's reign, the most important being that of 1601. This ordered the levying of a parochial poor rate, and authorised the parish officers to provide material for the able poor to work on, and to make provision for the disabled poor. It also provided that the relations of the pauper should contribute to his maintenance according to their means.[17] The Mayor and two Jurats of Sandwich gave a warrant for the assessment of this rate, when they visited Brightlingsea in 1601.[18] This compulsory rate did not stop charitable bequests. 20*s*. and 40*s*. were usual amounts for a bequest. There were two of 5*l*. each, and a cottage was left by John Hutt in 1673 to the Churchwardens and Overseers to sell for the benefit of the poor.[19] In the Manor Court Roll for 1665 is the record of a fine of 2*d*. ordered to be paid to the use of the poor.

Thomas Simpson, M.A., Rector of St. Olave's, Hart Street, London, and Prebendary of Hoton, made this bequest in his will dated 24th November, 1632. "I doo give unto the poore of the parish of Brikelsea in Essex where I was borne two and fiftie shillings a year for euer whereof twentie six shillings shalbe paid at the feast of the Blessed Virgin Marie (Lady Day) and twentie six shillings at the feast of St. Michaell, these paymentis to be made to the Vicar and Churchwardens of Brikelsea aforesaid, the first payment to begin at the first of the feasts beforenamed that shall first fall out after my decease, and so to be continued from feast to feast for ever toward the reliefe of twelve poore people weekelie as it hath alreadie since the yeare 1618 unto this present year 1632, and I will the foresaid poore twelve people of Brikelsea to be appointed and nominated by the Vicar, Deputie and Assistants of the aforesaid parish of Brightlingsea for ever."[20] The bequest was in abeyance for a time, and would have been lost but for Mr. Pertwee. The owner of the estate at Kirby had died intestate, and the heir was unknown for a time. When the heir was found, there was no record known on which to base a claim. The record of the orginal bequest was found in 1880, and the claim was recognised and the arrears paid.

144. A very important addition was made to the poor law in

1662. Any person who had come to a parish and settled in a residence worth less than 10*l.* a year could be sent back to the parish, where he was last legally settled as a native, householder, sojourner, apprentice, or servant for not less than forty days, on a Justice's certificate if applied for within forty days of his taking up his residence, unless he gave security for the discharge of the parish.[21]

Poor people, as a result, had a rough time. It was to the advantage of a parish to keep out every doubtful person. Our parish records are full of papers dealing with these questions. Some are records of the examination of the poor person before a magistrate to ascertain their last settlement. Others are orders for their removal to their last settlement. Some are acknowledgments by the overseers of settlement in other parishes, and some of acknowledgments of settlement in Brightlingsea.

The parish officers were allowed to hire or purchase a house in which the paupers were to live. They were allowed to arrange with some one to take charge of and maintain the paupers in the house.[22] There was such a house here. It stood on Hurst Green, and has since been made into the tenements, 6 to 10 Hurst Green. An agreement made in 1781 for the maintenance of the inmates of this workhouse is extant. The master was to be paid 200*l.* a year for their maintenance and clothing. They were to have three good hot meals a week " such as good Meat and Pudding " and on other days cold meat with bread and cheese for their breakfast. He was to keep them in decent clothing, and pay the cost of taking any of them before a magistrate, and those not belonging to Brightlingsea to their last settlement. He was to find them with a surgeon and apothecary and " be at the expence of Small Pox and broken Bones." Any dispute was to be settled at a vestry meeting on the next Sunday.[23] The treatment the poor had received, may be guessed from the fact, that in 1816 it was made illegal for the master of a workhouse to confine any sane pauper by chains or manacles.[24] There were sometimes as many as twenty-two inmates in the house, and 2*s.* 6*d.* each a week was paid for them in 1827.[23] This would be for all maintenance except rent and clothing.

Outdoor relief was not given until 1795.[25] Those in receipt of relief had to wear on the right sleeve a P and the first letter of the name of their parish until 1810.

Removing persons to their last settlement was sometimes expensive. A man, his wife, and seven children, were sent from Brightlingsea to Sunderland by steamer in 1830. They were accompanied by a solicitor. The charge for passage money to

Sunderland, board, grog, *etc.*, for the ten was 16*l.* 11*s.* 0*d.* The total cost was 49*l.* 7*s.* 0*d.*[23] A few cases such as this would soon make the rates go up. The poor rate was as high as 5*s.* 9*d.* in the pound in 1803, and 3*s.* 9*d.* in 1806.[26]

[[1] If   [2] Jg, 27.   [3] Jg, 7.   [4] Ej, xix., 462.   [5] Ig.   [6] Ih.   [7] Ik, 3.   [8] Ju.   [9] Ju, John Assheley, 1556.   [10] Ju Ric. Garritt.   [11] Ju, Edw. Bulvan.   [12] Ju Ric, West.   [13] Fk.   [14] M, i., 33-4.   [15] Ci, iv., 262.   [16] Ea, i., 278.   [17] Ej, xix , 465.   [18] Ld, 318.   [19] Ik, 273.   [20] Iy.   [21] Ej, xix., 466.   [22] Ej, xix., 467.   [23] Mg.   [24] Ej. xix., 469.   [25] Ej, xix., 468.   [26] Aw, Dc, i., 93.]

## ROADS AND BRIDGES.

145   The old highways could have been but little different from the present roads, save of course where new have been added of late. Some have lost their importance, and become byeways or drifts.

From the landing place on Gandergoose Creek there was almost certainly a way crossing Gandergoose (or Salcot) Green to Lower or Street Green. These Greens must have been continuous, and much larger than they are now. Gandergoose Green has been encroached on to the east. The site of the National School is another encroachment, and a big encroachment has been made on the west side of the Lower Green. The Green has been much reduced also by taking pieces into the roadway; at one time the grass reached to the Swan. On the opposite side to the Swan there was a big encroachment. Part of what was called the "Street" extended from the present Queen Street as far as the original Park gates (south of the present Waterworks). Queen Street was at one time called Wells or Rowlands Reach. Wells is I believe a corruption of Wields, the name of some property on the west side. Just west of the Spring was a way leading to the marshes, and called the Chase. This part of the parish was called Westend. The land from about Strangers Corner (it should be Stranges) to Morses was the Northend. At the Church the road divides, one part going to Thorington. At one time there must have been a ford, where it crosses into Thorington, and probably a bridge later. The Green, east of the Church, was called Hall or Church Green. It was much larger than it is now, a big slice having been added to the field on the south. A pound stood here, which gave its name to the field adjoining. After the encroachment, the pound was of necessity moved, and was placed just beyond the north end of the east wall of the Churchyard. A now objectless post may be seen sticking out of some brambles at this spot. It is a relic of the pound. There are four fields and marshes named Pound, suggesting the ancient grazing grounds so widespread as to need pounds in different parts of the Island.

The other branch of the road goes to Moverons and the Ford, where it crosses Alresford Creek. Near the Ford is the ancient Thicks Wood (thick=wood with close underwood).[1] The branch that goes to Moverons is continued to Wapping, which is now represented by two cottages.

The rest of the " Street " extended as far as the present Mill Street or Cook's Lane. The old Waterside Lane (now New Street) led from the Street to the Waterside, where the Hard and Shipyard are, and the Copperas Works were. From the Copperas Works a byeway joined Backwaterside Lane.

Hog Lane led northward from the Street to the fields. There was a lane, mentioned in the Extent called Haddeslane and Heddeslane and in the Ministers' Accounts in 1557, Hoddeslane.[2] Whether Hoddeslane was corrupted into Hoglane or not cannot be said. In any case the name had probably nothing to do with pigs. It appears to have been a common street name in old towns; it was found in Colchester,[3] Faversham,[4] and Hythe (Kent).[5]

Backwaterside Lane led to the head of a now dried up creek which once would float a boat, to the marshes, and to the Waterside. Hurst Green was spelt Hearst, and Hearse. It is spoken of by the older inhabitants as the Hurst or the Herse. In 1673 it was referred to as " le long hearse·"[6] Possibly long was used in the sense of great.[7] It has been suggested that Hurst is the Saxon for wood, and that it got its name from a wood near by. A ghostly funeral said to proceed round the Green once a year, has been given as an explanation of the name. I think it is in the form hearse and the triangular shape of the green, that the origin is to be found. The name herse was anciently given to things triangular in shape.[8] When the hearse became exclusively associated with funerals, the old meaning was forgotten. The ' t ' was added perhaps to get rid of the association of ideas and perhaps from an idea that a colloquial word was a sign of ignorance.

Little Lane, leading from Cook's Lane, was another of the numerous ways to the marshes, a reminder of the days when they were so important as common grazing ground. There is a spring close by, and boats used to come up a fleet to this lane to fill smacks' breakers with water.

146. A road leads eastward from East End Green and ends on the marshes. A grass-grown way leads from it to the marsh, about half-way from the Green, making in all five ways to the marshes on the south.

The Back Road extends from the north-west corner of this Green
to Bell or Capon's Green.  This must have been much larger than
it is now, for the present minute patch of grass would never have
been called a green.  A byeway leads to Jewers, and from here
there was most probably a way leading across the marshes to St.
Osyth.  The Back Road is continued as far as Samson's Corner,
where it joins the main road.  Folkard's Lane was an old road,
now a byeway, down to East Marsh Farm and to the marshes.  On
the marshes there may be seen the remains of a raised roadway
continuous with the lane, and going to within about thirty yards of
the Parish boundary fleet.  The marsh, which it crosses, was liable
to be submerged, until the two embankments across the boundary
fleet were made.  Hence the need of raising the roadway and ending
it before it reached what is now a fleet, but which must have been a
fair-sized channel then.  No doubt a bridge carried the way over
the channel to the embankment on the other side.  Another byeway
leads from the Back Road to Morses and to the marshes.  It is
continued as a foot-path to Thorington with a foot-bridge over the
fleet.

The highways were repairable by the parishioners.  Surveyors of
highways were appointed under a Statute of 1555-56.  The Surveyors and the Churchwardens were to appoint days, on which
parishioners were to repair the roads.[9]  Bequests were often made
for the repair of the highways, especially before the Reformation.
Twenty or forty shillings was the usual amount.  Sometimes the
part to be repaired was specified.  Forty shillings was left in 1537
to repair the Churchway in the Southend and Eastend.[10]  By this
was probably meant the present Church Road and the Back Road.
Twenty shillings was provided in 1539 for the repair of the foot-path
between Cowpers and Hearste End "at the wante."[11]  Wante
would appear to mean where required ; it, however, also meant a
cross road.[7]  The path was probably between 12 and 13 Lower
Green and the White Lion corner.  Thomas Beriffe left 3l. 6s. 8d.
for the repair of highways, bridges, and " steepes,"[3] and John Beriffe
the like sum to repair the road from Goodriches Brigge to the
Church.[14]  The " steepes " might have been the steps of a quay or
stepping stones across a fleet.[15]  Goodriches Brigge is difficult to
place.  The land at the east corner between New and High Street,
was called Goodriches.  There was a channel along the north side
of High Street, which crossed the street about this point.  Possibly
the stream was then large enough to need a bridge, though any but
a small one was not likely.  John Ayre in 1537 left 6s. 8d. to mend
the " bregge otherwise called the Newbregge."  Did the new bridge

replace or supplement the old one? In 1556-57 there is a note of a bridge called the Lady's Bridge, in the common outmarsh.[16] One of the landing places noted in 1576 was the bridge. There is a tradition of the existence of a sort of pier on the Hard, which was called the "Town Bridge." "The Bridge" may have been the forerunner of the Town Bridge. As the Lady's Bridge was on the common outmarsh, it must have crossed one of the fleets on the north shore of Borefleet; but which is difficult to say. There might have been a bridge between the Copperas land and the land, now an arable field, eastward of the Syndicate yacht stores. The strip of low-lying land was submersible by the sea, and the present arable field would have become an island at high water before the embankments were made. Near by there was some land called Bridgland, possibly so called through having a bridge on it, or because it was burdened with the repair of a bridge (see section 6).

In 1548, two Brightlingsea bridges "leading over the Salte water" were repaired, and Thorington mended a bridge called Borefleet bridge "which standeth in daunger of the sea."[17] Most probably Borefleet bridge joined Brightlingsea and Thorington over Borefleet opposite Jewers, or was the bridge which carried the road from East Marsh Farm over the channel to Thorington. A bridge crossing the boundary between two parishes would be repaired by both.

[[1] Co, Thick. [2] Fu, 99. [3] An, map. [4] Bj, i., 223. [5] K, iv., appendix, 431. [6] Nb, 154. [7] Co. [8] Bj, x., 733, Dk, 175. [9] Bv, 107-9. [10] Ig. [11] Ie. [13] Ih. [14] Ib. [15] Cn, steap. [16] Nb, 169. [17] Fx, xix., pp. 53, 64.]

## EDUCATION.

147. Education was in the hands of the monks and priests before the Reformation. In villages knowledge was imparted by the priest or a chaplain. Probably the Chantry priest taught here. Before the suppression of the Chantry, no instance appears in the wills examined of provision for children's education, but they occur later.

Thomas Beriff, yeoman, in 1563 left 3*l*. 6*s*. 8*d*. "towardes the mayntenaunce of a schole master to teach and instruct the youthe of the parishe of Brightlingsea duringe five yeares."[1] Richard Wade in 1575 stipulated that his son should be kept at the school till he could read and write, while his two daughters were to be taught until they could read English.[2] Nicholas Sallowes provided for his children's schooling in 1589.[3] John Walker in the same year ordered, that his daughter should be kept at school. The

executors of Roger Carewe, in 1590, were to see that his children
were brought up in "learning and godly knowledge." He was
a wealthy man, for his "goods chattells and moveables" were
expected to be worth 1800l.[4]  Roger Hempson, in 1669, provided
for his daughters' schooling.[5]  Ellis Markant's executrix (1630)
was to bring up his son "in the form of God and trayne him up in
learning and make him a Scholer if he be capable of learning and
desire the same, or otherwise that shee shall bind him apprentice to
some Trade fitt for him."[6]  Richard Simson, yeoman, in 1574, left
his son Esdras 30l. to be spent on his learning at Cambridge.[7]  He
(Richard) had a brother Thomas, who was probably the Vicar of
that name.

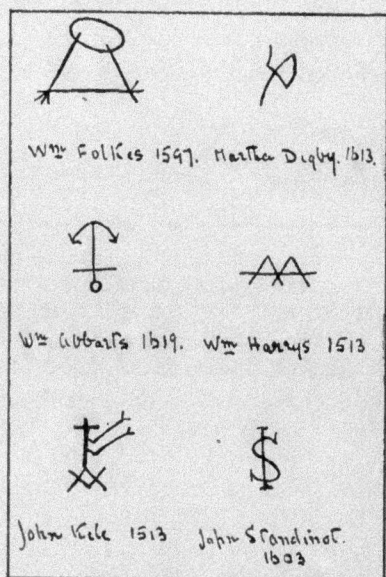

WM Follkes 1547.  Martha Digby. 1613.

WM Abbarts 1619.  WM Harrys 1513

John Kele 1513   John Scondinot.
                               1603

FIG. 8.
MARKS USED IN PLACE OF SIGNATURES.

A school in Brightlingsea is
mentioned in an affidavit dated
1713.  In this a relation is
made by a man of an event
which happened when he was
a scholar at Brightlingsea
School.  The School evidently
attracted non-residents for he
boarded with the Vicar while
there.[8]

Thomas Luck, Vicar, in
1731, gave a house standing
on the Lower Green for a
school.  Two children were
to be taught free reading,
writing, and "casting accompt."
The trustees were to be the
Lord and Lady of the Manor,
the Vicar, the Deputy Mayor
and Assistants, and the Churchwardens.[9]  In 1763, the School
was stated to be endowed with

6l. a year.[10]  An addition to the foundation was made in 1773.
Elizabeth Magens, Lady of the Manor, sold to the trustees, for 10s.
the newly erected dwelling house and garden lately paled "containing by estimation 10 rods adjoining to the charity school," to
be held in trust for the schoolmaster to live in.  The master was
to teach three such children to "read write and cast accompt as
by the Lord or Lady of the Manor should be appointed.  If at any
time there should not be so many children for writing then he was
to teach reading to two children for each writer wanting."[11]  By

1834 the free scholars were in number sixteen boys, and the yearly income had been raised to 16*l.* by 1848.[1][2]

[[1] Ib. [2] Im, 4. [3] Iq. [4] Is [5] Ju. [6] Ju. [7] Ju. [8] Kb, 42. [9] Mb. [10] Hf. [11] Fb. 13, Geo. III., pt. 16, no. 25. [12] As, Aq, 451.]

## FOLKLORE AND DIALECT.

148. A few old beliefs are still remembered, of which the following are some:—

It is unlucky for a man starting on a voyage to see a woman on his way to the water.

A wife should not pack her husband's clothes for him to take to sea, as he will in such case lose them.

A crow or rook seen at sea is unlucky. If it flies over the weather bow, the vessel will have a head wind with which to contend.

The new moon should be seen over the right shoulder.

Convalescents and newborn babies must take their first journey in an upward direction. A baby's nails must not be cut, but bitten down until it is a year old, otherwise it will grow up a thief. A baby must not be allowed to see itself in a mirror.

Wounds are claimed to be healed by being "blessed" by saying certain words over them. Thanks must not be given for the treatment. Cramp is said to be cured by turning the sufferer's shoes uppermost before going to bed. A piece of black flint suspended over the head of the sufferer's bed is an equally sure cure for nightmare.

An ancient custom, which is well remembered, is the game of rounders formerly played on the Church Green on Good Friday. Ball games or contests about Eastertide were common, and still survive in some places.[1] This appears to be an instance of such a game. An important point is the fact that it was on the Church Green (one and half mile away) that it was played, instead of on one of the greens available close at hand. This suggests a religious connection. The custom may have been a pagan one, the ball representing an egg, an emblem of life, and spring, the period of renewed life in the animal and vegetable world. Pagan customs were not abolished on the introduction of Christianity, but were given a Christian meaning. Possibly in this case the custom became associated with Eastertide, and the idea of renewal of life with the Resurrection. An objection to such an explanation is that Good Friday is not the day to celebrate the Resurrection. It may be that the day was changed after the intention of the custom was forgotten

It used to be the custom to have a "raising treat," a festive meal, when the roof of a building was put on. Was this a modification of the old sacrifice required for every building of importance to ensure its stability?

149. The devil appears in two local phrases—"as hard as the devil's backbone," and "as sure as the devil is at Bentley." The first is easily understood, but there is not much point in the latter; possibly it is one of those uncomplimentary pleasantries exchanged between neighbouring places.

"Sudbury, mate," is used as a hint to stand out of the light. Possibly some old word has been corrupted into Sudbury. There does not seem to be any reason for attributing undue opacity to Sudbury people.

The following is a list of the dialect words known to be or to have been in use in the last few years, except some well-known Essex words such as wonderful (very).

Acold, cold.
As ter was, as it was.
Attact, attack.

Bantie, bantam
Between lights, twilight.
Bibble, to drink in sips.
Bird, pupil of eye.
Blare, to cry noisily.
Botty, stuck up.
Breeder, abscess.
Bulk, to throb.
Bush, thorn.
Buskins, gaiters.
Buzz, blow (on the head).

Chates, scraps.
Chance time, on occasion.
Chissick, pinch of salt or other substance.
Choice, pinch of salt or other substance.
Clod, clot.
Clout, cloth.
Cluttered, muddled
Coarse, rough, applied to the weather.
Coase, to stroke, caress.
Cob, an oblong basket.
Count, to consider.
Crock, small piece of soot.
Crowm, to crawl along on a stooping gait.

Cuff, a tough yarn.
Culch, rubbish.
Curren, cunning.
Cut in, to carry on.

Daled, used for emphasis.
Daunt, to toss, said of a cow.
Dausey, stupid.
Deg, dew.
Doddy, little.
Doke, dent.
Dowl, to sit over the fire.
Doss, hassock
Dreening, dripping (wet).
Dringle, to dawdle.
Duller, crying noise.
Dunted, depressed.

Fantig, fluster.
Fare, to do, to seem.
Fierce, inflamed.
Flee, to flay.
Fleet, a drain is said to be fleet enough when it has fall enough, also shallow.
Force put, emergency.

Gag, to retch.
Girt, leap.
Good tightly, properly.
Guy up, to work up (for a storm).

Haggy daggy, mist.

Have a right to, ought to.

Head, used to express the superlative.

Hocket, to laugh heartily.

Hoglin, turnover (pastry).

Hog's court, pig's stye

Hold in with, to agree with.

Hoo roo, a row, fluster.

Housen, houses.

Hull, to throw.

Imitate, to attempt.

Illconvenient, inconvenient.

Instrip, instep.

Jack at a pinch, to fill a gap at an emergency.

Jown, joined.

Jubell, cheek.

Largess, an extra reward.

Lessest, least.

Levener, light refreshment between breakfast and dinner.

Little people, fairies.

Look for, expect.

Lope, leap.

Mavis, thrush.

Mawther, a girl.

Mouldy, bad tempered.

Musheroon, mushroom.

Music, a musical instrument.

Noddle, nape of the neck.

Out of kilter, out of gear.

Pharisees, fairies.

Pingle, to play with food, rather than eat it.

Pork cheese, brawn.

Pucker, worry.

Puggle, to prod, to mess about.

Pulk, tart.

Push, abscess.

Quilt, to swallow.

Ravenish, ravenous.

Releet, cross road.

Rench, to rinse.

Rimple, ripple.

Rub, a scab.

Scalt, scalded.

Scarp, sharp (mentally).

Scivering, slanting.

Scrowge, to crowd up.

Seel, time (of day or night).

Sere, withered.

Sewed up, set with fast (with pain)

Shale, to scale.

Sheer, tense and shining (skin).

Shew, showed.

Shiftening, change of clothing.

Shiver, a slice.

Shruf, shavings and other waste from a workshop.

Siss, hiss.

Sloamy, lazy, stupid.

Snap, to blink (the eyes)

Snarled, tangled.

Sneer, to wince.

Snug, to cuddle.

Soss-cheese, brawn made of odd scraps of meat.

Spade bone, shoulder blade.

Sparched, parched.

Squench, quench.

Squiggle, to wriggle through.

Squit, anything small or insignificent.

Stam, to astonish.

Steddle, bedstead.

Stilt, crutch.

Suffer shipwreck, to suffer severely.

Taffety, dainty, nice.

Take to, to eat.

Tant, aunt.

Tempest, thunderstorm.

Tendle, basket of bent twigs.

Terrify, to irritate.

Tissick, irritating (cough).

Topping, excellent.

Thribble, treble.

Trinkle, to dribble.

Truck, food, stuff, used contemptuously.

Ugly tempered, bad tempered.

Vexed for, troubled about.

Vods, thick woollen stockings worn with water boots.

Whole footed, flat footed.

# Index and Glossary.

NOTE.—(m) before a number indicates that the meaning or explanation of a word will be found on that page. The list of properties on pp. 41-5 is not indexed. Persons are only indexed under their surnames, except in a few cases.

Churchwardens' accounts, 62, 163.
Cindery Island, 1, (m) 2.
Cinque Ports, 75, 81, 83-4, 97-9, 100-1, 112-23.
Clacton, 107.
Clare, 113, 122, 143.
"Classes," 66.
Clerk of the market, 121-2.
Clerks, 23
Clock, 151.
Coats of arms, 68.
Cod, 139.
Colchester, 5, 11, 24, 73, 81, 96-7, 106-7, 111, 116, 120, 124-5, 131-2, 135-6, 156, 160, 167.
Colchester Archdeaconry, 119.
Colchester Carriers, 134.
Cole, 98.
Collins, 145.
Collision at sea, 112.
Colne, river, 1, 11, 12, 107-8, 111-2, 114, 116, 118, 127, 130-2, 135-7, 139.
Colt, 34, 47.
Commission for passage, 122.
Common drivers, 29, 30.
Common fine, 26, 29.
Common land, 9, 11, 30-1, 33, 36-7.
Common of fishing, 131.
Conduct money, 109, 116.
Consent, 115-6.
Constable, 24, 29, 39, 88, 90, 113, 117.
Contributions to Sandwich, 80, 83-4, 89, 92.
Copperas manufacture, 141.
Cornish, 134-5.
Coronations, 83-4.
Coroners, 86, 93.
Cottier, 13, 18, 20.
County rates, 93.
Cowper, 45, 59.
Crayer, (m) 111.
Crecy, 106.
Creeks, 2, 3, 28, 116, 137.
Criminal jurisdiction, 16-7, 25, 87.
Cripps, 85.
Crofts, 23.
Cromwell, 25-6, 61.
Cros, 106.
Cross, at, 43.
Crouch, 138.
Cullicance, 123.
Curate, 53, 70.

M

Curate, stipend, 70.
Curtis, 44.
Curtoys, 106.
Customary tenants, 20, 23, 39, 32.
Customs, 19, 127.

Dairy, 14, 21.
Danes, 11.
Darcy, 47, 66, 87, 91, 113-4, 134-5.
Dawson, 93.
Deal, 90, 92.
Death, 115.
Demesne, 10, 13, 14, 20-1, 26, 28, 36, 40, 49, 142.
Denny, 53.
Deodand, (m) 28.
Deptfordstrand, 114.
Deptford, 109.
Deputy, 67, 83, 85-98, 121-2, 125, 133-5, 150-1, 153, 155, 163-4.
Deputy Mayor, 92, 94, 96, 170.
Dialect, 172.
Diary, 1849, 129, 160.
Dock, 115-6.
Dogs, unlawed, 18.
Domesday, 1, 12, 49, 142.
Dover, 98, 92, 102, 122-4.
Dredgermen, 132.
Dredging boats, 121, 138.
Dredging, illegal, 85, 138-9.
Dredging, summer, 121-2, 133-5, 137.
Dress, 147, 152, 155-6.
Drinker acre, 27.
Droitgatherer, 122, 123.
Drury, 145.
Duke, 151-2.
Dyam, 43.

Eastend, 168.
Eastheye, 51.
East Marsh Farm, 39, 168-9.
Ecceforthe, 106.
Education, 109.
Edwards, 143, 151.
Elmstead, 55.
Elliott, 134.
Erasmus's Paraphrasis, 61, 151.
Escheat, 25, 33 (forfeiture of land for want of heirs or through treason).
Essex, 124, 131-2.
Essex, Earl of, 123.
Essex, forest, 18, 46

9 789353 602772